Letters of Great Women

This book is dedicated to my oldest friend, Katie Chang, who has been there at every twist of life since we were four years old.

It is also for all the other Great Women in my life – and for those still to be born. May we all take the examples of the women in this book and look at how we can improve the world around us.

Published in 2021 by Welbeck
An imprint of Welbeck Non-Fiction Limited, part of
Welbeck Publishing Group
20 Mortimer Street
London W1T 3JW

A CIP catalogue for this book is available from the British Library.

ISBN 978-1-78739-449-0

Printed in Dubai

10 9 8 7 6 5 4 3 2 1

Letters
of Great
Women

Extraordinary correspondence
from history's remarkable women

Lucinda Hawksley

WELBECK

CONTENTS

[Top-left panel]

3.34

Hill, nr. Ockover

[Nov 29. 1857]

[re Mr Nissam miss...]

Dear Miss Nightingale.

I hope you have now received the official receipt of our treasurer Mr Sheen for your kind donation to the fund for the little orphans. — But I must write myself & thank you for it individually. — Each among the large number who knew her must feel that they held their own special place with that noble friend who is gone from among us. how deeply I felt this few if any can ever know. That magnificent grasp of the noblest spirit in act; life can be conceived, or action planned; that sympathy with utter unselfishness; that sweetness that never failed; a generosity that knew no bound are not so much lost for their memory remains to us for ever; but the response to the

[Top-middle panel]

FACULTÉ DES SCIENCES DE PARIS

INSTITUT DU RADIUM
LABORATOIRE CURIE
1, Rue Pierre-Curie, Paris (5e)
TEL. GOBELINS 14-65

Paris, le November 3, 1929
New York

My dear Mr. President,

The first letter I have the opportunity to write during my sojourn in the United States, I wish to address to you. My visit to the White House I shall always remember as a great honor and a pleasure. I feel that it was very kind of you and Mrs Hoover to give time and thought to me in those particularly worried days.

I shall keep in memory your work at the Academy of Science and I am sure your address will be a precious document for the archives of the Radium Institute in Poland.

I beg you to believe that my good wishes shall follow you in your important work for peace and for the improvement of the world.

Sincerely and gratefully yours

Marie Curie

[Top-right panel]

My darling Mother

Just a few lines to tell you how glad I was to get your letter of June 24th and to know you were well and all the family after so long a silence. There are fewer & fewer opportunities of sending but you may rest assured that all goes on here as usual. And that we are very well. Prairie is better again but I fear not permanently. Will you let her father know I received the money he sent, it was handed over to me by the ...

[Middle-left panel]

50

On Apr 15 1862

Mr Higginson

Are you too deeply occupied to say if my verse is alive?

The Mind is so near itself it cannot see distinctly, and I have none to ask.

Should you think it breathed, and had you the leisure to tell me, I should feel quick gratitude.

[Center panel]

Dear Langston —

London, Sunday night
July

I've owed you this letter for some time now — so I'm finally doing it.

Thank you — thank you for the books (your autobiographies) you gave us — I'm reading "The Big Sea" right now and it gives me such pleasure — you have no idea! It is so funny — I read chapters over & over again — 'cause certain ones paint complete pictures for me And I get completely absorbed.

Then too, if I'm in a negative mood and want to get more negative (about the racial problem I mean) if I want to get down right mean And violent I go straight to this book And there is ALSO material for that. Amazing —

I use the book — what I mean is I underLine All meaningful sentences to me — I make comments in pencil

TWENTY HERTFORD STREET
PARK LANE. LONDON. W.1.
GROSVENOR 1881-2-3

[Middle-right panel]

THE WHITE HOUSE
WASHINGTON

March 19, 1936

My dear Mr. White:

Before I received your letter today I had been in to the President, talking to him about your letter enclosing that of the Attorney General. I told him that it seemed rather terrible that one could get nothing done and that I did not blame you in the least for feeling there was no interest in this very serious question. I asked him if there were any possibility of getting even one step taken, and he said the difficulty is that it is unconstitutional apparently for the Federal Government to step in in the lynching situation. The Government has only been allowed to do anything about kidnapping because of its interstate aspect, and even that has not as yet been appealed so they are not sure that it will be declared constitutional.

The President feels that lynching is a question of education in the states, rallying good citizens, and creating public opinion so that the localities themselves will wipe it out. However, if it were done by a Northerner, it will have an antagonistic effect. I will talk to him again about the Van Nuys resolution and will try to talk also to Senator Byrnes and get his point of view. I am deeply troubled about the whole situation as it seems to be a terrible thing to stand by and let it continue and feel that one cannot speak out as to his feeling. I think your next step would be to talk to the more prominent members of the Senate.

Very sincerely yours,

[Bottom-left panel]

Office of Correspondence with the Friends of the
Missing Men of the United States Army.

Washington, D. C., Dec. 8th, 1865.

Dear friends

A letter of Dec. 4 asking information of your son, D. H. Wareham, last heard of at Fort Magruder is before me. Ordinarily, I should reply to your inquiry by saying, that I would place the name upon my roll of Missing Men, and search as best I could. I will do so. But your letter draws upon my recollections for a few words more. Not that I remember your son. I wish I did; but I remember the charge on Magruder, that terrible night of the 18th of July 1863 — Only those whose eyes took in that scene will ever realize it. — Dawn; four long hours preceding that charge; I watched those doomed men marching, unto commands, a file in solid phalanx, unto that charge of death. Then four other hours of carnage such as God grant you may never realize, when the rolling volleys of destruction alone lit up the mists' blackness of the night; then the long line of wounded back along the now wasted beach, and the surging ocean sung its solemn requiem for the dead.

They lay by hundreds, wounded and bleeding,

[Bottom-middle panel]

July 3, 1974

R.S. Ikonen, M.D.
Central Hospital of Tampere
33520 Tampere 52
Finland

Dear Doctor Ikonen:

Never before has a doctoral thesis been written about the newborn scoring system which I reported in 1952! I do hope it helped you attain your degree, and not the opposite.

It interests me to read how often the scoring system is expected to forecast conditions for which it was never intended. As stated in 1953, the system was devised, as described on page 260 of your reference 87, "as a basis for discussion and comparison of the results of obstetric practices, types of maternal pain relief and the effects of resuscitation." Actually, its uses were: 1) to predict infant mortality and 2) to point out to the physician the need for active resuscitation if the total score was four or less.

Now, 22 years later, the score is being examined for association with I.Q. at school age, behavioral disorders, fatal infant diseases such as Tay-Sachs, autism, and length of time in the intensive care unit! I would not expect that there would be either a positive or negative association with those parameters. However, it does no harm at all to investigate under what conditions the score is useful or useless.

Dr. Erich Saling of West Berlin, who has quantitated the degree of asphyxia and acid-base balance, and I are attempting to combine our methods and hope to have something published soon.

Thank you for the autographed thesis. Please give my best regards to Dr. Ahvenainen. I had hoped to visit you during the Helsinki meeting of the European Teratology Society, but had to go to California instead.

With best wishes.

Sincerely yours,

VA:bs

Virginia Apgar, M.D., M.P.H.

[Bottom-right panel]

Mr Cook

Notes your desire

Radiophysics Laboratory
University Grounds
Chippendale

20/2/50

Dear Dr. Ross

Your letter to me came while I was away on holiday, & with the mass of unprecedented other activities of the last few weeks to seem to have mislaid it, so I will have to reply from memory.

Thank you for your opinion on my behalf, but when I spoke to you about my marriage I was in effect asking you whether the Executive realises that the customary penalty of women officers on their marriage — the status of "temporary" has not appeared to be applied in the Act & whether the Executive of with this provision or not. Whether or not there are any material disadvantages to the women concerned by this procedure, all the learned women research officers I have met have felt that this classification as "temporary" puts them at a considerable psychological disadvantage in their work.

Personally I feel no legal or moral obligation to have taken any other action than I have in ...

INTRODUCTION

To be able to write a letter is, in itself, to be in a position of privilege. To have your reputation considered one of such importance that your letters are preserved for generations to come is even more of a privilege. Choosing the women to appear in this book was a very difficult task, because there are so many great women throughout history whose voices have been lost or whose lack of formal education meant they were never able to record their own words. This book is a small sample of the many women from all over the world whose lives and work have been – and continue to be – inspiring, but they form an infinitesimally tiny fraction of all the women who deserve to be in a book such as this.

Letters of Great Women is a glimpse at remarkable women whose lives have spanned many centuries, living under a vast array of societal norms, belief systems, prejudices and experiences. Many of their letters reveal struggles to achieve what seem to us today the most basic of needs or human rights. The lives featured in this book echo the adage that Ginger Rogers achieved everything Fred Astaire did, except she performed it all backwards and in high heels. Some of the women in this book were pioneers in their fields,

while others exhibited extraordinary creative talent or a high level of skill. Some devoted their lives to improving the world around them, and some showed phenomenal courage and bravery at a level unimaginable to most of us. From Cleopatra to Greta Thunberg, this book aims to bear witness to the experiences of women throughout the ages, across the globe and of all generations. We have tried to encompass as many geographic regions and fields of work and life experience as possible, while we acknowledge that the nature of recorded history itself has created its own inbuilt biases.

The letters in this book are all wonderfully different from one another. Some are amusing, others are heartbreaking; some will make you furious, while others will make you feel empathy or happiness or awe. Each of these letters echoes a life experience of a woman whose voice cannot be silenced – diverse women of all backgrounds and experiences, many of whose causes, careers or choices have resonances for every woman and man alive today. It is a book that celebrates the resilience of the human spirit and, I hope, will inspire a future generation of great women and girls, as well as the great men and boys who support them.

Lucinda Hawksley, 2021

Author's note
I am extremely grateful to my dear friend and colleague Julie Charalambides, who stepped in when I was overwhelmed by unexpected caring responsibilities and wrote four of the biographies (Emmy Noether, Bev Ditsie, Manuela Sáenz and Edmonia Lewis). That kind of support and friendship is what Great Women do!

Opposite Top Octavia Hill, Marie Curie, Edith Cavell
Opposite Middle Emily Dickinson, Nina Simone, Eleanor Roosevelt
Opposite Bottom Clara Barton, Virginia Apgar, Ruby Payne-Scott

CLEOPATRA

Queen of Egypt, *c.*69–30 BCE (reigned 51–30 BCE)
A royal ordinance, 33 BCE

Cleopatra VII was the last ruler of Egypt from the Greek-speaking Ptolemaic dynasty. Following the death of her father, the pharaoh Ptolemy XII, in 51 BCE, 18-year-old Cleopatra and her ten-year-old brother Ptolemy XIII were named the new rulers of Egypt. As was tradition, they were also expected to marry – but when the brother and sister/husband and wife became political rivals, Egypt descended into civil war.

In 48 BCE, the Roman general Julius Caesar arrived in Alexandria. At that time, the Roman Republic was also in the middle of a civil war as Caesar struggled for power against his former ally, and fellow famed general, Pompey. Caesar knew that Pompey had travelled to Egypt hoping to enlist support, but instead had been executed on the orders of Ptolemy XIII. Once in Egypt, Caesar attempted to broker peace between the two ruling siblings, a process that foundered after Caesar and Cleopatra became lovers. Caesar appointed Roman troops to guard and fight on behalf of the queen, and Ptolemy XIII was killed in battle. He was succeeded by his and Cleopatra's younger brother Ptolemy XIV, who became his sister's second husband and co-ruler.

Cleopatra and Caesar had a child, a son named Caesarion, which gave Cleopatra even greater power. After Julius Caesar was assassinated in 44 BCE, however, Cleopatra's position became precarious until she formed a relationship with Caesar's ally and military chief Mark Antony. In this royal ordinance, dating from 33 BCE, Cleopatra grants tax privileges to a wealthy Roman landlord, emphasising her close connections with Rome and its eminent citizens.

Caesar's death plunged the Roman Republic back into civil war, as Mark Antony and Caesar's great-nephew Octavian vied for power. When Mark Antony fled to Egypt to join Cleopatra, they were both pursued by Octavian's army. They were eventually defeated at the Battle of Actium in 31 BCE. In the August of the following year, 30 BCE, both Mark Anthony and Cleopatra committed suicide. Octavian ordered the death of Cleopatra's son, Caesarion, who was also Octavian's rival heir. By this time, Cleopatra's younger brother Ptolemy XIV and her younger sister Arsinoe were also dead; their deaths are believed to have been ordered by Cleopatra. The death of Cleopatra ended three centuries during which Egypt was ruled by leaders descended from the Macedonian general Ptolemy I, an ally of Alexander the Great. Meanwhile, Rome's five-century-long Republic was replaced by an empire, as Octavian changed his name to Augustus and became the first Roman emperor.

The fact that history has recorded the name of Cleopatra's father, but not of her mother, seems to have set the scene for the dumbing down of Cleopatra's own reputation. Despite having been one of the most important and influential rulers of her era and beyond, history prefers to remember Cleopatra as a Hollywood-style sex kitten. Her intelligence, knowledge of diplomacy and political skill, as well as her ruthlessness, are constantly ignored in favour of comments about her 'beauty' and 'desirability', and many modern-day interpretations seem to suggest that she was a seductress who merely played at being a ruler. The name of Cleopatra remains famous all over the world, and she has inspired plays, paintings, books and films, most of which focus on her love affairs.

Opposite A depiction of Cleopatra and her son Caesarion at a temple to the goddess of love and fertility, Hathor, at Dendera on the banks of the River Nile.

We have granted to Publius Canidius and his heirs the annual exportation of
10,000 artabas [300 tonnes] of wheat and the annual importation of 5,000 Coan amphoras
[ca. 15,500 litres] of wine without anyone exacting anything in taxes from him or any
other expense whatsoever. We have also granted tax exemption on all the land he owns in
Egypt on the understanding that he shall not pay any taxes, either to the state account or
to the account of me and my children, in any way in perpetuity. We have also granted that
all his tenants are exempt from personal liabilities and from taxes without anyone exacting
anything from them, not even contributing to the occasional assessments in the nomes
[territories of Egypt] or paying for expenses for soldiers or officers. We have also granted
that the animals used for ploughing and sowing as well as the beasts of burden and the ships
used for the transportation [down the Nile] of the wheat are likewise exempt from 'personal'
liabilities and from taxes and cannot be commandeered [by the army]. Let it be written to
those to whom it may concern, so that knowing it they can act accordingly.
Make it so!

KATHERINE OF ARAGON

Queen of England, 1485–1536
To King Henry VIII, 16 September 1513

Katherine was the youngest child of Queen Isabella of Castile and King Ferdinand of Aragon. She was born at the Archbishop's Palace of Alcalá de Henares, near Madrid in Spain, but was destined to spend most of her life in England – and to become a figure of huge controversy. As a royal female child, the question of her marriage was considered a strategic political deal from the moment of her birth. Her first husband was Arthur, Prince of Wales and heir to the throne of England, in a marriage arranged by the two sets of parents when both were still children. Until she was old enough to marry, Katherine lived with her parents and was given a wide-ranging education fitting for a future queen, learning about the law, military strategy, philosophy and religion. She was fluent in several languages, including English as this letter demonstrates, although she spoke very little English on her arrival in her adopted country.

Katherine married Prince Arthur in London on 14 November 1501. The bride was 16 and the groom 15, but despite their youth, the marriage was destined to be short-lived. After contracting what was believed to be consumption (tuberculosis), Arthur died the following April. Following his death, his widow was watched carefully in case she was pregnant with an heir to the throne, but it was soon realised that she was not. Speculation about whether or not the marriage had been consummated was to dramatically affect the future of Europe.

For seven years, Katherine was stranded in England, where her father-in-law King Henry VII allowed her very little money, despite

Right Dating from 1511, this painting shows a young Henry VIII competing in a tournament in front of his new wife, Katherine.

her having endowed his family with a large dowry. Queen Isabella and King Ferdinand wanted their daughter to return to Spain, but that would have meant returning her dowry, so it was in the king's interest to keep her in England, while ensuring that she did not have enough funds for independence. In 1509, resigned to life in England, Katherine married Arthur's younger brother, the newly crowned King Henry VIII. He was six years her junior and infatuated with her.

Initially it was a strong marriage, in which Katherine acted as her husband's political advisor. They had six children, but five were still-born or died in infancy. Only one survived to adulthood: the future Queen Mary I. Thwarted in his desire for a son, Henry blamed his wife. In later years, he decided that he wanted a new,

younger wife who he was sure would give him a son, so he tried to insist on an annulment. Even though Katherine had always maintained that she was still a virgin after her first marriage, Henry insisted that his brother's marriage had been consummated, and therefore his marriage to Katherine was never legal. The Church refused to sanction Henry's wishes, leading the king to sever his country's ties with Catholicism. In 1533, he declared himself Supreme Head of a newly created religion, the Church of England. His marriage to Katherine was declared illegal, and Henry promptly married Anne Boleyn.

Katherine was exiled from the royal court in 1533. She died aged 50 just three years later at Kimbolton Castle, Cambridgeshire, amid rumours that she had been poisoned.

Sir,

My Lord Howard hath sent me a letter open to your Grace, within one of mine, by the which you shall see at length the great Victory that our Lord hath sent your subjects in your absence; and for this cause there is no need herein to trouble your Grace with long writing, but, to my thinking, this battle hath been to your Grace and all your realm the greatest honor that could be, and more than you should win all the crown of France; thanked be God of it, and I am sure your Grace forgetteth not to do this, which shall be cause to send you many more such great victories, as I trust he shall do. My husband, for hastiness, with Rougecross I could not send your Grace the piece of the King of Scots coat which John Glynn now brings. In this your Grace shall see how I keep my promise, sending you for your banners a king's coat. I thought to send himself unto you, but our Englishmens' hearts would not suffer it. It should have been better for him to have been in peace than have this reward. All that God sends is for the best. My Lord of Surrey, my Henry, would fain know your pleasure in the burying of the King of Scots' body, for he has written to me so. With the next messenger your Grace's pleasure may be herein known. And with this I make an end, praying God to send you home shortly, for without this no joy here can be accomplished; and for the same I pray, and now go to Our Lady of Walsingham that I promised so long ago to see. At Woburn the 16th of September.

I send your Grace herein a bill found in a Scotsman's purse of such things as the French King sent to the said King of Scots to make war against you, beseeching you to send Mathew hither as soon as this messenger comes to bring me tidings from your Grace.

Your humble wife and true servant,

Katherine

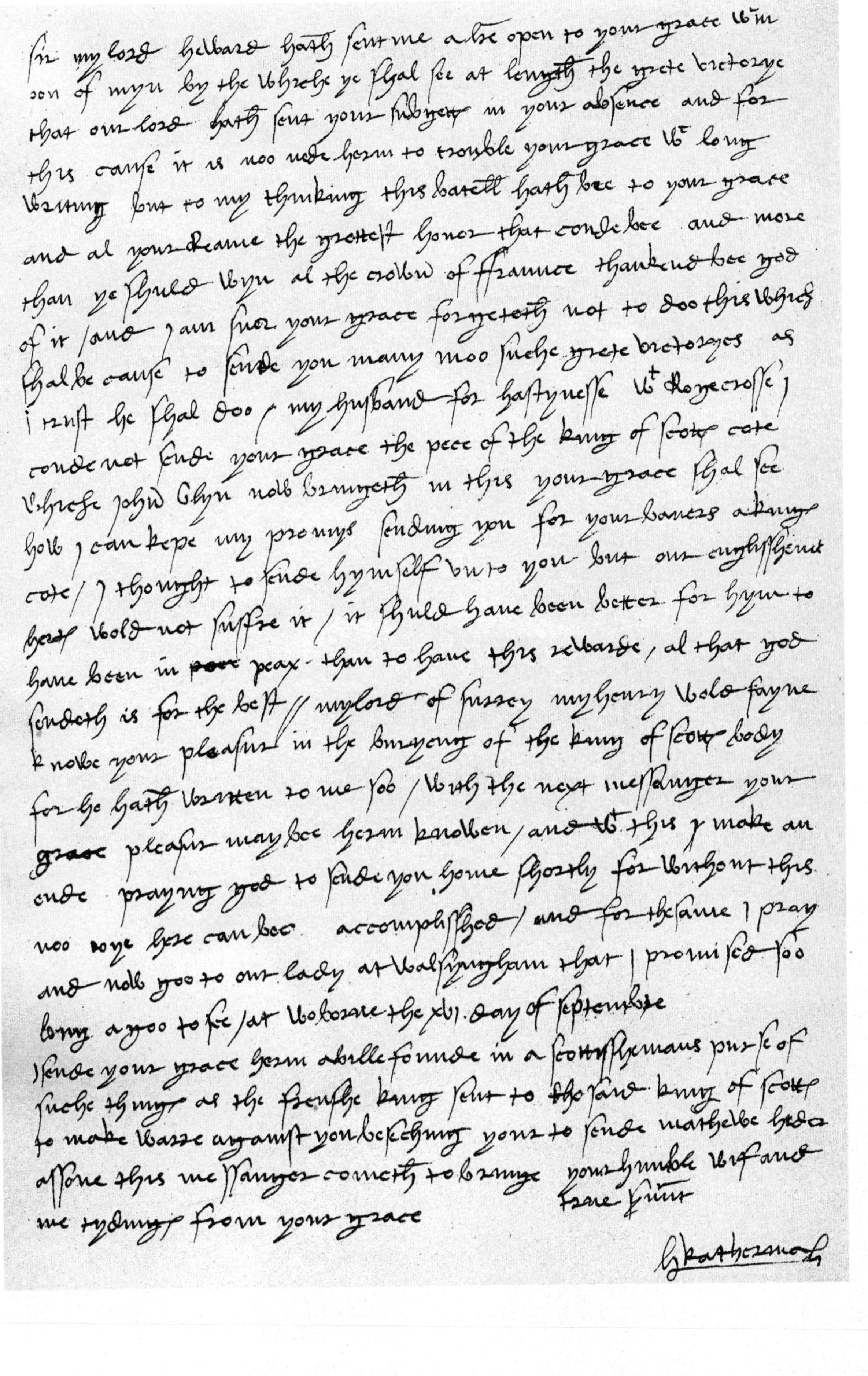

Sir my lord hilbard hath sent me a lre open to your grace wt in
son of myn by the whiche ye shal see at length the grete victorye
that our lord hath sent your subyett in your absence and for
this cause it is noo nede herin to trouble your grace wt long
wryting but to my thinking this batell hath bee to your grace
and al your reame the grettest honor that coude bee and more
than ye shuld wyn al the crown of ffraunce thanked bee god
of it and I am sure your grace forgeteth not to doo this whiche
shalbe cause to sende you many moo suche grete victoryes as
I trust he shal doo / my husband for hastynesse wt Rogecrosse
coude not sende your grace the pece of the kyng of scottys cote
whiche John Glyn now bryngeth in this your grace shal see
how I can kepe my promys sending you for your baners a kynges
cote / I thought to sende hymself vnto you but our englishmens
herts wold not suffre it / it shuld have been better for hym to
have been in peax than to have this rewarde / al that god
sendeth is for the best // my lord of surrey my henry wold fayne
knowe your pleasur in the buryeng of the kyng of scottys body
for he hath wryten to me soo / with the next messanger your
grace pleasur may bee herin knowen / and with this I make an
ende praying god to sende you home shortly for without this
noo Ioye here can bee accomplished / and for the same I pray
and now goo to our lady at walsyngham that I promised soo
long agoo to see / at woborne the xvi day of september
I sende your grace herin a bille founde in a scotyshmans purse of
suche thyngs as the frenshe kyng sent to the said kyng of scottys
to make warre agaynst you beseching yow to sende mathewe heder
assone this messanger cometh to bryng me tydyngs from your grace

your humble wif and
true servant
Katherine

LADY JANE GREY

Queen of England, 1537–1554
To William Parr, Marquess of Northampton, 10 July 1553

Lady Jane Grey was the daughter of the Marquess of Dorset and Lady Frances Brandon. It was through her mother's family that Jane found herself in line for accession to the English throne, and a pawn in a bloody inter-familial, religious and societal conflict. Jane's mother was the niece of King Henry VIII (a daughter of his sister, Princess Mary). When Henry VIII broke away from the Catholic throne over Rome's refusal to grant him a divorce from his first wife, he set in motion the chain of events that would lead to the death of his great-niece at the age of just 17.

When Lady Jane was 10 years old, she was sent to live with Thomas Seymour and his family. Thomas was the brother of Jane Seymour, the third wife of Henry VIII, who had died shortly after giving birth to her only child, the future King Edward VI. When Henry VIII died in 1547, his nine-year-old son Edward was crowned king. Thomas Seymour subsequently married Henry's widow, Katherine Parr. He had great ambitions for Lady Jane, intending that she should become queen by marrying Edward VI. This plan was scuppered when Thomas Seymour fell foul of the boy-king and was executed.

Edward VI was a very sickly child, and was destined to die in 1553, at the age of 15. As Edward did not believe a woman should be a monarch, his will deliberately went against the accepted rules of accession by taking away the rights of both of his sisters – the future queens Mary and Elizabeth. Instead, he named as his successors Lady Jane Grey and the male children he hoped she would have. Edward was especially keen that his eldest sister Mary should not accede to the throne, because she was Catholic. Jane had recently married Lord Guildford Dudley, the son of the

King's Protector, John Dudley, Duke of Northumberland. The dying king pinned his hopes on Jane having male children – and if she did not, his will stipulated that the throne should pass from Jane to a male relative.

Lady Jane was a well-educated and intelligent young woman, who studied the Classics and spoke several languages. Crucially, in King Edward's view, she was also a devout Protestant. As she was a great-granddaughter of King Henry VII, there were some who believed she had a rightful claim to the throne, although there were far more who believed that changing the line of accession was going against God's will.

When Lady Jane was informed that she had been chosen as Edward's successor, she cried in front of her bewildered courtiers. She knew her father-in-law had played a very dangerous political game, in which she had been a pawn. Although in this letter to Katherine Parr's brother, William, she writes confidently, dismissing Mary as the 'bastard daughter' of her great-uncle, her entreaty that Parr show his allegiance to her demonstrates how aware she was of the dangerous position in which she had been placed. The letter is believed to be written in a secretary's hand, with Jane's signature at the top.

The supporters of Princess Mary rallied an enormous army, which easily defeated the army assembled by Jane's father-in-law. The newly named queen and her young husband were confined to the Tower of London after Jane had reigned for a mere nine days, from 10–19 July 1553. Both she and Guildford Dudley were executed for high treason at the Tower of London on 12 February 1554.

Opposite *The Execution of Lady Jane Grey*, by French artist Paul Delaroche, which today hangs in the National Gallery, London.

Jane the Quene

Right trusty and wellbiloved, we grete you well, advertiseing you that, where it hath pleased Almighty God to call to his mercye out of this life our derest cousin the King your late Sovereigne Lorde, by reason whereof and such ordonaunces as the sayd late King dyd establishe in his life tyme for the securitie and welthe of this realme, we are entred into our rightfull possession of this kingdome, and by the last will of our sayd derest cousin our late progenitor and other several instruments to that effect, signed with his owne hande and sealed with the greate seale of this realme in his own presence, whereunto the nobles of this realme for the most parte and all our Counsail and Judges, with the Mayour and Aldermen of our cities of London and diverse other grave personages of this our realme of England, have also subscribed their names, as by the same will and instrument it may more evidently and planely appere, we therefore do you to understand that, by the ordonaunce and sofferaunce of the hevenly Lorde and by the assent and consent of our sayd nobles and counsailours and others before specified, we do this daye make our entree into our Tower of London as rightfull Quene of this realme and have accordingly set fourth our proclamacions to all our loving subjects, gyveng them therby to understande their dieutes of allegiance which they nowe owe unto us as more amplye by the name ye shall briefly perceive and understande, nothing doubting right trusty and wellbiloved but that ye will endevour yourself in all things to the uttermost of your power, not only to defende our juste title but also assist us in our rightfull possession of this kingdom and to disturbe, repell and resist the fayned and untrewe clayme of Lady Marye, bastard daughter to our greate ungle Henry the eighth of famous memorye. Wherin as ye shall doe that which to your honour, trewth and dieutie apperteyneth, so shall we remember the same unto you and yours accordingly. And our further pleasyr is that ye shall contiynue, doo and execute every thing and thinges as our Lieutenaunt within all places according to the tenour of the commission addressed unto you from our late cousin King Edwarde the Sixte in such and lyke sorte as if the same had been, as we mynde shortely it shall be, renewed and by us confirmed under our greate seale unto you. Given under our signe at our Tower of London, the xth of July, the first yere of our reign.

To our right trusted and right wellbeloved cousin and counsailour the lorde Marques of Northampton, our Lieutenaunt of our Counties of Surreye, Northamton, Bedford and Berkshire.

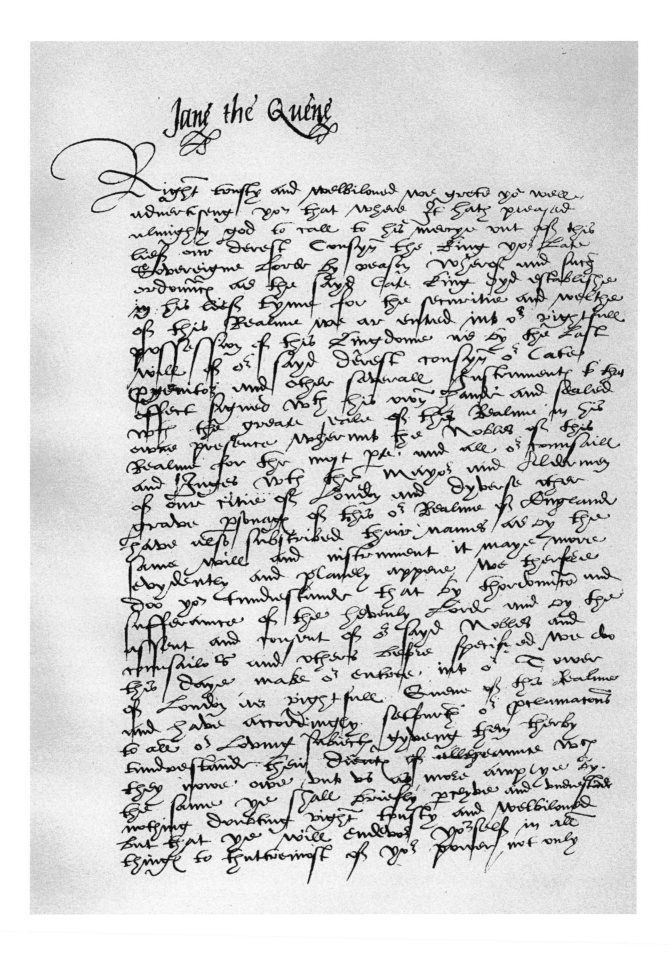

QUEEN ELIZABETH I

Queen of England, 1533–1603
To King James VI of Scotland, 5 January 1603

Princess Elizabeth, the daughter of King Henry VIII and his second wife Anne Boleyn, never expected to become Queen of England. Not only was she born into a society that expected a male monarch, she also had an older half-sister, Mary, who was considered legitimate in the eyes of the Church, whereas Elizabeth was considered by many to be illegitimate. Elizabeth grew up in fear, with the horror of knowing that her mother had been beheaded on the orders of her father. Mary was raised a Catholic, while Elizabeth was raised a Protestant. As England battled between its Catholic past and its Protestant future, Elizabeth's life was often in great danger.

When Henry VIII died, his young son – the child of Jane Seymour, his third wife – was crowned King Edward VI. He was just nine years old and reigned for only six years. Before his death, Edward named his first cousin once removed, Lady Jane Grey, as his successor instead of Mary. Jane reigned for just nine days before she was deposed and executed. Mary I acceded to the throne and reigned for five years, a time of great brutality that earned her the nickname of 'Bloody Mary'. This was also a very dangerous time for Elizabeth, who was imprisoned and feared execution.

When Mary I died in November 1558, Elizabeth became queen. She was an intelligent woman who spoke five languages and understood the art of diplomacy. She chose not to risk her sovereignty by marrying, but was a great admirer of men and those who became her 'favourites' were given important positions in court and politics. Although commonly called the 'Virgin Queen', it is widely believed that Elizabeth had lovers amongst her favourites.

Queen Elizabeth I, the last of the Tudor monarchs, reigned for 45 years. During her reign, the Church of England became fully established – a shrewd political act, as the Church was considered a middle ground between Catholicism and Protestantism. This first Elizabethan era was seen as a golden age for England, a time of exploration and discovery, and of a renaissance for English culture in theatre, art, literature, music and the sciences. It was also a time of war and uncertainty. England lived in fear of attacks from Spain, and Elizabeth lived in fear of assassination by the supporters of her Catholic cousin, Mary, Queen of Scots. The supporters of Mary considered Elizabeth illegitimate because her father had divorced his first wife to marry her mother, and therefore unfit to be queen. Their plots against her life caused Elizabeth to turn away from her earlier religious tolerance and to pass tough laws against Roman Catholics.

Elizabeth I died on 24 March 1603, at Richmond Palace on the banks of the River Thames. The death of the queen at the age of 69 led to vast changes in Britain. Her throne was inherited by her cousin, King James VI of Scotland, thereby uniting the countries of Scotland and England, where he became known as King James I. In this letter from Elizabeth to James, written just a few weeks before her death, the queen addresses her cousin as 'My verie good brother'.

My verie good brother.

It pleaseth me not a little, that my trew intents (without gloses or guyles) are by you soe
gratefully taken, for I am nothinge of the vile disposition of such, as whyle their nighbours
howse is or likely to be a fyre, will not only not helpe, but not afford them water to quench
the same. Yf any such you have heard of towards me, God graunt he remember it not to
well for them; for the Archduke [of Austria] Alas poore man, he mistaketh everye bodye
like himselfe, except his bonds, which without his brothers helpe, he will soone repent...
I suppose (consideringe whose apart enemy the kinge of Spayne is) you will not neglect
your owne honour, soe much to the world, (though you had noe perticuler love to me) as
to permitt his Embassador in your land, that soe cause [...] prosequtes such a Princess, as
never harmed him; yea such an one as if his deceased father had been rightly informed) did
better merit at his hands then any Prince on earth, ever did to other: for where hath there
been an example, that any one kinge, hath ever denyed soe soe fayre a present, as the whoale
Seaventeen Provinces, of the Low Countreyes, yea whoe not only would not have denyed
them, but sent a dosen gentlemen, to warne him of their slydinge from him, with offer of
keepinge them from the neere nighbours hands and sent treasure to pay the shakinge townes
from [...] Deserved I such recompence, as many a complot, both for my life and kingdome.
Ought not I to defend and bereave him of such weapons as might innoye my self? He will
say I helpe Holland and Zeland from his handes. Noe, if ether his father or himselfe would
observe such oath, as the Emperour Charles obliged himselfe and soe in sequell his soonn,
I would not delt with others territory but they hould those by such couvenantes, as not
observinge, by their owne grauntes, they are noe longer bound unto them. But though all
this weare not unknown to me, yet I cast such right reasons, over my shoulder, and regarded
their good, and have never defended them in a wicked quarrel, And had he not mixt that
Government contrarye to his owne lawe, with the Rule of Spaniardes, all this had not

Continued overleaf

Continued from overleaf

needed. Now for the warning, the Frenche gave you, of Besons Embassadge to you, methinkes the kinge (your good brother) hath given you a caveat, that beeinge a kinge he supposes by that measure that you would deny such offers. And since you will have any counsayle, I can hardly believe, that (beeinge warned) your own subject shalbe suffered, to come into your Realme, from such a place to such intent. Such a Prelate (if he come) should be taught a better a lesson, then play soo presumptuous and bould a part, afore he knew your good liking thereof, which I hope is farr from your intent, soe will his comminge verify to much, good Mr Symples asservations at Rome, of which you have or now here warned enough. Thus you see, how to fullfill your trust reposed in me, (which to infringe I never mynde) I have sincerely made patent my sincerity. And though not fraught with much widome, yet stuffed with great goodwill. I hope you will beare with my molestinge you to [too] longe, with my seratting hand, as proceedinge from a hart, that shalbe ever filled, with the sure affection of

your lovinge and frendly systar
Elizabeth R.

Opposite Queen Elizabeth I in her coronation robes. She wears her hair loose, as is traditional for the coronation of a queen, perhaps also as a symbol of her virginity. This painting, by an unknown artist, dates from around 1600.

APHRA BEHN

Writer, *c.*1640–1689
To Zachary Baggs, 1 August 1685

Aphra Behn was the first Englishwoman to make her living as a professional writer. As a woman writing about subjects such as sex and political intrigue, her works were often considered scandalous. Much of her life remains shrouded in mystery and very little is known about her childhood. Even the identity of her parents is unknown, although several theories have been suggested by biographers. Aphra lived for a while with a Mr and Mrs Johnson, with whom she travelled to Surinam in the 1660s. She remained there for several months before returning to England. Behn is believed to be her married name, and it has been suggested that her husband was a Dutchman who died young, shortly after their marriage.

By the mid-1660s, Aphra had been widowed and was struggling financially, so she accepted a poorly paid job as a spy for King Charles II. In this capacity, she travelled to Antwerp, but the king left her very short of money. On her return home, she was arrested for debt and incarcerated in a debtors' prison. It was at this time that her writing career truly began.

Behn wrote plays, poetry and novels, beginning with her first play, *The Forc'd Marriage*, which was produced in 1670, and continuing with *The Amorous Prince* and *The Dutch Lover*. She did not encounter commercial success with her plays until her 1677 production *The Rover*, which made her name. Many people were angered by the very notion of a female playwright, but Aphra Behn fought against this prejudice to make her name famous. Indeed her name became so controversial that she was both held up as an example to all women and cursed with a depraved collection of threatened 'divine' punishments. Despite achieving such fame (or notoriety), however, Aphra's finances were seldom secure. This letter is a promissory note, dated 1885, for a debt of £6, which she owed to a Zachary Baggs.

Some of her works were published anonymously, and the most sexually explicit of them were usually believed to have been written by a man. Her novel *Love Letters Between a Nobleman and His Sister* (1684–87) was not published under her name until the late twentieth century. Her most famous book is her powerful novel *Oroonoko*, published in 1688 and hailed today as a protest against slavery. It was highly unusual for its time, its hero an African man who has been captured as a slave and taken to South America, where he becomes a military leader. The novel, which is written through the eyes of an admiring female narrator, is believed to have been inspired by Behn's months in Surinam. Ever since its publication, speculation has continued about the identity of the person who inspired Behn to create the character of Oroonoko.

Aphra Behn died on 16 April 1689 after several years of ill health amid increasing and debilitating poverty. She was buried in Westminster Abbey in London beneath a gravestone carved with the epitaph 'Here lies a Proof that Wit can never be Defence enough against Mortality'.

Whereas I am indebted to Mr Bags [sic] the sum of six pound for the payment of which Mr Tonson has obliged himself – now I do hereby empower Mr Zachary Baggs, in case the said debt is not fully discharged before Michaelmas next, to stop what money he shall hereafter have in his hands of mine, upon the playing my first play till this aforesaid debt of six pound be discharged.

Witness my hand this 1st August 85

A. Behn

MARIA SIBYLLA MERIAN

Naturalist and scientist, 1647–1717
To Christian Schlegell, 2 October 1711

Maria Sibylla Merian was born in Frankfurt, to a Swiss father and German mother. From a very young age, her passion was the study of insects. She has become known as one of the world's greatest entomologists, even though she was studying the subject decades before entomology was recognised as a science.

When Maria was three years old, her father, the illustrator Matthias Merian, died. Maria had eight older half-siblings from her father's first marriage. Her mother Johanna remarried a year after being widowed. Johanna's second husband was the artist Jacob Merrel, who taught his little stepdaughter how to draw, paint and engrave. This artistic background ensured she was able to create detailed illustrations of her insect collections. Maria bred silkworms and caterpillars and collected other insects. She made notes about the effects of climate and diet on the growth of the insects that she bred. She kept intricately detailed records and drawings of their life cycles and the plants on which they fed and bred.

At the age of 18, Maria married one of her stepfather's apprentices, Johann Andreas Graff, with whom she had two daughters, Johanna and Dorothea. Together, the couple worked as artists, setting up a studio in Nuremberg, where Maria worked on her illustrations of flowers and insects. In 1675, the year in which she turned 28, Maria published her first volume of engravings. Her second and third volumes were published within five years and started to make her name. Although the majority of her customers were buying the engravings for the illustrations of flowers, almost every flower was accompanied by accurate depictions of insects.

In 1679, Maria published a book about European butterflies, translated as *The Wonderful Transformation of Caterpillars and Their Particular Plant Nourishment*. Her work differed from all the other books available because the insects she painted were not desiccated, dead specimens, but were the live caterpillars and butterflies she collected and bred. The book did not make her name in the scientific world because it was written in Maria's native German, whereas the language of science was Latin. It did, however, sell relatively well. This gave her financial independence. In 1681, Maria's stepfather died and Maria took the opportunity to leave her now unhappy marriage and return with her children to live with her mother. Ten years later, she and her daughters, by now also both working as artists, moved to Amsterdam, where Maria took full advantage of the natural and scientific wonders brought to the port by ships arriving from all over the world.

Life in Amsterdam encouraged Maria, aged in her early fifties, to travel to Surinam (then a Dutch colony) in 1699. She travelled with her younger daughter, Dorothea, on an arduous and dangerous journey, and at a time when very few women were able to travel. In Surinam, she studied and collected the native insects. This resulted in her 1705 book *Metamorphosis insectorum Surinamensium*, or *Insects of Surinam*.

This letter, describing her books to an interested buyer, was written six years before Maria Sibylla Merian died. Long after her death, her work continues to inspire naturalists and entomologists – and her name lives on in the insects that have been named in her honour.

Opposite A plate from *Metamorphosis Insectorum Surinamensium*, titled 'Grenadier'.

To Monsieur
Monsieur the generous Gentleman
Mr Christian Schlegell
in Rastadt

Amster[dam], October 2nd 1711

My lord!

With regard, most esteemed Sir, to your kind letter of September 19th, which was received in good condition and from which is understood that you wish to have a copy of my Indian Insects, curiously illuminated, I kindly reply that such an illuminated copy may now be obtained at the price of 45 florins, in other words forty-five Dutch guilders, and from the Ambon [book] I still have one copy left, also curiously illuminated, which can be had for 60 fl, in other words sixty Dutch guilders. I will not make more copies of the Ambon [book], but I also [do have available] a volume I have published in high German in a quarto edition, curiously illuminated too, 10 guilders a volume. When, however, one wants them painted, the Indian [book] [amounts to] 75 Dutch fl and the quarto [book] 20 Dutch fl.

[I] have made this offer in honest hope and therefore expect an affirmative reply, so that, if indeed required, the books may be delivered to Mister Van der Berg against proper payment. Concluding with friendly greetings and commended with God's blessing, [I] remain faithfully my lord's obedient servant

Maria Sybilla von Merian

Opposite A plate from *Metamorphosis Insectorum Surinamensium,* titled 'Eichhornia Crassipes'.

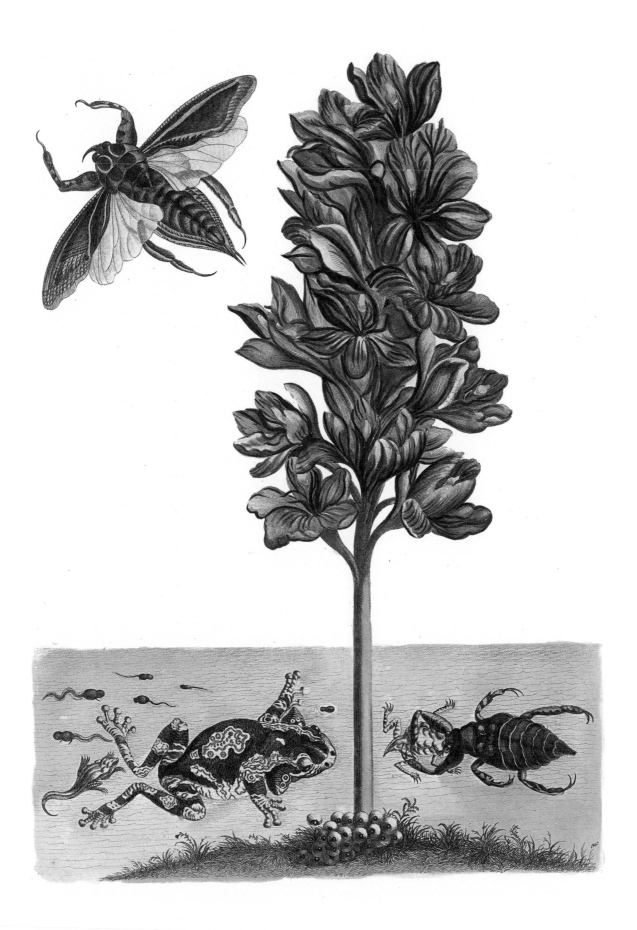

ABIGAIL ADAMS

First Lady and campaigner, 1744–1818
To John Adams, March–April 1776

History places Abigail Adams very much behind the scenes, as the wife of second US president John Adams. However, in addition to being the First Lady, Abigail Adams was also her husband's advisor, an activist against slavery and a campaigner for women's rights.

She was born in Weymouth, Massachusetts, the daughter of the Reverend William Smith and his wife Elizabeth (née Quincy). She grew up in a Congregationalist Christian family who were fervent about trying to make a difference in their local community. Throughout her childhood, Abigail helped her mother with charitable causes, and this desire to bring about change stayed with her into her adult life. Although Abigail was not sent to school, she was educated at home and was able to make use of her father's library, through which she educated herself further. As an adult, she would become known for her eloquent letters as well as her ability to formulate logical arguments in her writing.

Abigail Smith married John Adams in 1764. At the start of their marriage, they lived on a farm. While her husband was working as a lawyer, Abigail capably ran the farm, organised the family and business finances and gave birth to six children. They had three daughters, Abigail (known as 'Nabby'), Susanna and Elizabeth, and three sons, John Quincy, Charles and Thomas Bolyston. Susanna died in infancy and Elizabeth was stillborn.

John Adams' work frequently required him to travel, during which times the couple communicated by letter. It was through this correspondence that Abigail came to have such an influence on her husband. As this particular letter shows so well, Abigail was always actively involved in her husband's work, and he relied on her insights and perspicacity about legal and political situations, as well as their family finances.

Abigail had held abolitionist beliefs since childhood, and in 1774, she wrote to her husband saying that she wished slavery did not exist. The letter shown here exhorts him to consider women's legal rights, with the now-famous phrase 'Remember the Ladies, and be more generous and favourable to them than your ancestors'. At the time of this letter, which spans several days in 1776, her husband had recently been admitted to the Bar and was at the start of his political career. John Adams took full advantage of his wife's interest in his work, and their conversations and correspondence helped to form many of his political ideals.

In 1784, John Adams was given a diplomatic posting to Paris, after several years of working (away from his family) in Europe. This gave Abigail the chance to live in the French capital, where she recorded her observations of Parisian life. While in Europe, Abigail also travelled to The Hague and to the UK. In London, she and her daughter were presented to Queen Charlotte.

John Adams was elected president in 1797. This was just after Washington, DC, had been named the new capital city (replacing Philadelphia), so he and Abigail were the first presidential family to live in the White House. Abigail died in 1818, six years before her son John Quincy Adams was elected the sixth president of the United States.

Braintree March 31 1776

I wish you would ever write me a Letter half as long
as I write you; and tell me if you may where your Fleet are
gone? What sort of Defence Virginia can make against our
common Enemy? Whether it is so situated as to make an able
Defence? Are not the Gentery Lords & the common people vassals,
are they not like the uncivilized Natives Brittain
represents us to be? I hope their Rifel Men who have
shewen themselves very savage & even Blood thirsty; are not
a Specimen of the Generality of the people

I am willing to allow
the Colony great merit for having produced a Washington
but they have been shamefully duped by a Dunmore

I have sometimes been ready
to think that the passion for Liberty cannot be Eaquelly
strong in the Breasts of those who have been accustomed to
deprive their fellow Creatures of theirs. Of this I am certain
that it is not founded upon that Generous & christian principal
of doing to others as we would that others should do unto
us —

Do not you want to see Boston;
I am fearfull of the small pox, or I should have been in before
this time. I got Mr Crane to go to our House & see what state
it was in, I find it has been occupied by one of the Doctors of
a Regiment, very dirty, but no other Damage has been done to
it — the few things which were left in it are all gone. Crank has
the key which he never delivered up, I have wrote to him for it
& am determined to get it cleaned as soon as posible & shut it
up — I look upon it a new acquisition of property, a property
which one month ago I did not value at a single Shilling, and
could with pleasure have seen it in flames —

The Town in General is left in
a better state than we expected, more oweing to a percipitate
flight than any regard to the inhabitants, tho some individuals
discoverd a sense of honour & justice & have left the rent of the
Houses in which they were, for the owners & the furniture
unhurt, or if damaged sufficent to make it good —
others have committed abominable Ravages —
The Mansion House of your President is safe
and the furniture unhurt whilst both

the House and furniture of the Solister General have fallen a prey to their own merciless party – Surely the very fiends feel a reverential awe for virtue & patriotism, whilst they Detest the paricide & traitor —

I feel very differently at the ap-proach of spring to what I did a month ago, we knew not then whether we could plant or sow with Safety, whether when we had toild we could reap the fruits of our own industery, whether we could rest in our own Cottages, or whether we should not be driven from the Sea coasts to seek shelter in the wilderness but now we feel as if we might sit under our own vine and eat the good of the land – I feel a gaieti de Coar to which before I was a stranger, I think the Sun looks brighter the birds sing more melodiously, & nature puts on a more chearfull countananice we feel a temporary peace, & the poor fugitives are returning to their deserted habitations

tho we felicitate ourselves, we sympa thize with those who are trembling least the Lot of Boston should be theirs – But they cannot be in Similar circumstances unless pusilanimity & cowardise should take possession of them – they have time & warning given them to see the Evil & shun it – I long to hear that you have de-clared an independancy – and by the way in the new Code of Laws which I suppose it will be necessary for you to make I desire you would Remember the Ladies, & be more generous & favourable to them than your ancestors do not put such unlimited power into the hands of the Husbands. Remember all Men would be tyrants if they could. if perticuliar care & attention is not paid to the Laidies we are determined to foment a Rebellion, and will not hold ourselves bound by any Laws in which we have no voice, or Representation – That your Sex are Naturally Tyrannical is a Truth so throughly established as to admit of no Dispute, but such of you as wish to be happy willingly give up the harsh title of Master for the more tender & endearing one of Friend why then not put it out of the power of the vicious & the

                                    with impunity
Law ^ less to use us with cruelty & indignitey Men of sense in all
Ages abhor those customs which treat us only as the vassals of your
Sex Regard us then as Beings placed by providence under your protection
& in immitation of the Supreme Being make use of that power
only for our happiness —

                              April 5

                    Not having an opportunity of sending
this I shall add a few lines more; tho not with a heart so gay
I have been attending the sick chamber of our neighbour Trott whose
affliction I most sensibly feel but cannot discribe, striped of two
lovely children in one week George the Eldest died on wedensday &
Billy the youngest on fryday — with the Canker fever, a terible
disorder so much like the throat distemper that it differs but little
from it — Betsy Cranch has been very bad, but upon the recovery,
Becky Peck they do not expect will live out the day — Many grown
persons are now sick with it, in this street 5 — it rages much in other
Towns — the Mumps too are very frequent, Isaac is now confined with
it — our own little flock are yet well. my Heart trembles with
anxiety for them, God preserve them, —
                                            I want to hear much
ofter from you than I do march 8 was the last date of any
that I have yet had — you inquire of whether I am making
Salt peter, I have not yet attempted it, but after soap making
believe I shall make the experiment, I find as much as I can
                                                        which
do to manufacture cloathing for my family who would else be
Naked — I know of but one person in this part of the Town who
has made any, that is mr Tertias Bass as he is called who has
got very near an hundred weight which has been found to be
very good — I have heard of some others in the other parishes
mr Reed of weymouth has been applied to, to go to Andover
to the mills which are now at work, & has gone — I have
lately seen a small manuscrip, describing the proportions for the
various sorts of powder, fitt for cannon small arms & pistols
    — if it would be of any service your way I will get it
transcribed & send it to you — every one of your friends send
their regards, and all the little ones — your Brothers youngest child
lies bad with convulsion fitts — adieu I need not say how much
I am your ever faithfull friend —
                                                        [A]

Braintree March 31 1776

I wish you would ever write me a Letter half as long as I write you; and tell me if you may where your Fleet are gone? What sort of Defence Virginia can make against our common Enemy? Whether it is so situated as to make an able Defence? Are not the Gentery Lords and the common people vassals, are they not like the uncivilized Natives Brittain represents us to be? I hope their Riffel Men who have shewen themselves very savage and even Blood thirsty; are not a specimen of the Generality of the people.

I am willing to allow the Colony great merit for having produced a Washington but they have been shamefully duped by a Dunmore.

I have sometimes been ready to think that the passion for Liberty cannot be Eaquelly Strong in the Breasts of those who have been accustomed to deprive their fellow Creatures of theirs. Of this I am certain that it is not founded upon that generous and christian principal of doing to others as we would that others should do unto us.

Do not you want to see Boston; I am fearfull of the small pox, or I should have been in before this time. I got Mr. Crane to go to our House and see what state it was in. I find it has been occupied by one of the Doctors of a Regiment, very dirty, but no other damage has been done to it. The few things which were left in it are all gone. Cranch has the key which he never deliverd up. I have wrote to him for it and am determined to get it cleand as soon as possible and shut it up. I look upon it a new acquisition of property, a property which one month ago I did not value at a single Shilling, and could with pleasure have seen it in flames.

The Town in General is left in a better state than we expected, more oweing to a percipitate flight than any Regard to the inhabitants, tho some individuals discoverd a sense of honour and justice and have left the rent of the Houses in which they were, for the owners and the furniture unhurt, or if damaged sufficent to make it good.

Others have committed abominable Ravages. The Mansion House of your President is safe and the furniture unhurt whilst both the House and Furniture of the Solisiter General have fallen a prey to their own merciless party. Surely the very Fiends feel a Reverential awe for Virtue and patriotism, whilst they Detest the paricide and traitor.

I feel very differently at the approach of spring to what I did a month ago. We knew not then whether we could plant or sow with safety, whether when we had toild we could reap the fruits of our own industery, whether we could rest in our own Cottages, or whether we should not be driven from the sea coasts to seek shelter in the wilderness, but now we feel as if we might sit under our own vine and eat the good of the land.

I feel a gaieti de Coar to which before I was a stranger. I think the Sun looks brighter, the Birds sing more melodiously, and Nature puts on a more chearfull countanance. We feel a temporary peace, and the poor fugitives are returning to their deserted habitations.

Tho we felicitate ourselves, we sympathize with those who are trembling least the Lot of Boston should be theirs. But they cannot be in similar circumstances unless pusilanimity and cowardise should take possession of them. They have time and warning given them to see the Evil and shun it. — I long to hear that you have declared an independency — and by the way in the new Code of Laws which I suppose it will be necessary for you to make I desire you would Remember the Ladies, and be more generous and favourable to them than your ancestors. Do not put such unlimited power into the hands of the Husbands. Remember all Men would be tyrants if they could. If perticuliar care and attention is not paid to the Laidies we are determined to foment a Rebelion, and will not hold ourselves bound by any Laws in which we have no voice, or Representation.

That your Sex are Naturally Tyrannical is a Truth so thoroughly established as to admit of no dispute, but such of you as wish to be happy willingly give up the harsh title of Master for the more tender and endearing one of Friend. Why then, not put it out of the power of the vicious and the Lawless to use us with cruelty and indignity with impunity. Men of Sense in all Ages abhor those customs which treat us only as the vassals of your Sex. Regard us then as Beings placed by providence under your protection and in immitation of the Supreem Being make use of that power only for our happiness.

April 5

Not having an opportunity of sending this I shall add a few lines more; tho not with a heart so gay. I have been attending the sick chamber of our Neighbour Trot whose affliction I most sensibly feel but cannot discribe, stripped of two lovely children in one week. Gorge the Eldest died on wednesday and Billy the youngest on fryday, with the Canker fever, a terible disorder so much like the throat distemper, that it differs but little from it. Betsy Cranch has been very bad, but upon the recovery. Becky Peck they do not expect will live out the day. Many grown persons are now sick with it, in this street 5. It rages much in other Towns. The Mumps too are very frequent. Isaac is now confined with it. Our own little flock are yet well. My Heart trembles with anxiety for them. God preserve them.

I want to hear much oftener from you than I do. March 8 was the last date of any that I have yet had. — You inquire of whether I am making Salt peter. I have not yet attempted it, but after Soap making believe I shall make the experiment. I find as much as I can do to manufacture cloathing for my family who which would else be Naked. I know of but one person in this part of the Town who has made any, that is Mr. Tertias Bass as he is calld who has got very near an hundred weight which has been found to be very good. I have heard of some others in the other parishes. Mr. Reed of Weymouth has been applied to, to go to Andover to the mills which are now at work, and has gone. I have lately seen a small Manuscrip describing the proportions for the various sorts of powder, fit for cannon, small arms and pistols. If it would be of any Service your way I will get it transcribed and send it to you. — Every one of your Friends send their Regards, and all the little ones. Your Brothers youngest child lies bad with convulsion fitts. Adieu. I need not say how much I am Your ever faithfull Friend.

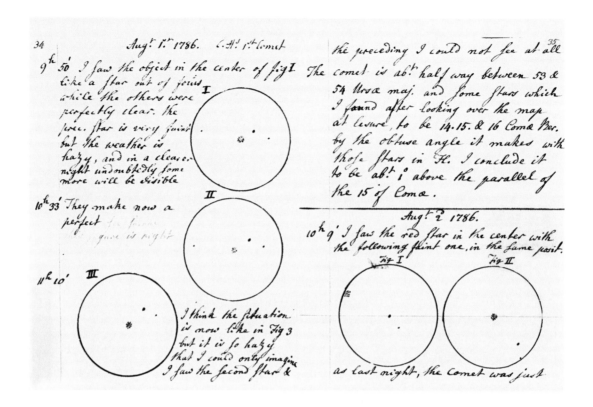

April 19th, 1790

Sir,

I am very unwilling to trouble you with incomplete observations, and for that reason did not acquaint you yesterday with the discovery of a comet. I wrote an account of it to Dr. Maskelyne and Mr. Aubert, in hopes that either of those gentlemen, or my brother, whom I expect every day to return, would have furnished me with the means of pointing it out in a proper manner.

But as perhaps several days might pass before I could have any answer to my letters, or my brother return, I would not wish to be thought neglectful, and therefore if you think, sir, the following description is sufficient, and that more of my brother's astronomical friends should be made acquainted with it, I should be very happy if you would be so kind as to do it for the sake of astronomy.

The comet is a little more than 3½° following α Andromedæ, and about 1½° above the parallel of that star. I saw it first on April 17th, 16h 24′ sidereal time, and the first view I could have of it last night was 16h 5′. As far as I am able to judge, it has decreased in P. D. nearly 1°, and increased in A. R. something above 1′.

These are only estimations from the field of view, and I only mention it to show that its motion is not so very rapid.

I am, &c.,
C.H.

CAROLINE HERSCHEL

Astronomer, 1750–1848
To Sir Joseph Banks, 19 April 1790

Caroline Herschel's introduction to Britain came when she left her native Hanover to join her older brother William, who had moved to Bath. Initially, both siblings planned to make their careers as musicians.

Caroline was the youngest of 10 children. In childhood, she almost died from typhoid, which left her blind in one eye and stunted her growth. Although her older siblings were given a good education, their mother Anna Herschel was adamant her youngest child should not be educated. Caroline was expected to take care of the house and her mother, and she was treated with contempt; this became worse with the death of her father, after which she was spoken to as if she were a servant.

William was 12 years older than Caroline. In 1766, he had moved to the UK, where he worked as a composer and musician. When Caroline arrived in Bath, at the age of 21, she spoke almost no English. She had been invited to run William's household, but he also gave her an education, coaching her in singing and mathematics. Soon she was appearing as a soprano in his concerts, and they started to work together on his hobby of astronomy and telescope design.

Caroline learned how to make telescopes and began to work on a new approach to mathematics and astronomy. In 1781, the siblings made history when they discovered the planet Uranus, which they initially named George, after the king. This brought William to the attention of King George III, who, in 1787, invited William Herschel to move to Windsor and become the King's Astronomer. This role provided him with a good salary and a pension, enabling him to give up music. Caroline was also employed by the king as William's assistant, making her the first woman to be paid for working as an astronomer.

Between 1783 and 1797, Caroline discovered three nebulae and eight comets. She also worked with Astronomer Royal Nevil Maskelyne at Greenwich, creating a catalogue of almost 3,000 stars, a work that has been an important reference for astronomers ever since.

Caroline Herschel discovered her first comet in August 1786 when William was away from home. She wrote to his friend Dr Blagden, 'last night … I found an object very much resembling in colour and brightness the 27 nebula of the Connoissance des Temps, with the difference, however, of being round. I suspected it to be a comet; but a haziness coming on, it was not possible to satisfy myself as to its motion till this evening.' She was the first woman to discover a comet. This letter to Sir Joseph Banks was also sent when her brother was away from home, on the date she discovered her third comet.

Throughout her long life, Caroline Herschel received significant awards usually given to men. At the age of 77, she was awarded a Gold Medal by the Astronomical Society, which gave her honorary membership. She was also made an honorary member of the Royal Irish Society, and the King of Prussia awarded her with a Gold Medal of Science. In the latter years of her life, she wrote her memoirs, before dying on 9 January 1848, at the age of 97.

Opposite Top Notes and drawings made by Caroline Herschel recording her discovery of a comet on 1 August 1786. This comet, now known as Comet C/1786 P1 (Herschel), was the first of eight comets she discovered.

ANNE LISTER

Diarist and activist, 1791–1840
To Eliza (schoolfriend and probable lover), 21 February 1808

In an age when a girl was expected to marry well and become the property and financial responsibility of her husband, Anne Lister broke all conventions. In her teens, she was suspended from school amid rumours of lesbianism. She continued to have lesbian relationships, and steadfastly refused to do what so many gay women of her era did – marry a man in order to become socially acceptable.

From the age of 15, Anne wrote extensive diaries, numbering almost 4 million words in total. She also wrote over 1,000 letters. In some of her earliest diary entries, she writes about her schoolfriend Eliza Raine, the recipient of this letter. They were pupils together at the Manor School in York, and Eliza appears to have been Anne's first love.

As a child, Anne was a regular visitor to her aunt and uncle, who lived in the Lister family's ancestral home, Shibden Hall in Yorkshire. As a young woman she moved in with them, and in 1826, following the death of her uncle, Anne took over the running of the estate. A decade later, following the deaths of her father and her aunt, Anne inherited Shibden Hall. She was so good at running the estate that she earned the respect of sceptical local landowners and became accepted as an intelligent and perspicacious businesswoman. Anne dressed in masculine clothing, always in black, and became known as 'Gentleman Jack'.

Anne was also a keen traveller, walker and mountaineer. Her love of travel had begun in 1819, when her aunt took her to Paris. It was to be the first journey of many, and Anne made regular overseas trips, defying convention by not travelling with a male guardian or chaperone. She lived her life just as she wanted to. Her diaries record her infatuations and love affairs with a number of women, including her two most significant lovers, Mariana Lawton and Ann Walker. With both women, Anne Lister went through an unofficial 'marriage' ceremony, and Ann Walker moved into Shibden Hall as her wife.

To keep her journal entries secret, Lister devised a code, which she called 'crypthand'. She created the code by combining her knowledge of ancient Greek and algebra, believing that no one else would ever be able to understand it. Many years after her death, however, in the 1890s, one of her family members, John Lister, who had inherited Shibden Hall, cracked the code and read her diaries. He was so worried about what would happen if they were made public that he concealed them behind a panel. They would not be discovered and deciphered again for many years to come.

Anne Lister's final journey was made to the Caucasus Mountains, travelling with Ann Walker. After contracting a fever seemingly from an infected insect bite, Lister died in Georgia. It took several months for her body to be sent back to Yorkshire. Today, Anne Lister's writing is considered so important to social history that in 2011 her diaries were added to the UNESCO Memory of the World register, an initiative to safeguard the world's documentary heritage.

Opposite Shibden Hall, West Yorkshire, home to the wealthy Lister family from the early seventeenth century.

Halifax – Sunday February 21st 1808

My dear Eliza,

      I shall begin with telling you that I cannot say much this week however I will not waste time in making apologies therefore to proceed – I thank you much for your last long letter which I wish it were in my power to answer more worthily but such pleasure I trust will not always be out of my reach and it has been of late the idea of seeing you so soon can alone reconcile me to it but in this most comfortable thought I find every needful consolation. I am glad that you esteem yourself so happily situated and equally so that you think me as affectionate as ever. I assure you Eliza I am very steady in my attachments and though not deemed of an affectionate disposition I feel that I can be strongly attached to my dear and kind friend ER – you still give an unfavourable account of your health indeed I cannot get the better of a thousand fears concerning you nor can I forget that tender yet painful anxiety which is to me the greatest proof how much I love you but I see it is in vain to tell you of my solicitude since you are so surrounded with gaiety that you have not time to think of your own complaints much less of those of your friend – I daresay WL is in no very great hurry for the worsteds but when I see her I will mention what you say. I have not heard my Mother speak of going Weighton in March. You make good resolves concerning your studies and I hope have as good a mind to keep them. You have had your share of Valentines. I had one, from whom I cannot guess, in singularity somewhat like one of yours I think. I shall have time to give you a copy of it.

I know nothing more dismal than the tolling of a death-bell therefore do not wonder that it should almost incline you to melancholy but, pleasing thought! if we live well we may joyfully expect death that will make to cease all care and trouble. Good night my dear friend and may you not wound the heart of that one to whom every pleasure is imperfect which Eliza does not share.

L

N.B.

For your information I give you a translation of the two Latin ornaments of my Valentine.

Latet anguis in herbâ – Deep in the grass the wary snake has hid.

Contra quam sentis solet Ironia jocari

You see against whom Irony is wont to joke.

Contra quam sentis solet Ironia jocari

All hail! Thou beauteous charming fair

Whose great designs thy noble mind declare

Permit a poet make in humble lays

To sing to thee an amazonian praise

With thy great* Drum oh! lead thy troops to war

And let its dreadful sound be heard afar

Thy needle distaff, puddings, and thy pies

Thy much liked cheesecakes and thy curds despise

Let nobler objects emulate thy mind

By grammar rules and classic laws refin'd

Let great Maeonedes with sounding lyre

Or softer Virgil all thy thoughts inspire

In thy charm'd soul let fam'd Anacreon sing

Or Roman Horace touch the lyre string

With these acquirements thou wilt lovers gain

And future ages shall immortalize thy name.   Eugenio

*Alluding to my beating the Drum which you will recollect that I sometimes used to do.

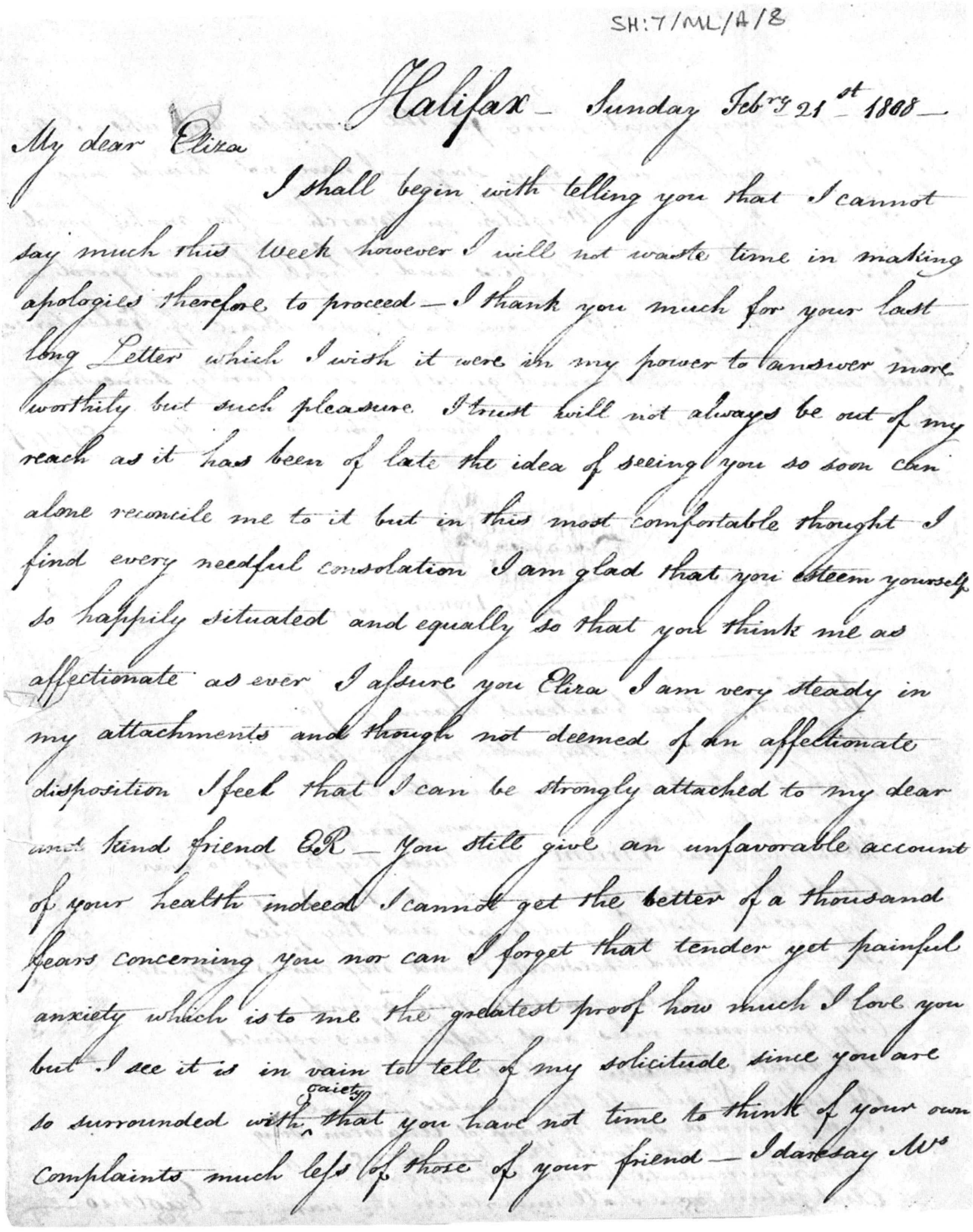

SH:7/ML/A/8

Halifax – Sunday Feb'y 21st 1808 –

My dear Eliza

I shall begin with telling you that I cannot say much this week however I will not waste time in making apologies therefore to proceed – I thank you much for your last long Letter which I wish it were in my power to answer more worthily but such pleasure I trust will not always be out of my reach as it has been of late the idea of seeing you so soon can alone reconcile me to it but in this most comfortable thought I find every needful consolation I am glad that you esteem yourself so happily situated and equally so that you think me as affectionate as ever I assure you Eliza I am very steady in my attachments and though not deemed of an affectionate disposition I feel that I can be strongly attached to my dear and kind friend ER – You still give an unfavorable account of your health indeed I cannot get the better of a thousand fears concerning you nor can I forget that tender yet painful anxiety which is to me the greatest proof how much I love you but I see it is in vain to tell of my solicitude since you are so surrounded with gaiety that you have not time to think of your own complaints much less of those of your friend – I daresay Mrs

41

L is in no very great hurry for the worsteds but when I se
her I will mention what you say — I have not heard my
Mother speak of going Weighton in March — You make good
resolves concerning your studies and I hope have as good a
mind to keep them — You have had your share of Valentin
I had one, from whom I cannot guess, in singularity somewhat
like one of yours I think I shall have time to give you a copy
it —

Contra quam sentis solet Ironia Jocari

All hail! thou beauteous charming fair
Whose great designs thy noble mind declare
Permit a poet male in humble lays
To sing to thee an amazonian praise
With thy great *Drum oh! lead thy troops to war
And let its dreadful sound be heard afar
Thy needle, distaff, puddings, and thy pies
Thy much liked cheesecakes and thy curds despise
Let nobler objects emulate thy mind
By grammar rules and classic laws refin'd
Let great Maonedes with sounding lyre
Of softer Virgil all thy thoughts inspire
In thy charm'd soul let fam'd Anacreon sing
Or Roman Horace touch the lyric string
With these acquirements thou wilt lovers gain
And future ages shall immortalize thy name — Eugenio —

* Alluding to my beating the Drum which
You will recollect that I sometimes used

I know nothing more dismal than the tolling of a death-bell & therefore do not wonder that it should almost incline you to melancholy but, pleasing thought! if we live well we may joyfully expect death that will make to cease all care and trouble — Good night my dear friend and may you not wound the heart of that one to whom every pleasure is imperfect which Eliza does not share

L

N.B. For your information I give you a translation of the two Latin ornaments of my Valentine —

Latet anguis in herbâ — Deep in the grass the wary snake lies hid.

Contra quam sentis solet Ironia jocari

You see against whom Irony is wont to joke ——

My dearest Frank!

Behold me going to write you as handsome a Letter
as I can. Wish me good luck. — We have had the pleasure of hearing
of you lately through Mary, who sent us some of the particulars of
Yours of June 18th (I think) written off Rugen, & we enter into the
delight of your having so good a Pilot. — Why are you like Queen
Eliz.th? — Because you know how to chuse wise Ministers. — Does not
this prove you as great a Captain as she was a Queen? — This may
serve as a riddle for you to put forth among your Officers, by way
of increasing your proper consequence. — It must be real enjoyment
to you, since you are obliged to leave England, to be where you are,
seeing something of a new Country, & one that has been so distinguished
as Sweden. — You must have great pleasure in it. I hope you may
have gone to Carlscroon. — Your Profession has it's douceurs to re-
-compence for some of it's Privations; — to an enquiring & observing
Mind like yours, such douceurs must be considerable. — Gustavus
Vasa, & Charles 12th, & Christina, & Linneus — do their Ghosts arise
up before you? — I have a great respect for former Sweden. So
Zealous as it was for Protestantism! And I have always fancied
it more like England than many Countries; — & according to the
Map, many of the names have strong resemblance to the English.
July begins unpleasantly with us, cold & showery, but it is often
a baddish month. We had some fine dry weather preceeding it,
which was very acceptable to the Holders of Hay & the Masters of
Meadows. — In general it must have been a good Haymaking Season.
Edward has got in all his, in excellent order; I speak only of Chawton;

JANE AUSTEN

Author, 1775–1817
To Frank Austen, 3 July 1813

Jane Austen was born a few days before Christmas in 1775, in the Steventon Parsonage in Hampshire, England. She was the seventh child in a family of eight children. Their father was a clergyman, the Reverend George Austen, while their mother Cassandra (née Leigh) was from an aristocratic family. This family background set the scene for so many of Jane Austen's novels, drawing upon the world she lived in, understood and observed so keenly.

Jane began writing as a child, crafting her novels throughout her teens and twenties, although she was not published until 1811, the year she turned 36. Her family and their acquaintances inspired many of her fictional characters and plots. Her brother Edward was adopted by a very wealthy couple, the Knights, whose fortune he inherited, while her other brothers followed their father into the Church or joined the navy, while Jane maintained a very close relationship with her only sister, Cassandra. All these careers and relationships are echoed in her books.

When the Reverend George Austen retired, the family moved to Bath, a place that has become synonymous with the name Jane Austen, featuring in several of her novels. Bath, however, was not Jane's favourite place. It was a difficult time in her life, coping with her father's increasingly fragile health, which allowed her very little writing time. Following Reverend Austen's death in 1805, Jane, her sister Cassandra and their mother struggled financially until Jane's brothers provided an income for the three of them. The Austen women left Bath, together with their friend Martha Lloyd, and lived for a while in the port city of Southampton, before settling in Chawton in Hampshire, close to Jane's wealthiest brother, Edward Austen Knight.

It was while living at Chawton Cottage that Jane Austen completed the six novels for which she is best remembered. Initially, her writing was kept a close family secret as writing was considered an unseemly occupation for a genteel woman. Mrs Austen, Cassandra and Martha took on the bulk of the household tasks, thereby allowing Jane ample writing time. The room in which Jane wrote was entered through an outer and then an inner door, and the hinges of the outer door were purposefully left unoiled so that they would squeak to warn Jane of any approaching visitors, giving her time to conceal her manuscript before they entered.

The first four of Austen's novels, *Sense and Sensibility* (1811), *Pride and Prejudice* (1813), *Mansfield Park* (1814) and *Emma* (1815), were published during her lifetime. She wrote this letter to her brother Frank in the year her second novel was published, mentioning the money she has started earning from her books. The letter shows how little she imagined the sensational fame she and her books would attain, with her comment about whether copyright of her books 'sh[ould] ever be of any value'.

After Jane Austen's death at the age of 41, her brother Henry ensured that *Persuasion* and *Northanger Abbey* were published. She also left behind unfinished works and juvenilia, including *Sanditon* and *Lady Susan*.

Chawton July 3[r]d 1813

My dearest Frank,

Behold me going to write you as handsome a Letter as I can. Wish me good luck. – We have had the pleasure of hearing of you lately through Mary, who sent us some of the particulars of Yours of June 18th (I think) written off Rugen, & we enter into the delight of your having so good a Pilot. – Why are you like Queen Eliz[abeth]? – Because you know how to chuse wise Ministers. – Does not this prove you as great a Captain as she was a Queen? – This may serve as a Riddle for you to put forth among your Officers, by way of increasing your proper consequence. – It must be real enjoyment to you, since you are obliged to leave England, to be where you are, seeing something of a new Country, & one that has been so distinguished as Sweden. – You must have great pleasure in it. – I hope you may have gone to Carlscisen. – Your Profession has its douceurs to recompense for some of its Privations. – to an enquiring & observing Mind like yours, such douceurs must be considerable. – Gustavus Vaza, & Charles 12th & Christiana, & Linneus – do their Ghosts rise up before you? – I have a great respect for former Sweden. So Zealous as it was for Protestanism! – And I have always fancied it more like England than many Countries; – & according to the Map, many of the names have a strong resemblance to the English. July begins unpleasantly with us, cold & showery, but it is often a baddish month. We had some fine days weather preceding it, which was very acceptable – to the Holders of Hay & the Master of Meadows. – In general it must have been a good Haymaking Season. Edward has got in all his, in excellent order; I speak only of Chawton;

[Interlined and upside down]

You will be glad to hear that every Copy of S[ense] & S[ensibility] is sold & that it has brought me £140 – besides the Copy right, if that sh[ould] ever be of any value. – I have now therefore written myself into £250. – which only makes me long for more. – I have something in hand – which I hope on the credit of P[ride] & P[rejudice] will sell well, tho' not half so entertaining, and by the bye – shall you object to my mentioning the Elephant in it, & two or three others of your old Ships? – I have done it, but it shall not stay, to make you angry. – They are only just mentioned.

but here he has had better luck than Mr Middleton ever had in the 5 years that he was Tenant. Good encouragement for him to come again; & I really hope he will do so another Year. – The pleasure to us of having them here is so great, that if we were not the best creatures in the world we should not deserve it. – We go on in the most comfortable way, very frequently dining together, & always meeting in some part of every day. – Edward is very well & enjoys himself as thoroughly as any Hampshire born Austen can desire. Chawton is not thrown away upon him. – He talks of making a new Garden; the present is a bad one & ill situated, near Mr Papillon's; – he means to have the new, at the top of the Lawn behind his own house. – We like to have him proving & strengthening his attachment to the place by making it better. – He will soon have all his Children about him, Edward, George & Charles are collected already, & another week brings Henry & William. – It is the custom at Winchester for Georges to come away a fortnight before the Holidays, when they are not to return any more; for fear they should over study themselves just at last, I suppose. – Really it is a piece of dishonourable accommodation to the Master. – We are in hopes of another visit from our own true, lawful Henry very soon, he is to be our Guest this time. – He is quite well I am happy to say, & does not leave it to my pen I am sure to communicate to you the joyful news of his being Deputy Receiver no longer. – It is a promotion which he thoroughly enjoys, as well he may; the work of his own mind. – He sends you all his own plans of course. – The scheme for Scotland we think an excellent one both for himself & his nephew. – Upon the whole his Spirits are very much recovered. – If I may so express myself, his mind is not a mind for affliction. He is too Busy, too active, too sanguine. – Sincerely as he was attached to poor Eliza moreover, & excellently as he behaved to her, he was always so used to be away from her at times, that her Loss is not felt as that of many a beloved wife might be, especially when all the circumstances of her long & dreadful Illness are taken into the account. – He very long knew that she must die, & it was indeed a release at last. – Our mourning for her is not over, or we should now be putting it on again for Mr Tho[mas] Leigh – the respectable, worthy, clever, agreable Mr Tho[mas] Leigh, who has just closed a good life at the age of 79, & must have died the possessor of one of the finest Estates in England & of more worthless Nephews & Neices than any other private Man in the united Kingdoms. – We are very anxious to know who will have the Living of Adlestrop, & where his excellent Sister will find a home for the remainder of her days. As yet she bears his Loss with fortitude, but she has always seemed so wrapt up in him, that I fear she must feel it very dreadfully when the fever of Business is over. – There is another female sufferer on the occasion to be pitied. Poor Mrs L.P. – who would now have been Mistress of Stenleigh had there been none of that vile compromise, which in good truth has never been allowed to be of much use to them. – It will be a hard trial. – Charles's little girls were with us about a month, & had so endeared themselves that we were quite sorry to have them go. We have the pleasure however of hearing that they are thought very much improved at home – Harriet in health, Cassy in manners. The latter ought to be a very nice Child – Nature has done enough for her – but Method has been wanting:- we thought her very much improved ourselves, but to have Papa & Mama think her so too was very essential to our contentment. – She will really be a very pleasing Child, if they will only exert themselves a little. – Harriet is a truely sweet-tempered little Darling. – They are now all at Southend together. – Why do I mention that? – As if Charles did not write himself. – I hate to be spending my time so needlessly, encroaching too upon the rights of others. – I wonder whether you happened to see Mr Blackall's marriage in the Papers last Jan[uary]. We did. He was married at Clifton to a Miss Lewis, whose Father had been late of Antigua. I should very much like to know what sort of a woman she is. He was a piece of Perfection, noisy Perfection himself which I always recollect with regard. – We had noticed a few months before his succeeding to a College Living, the very Living which we remembered his talking of & wishing for, an exceeding good one, Great Cadbury in Somersetshire. – I would wish Miss Lewis to be of a silent turn & rather ignorant, but naturally intelligent & wishing to learn; – fond of cold veal pies, green tea in the afternoon, & a green window blind at night.

July 6. –

Now my dearest Frank I will finish my Letter. I have kept it open on the chance of what a Tuesday's post might furnish in addition, & it furnishes the likelihood of our keeping our Neighbours at the G[reat] House some weeks longer than we had expected. – Mr Scudamore, to whom my Brother referred, is very decided as to Gm not being fit to be inhabited at present; – he talks even of two months more being necessary to sweeten it, but if we have warm weather I dare say less will do. – My Brother will probably go down. sniff at it himself & receive his Rents. – The Rent day has been postponed already. – We shall be gainers by their stay, but the young people in general are disappointed, & therefore we c[ould] wish it otherwise. – Our Cousins Col[onel] Tho[mas] Austen & Margaretta are going Aid-de-camps to Ireland & Lord Whitworth goes in their Train as Lord Lieutenant; good appointments for each. – God bless you. – I hope you continue beautiful – & brush your hair, but not all off. – We join in an infinity of Love. – Y[ours] very affec[tionately]

Jane Austen

Capt[ain] Austen
HMS. Elephant
Baltic

MARY ANNING

Palaeontologist, 1799–1847
To Sir Henry Bunbury, 26 December 1823

Mary Anning lived her entire life in the seaside town of Lyme Regis in Dorset, south-west England. The area has since become a prime destination for fossil hunters and is proudly named 'The Jurassic Coast'. That fame is largely due to Mary Anning and her discoveries.

Mary and her older brother Joseph were the only surviving children in what should have been a large family. Their father Richard was a cabinet maker, but in his spare time his passion was collecting fossils, which he sold to supplement his income. Richard took both his children on fossil-hunting trips, inspiring in Mary a passion for palaeontology from a young age. He taught her how to recognise, collect and clean fossils, lessons which would prove invaluable in her career. Richard died very suddenly of tuberculosis in 1810, leaving his wife Molly and their children in financial trouble. Joseph started working and Mary sold her collection of fossils to pay their debtors.

Anning had little formal education, but she was literate and her love of palaeontology encouraged her to read books about the natural sciences. She was also good at drawing, able to make detailed sketches of the fossils she discovered. Shortly after their father's death, Joseph found a strange fossil on the beach. Mary, aged 12, spent months carefully uncovering what turned out to be a full skeleton, over five metres in length. This entirely new species was later named *Ichthyosaurus*. A few years later, Mary also discovered the first complete skeleton of a *Plesiosaurus*; some years after that, she discovered the first pterodactyl. These finds were so unlike anything that had been uncovered before, that they were widely dismissed as fakes, not least because they had been discovered by a young woman.

For years, Mary Anning battled with hostility, opposition and accusations of fakery from male scientists. She was denied access to the Geological Society and her work and discoveries were repeatedly dismissed or denied. As this letter to the aristocratic historian Sir Henry Bunbury demonstrates, Anning's fossils were eagerly bought up by the scientific community, yet all the while the men who wrote to her to purchase them refused to admit her into their inner circle. Despite this hostility, Mary continued to make and record remarkable finds and her reputation slowly grew. Her breakthrough into the scientific world came when French scientist Georges Cuvier announced that her *Plesiosaurus* was genuine. However, she gained little fame during her lifetime. Only after her death would she be recognised as a world authority on fossils and coprolites (fossilised poo), the study of which she brought to prominence.

Anning struggled financially for most of her life, never earning the great rewards a male palaeontologist of the same calibre would have gained. In 1838, she was awarded an annuity by the British Association for the Advancement of Science, which helped her during the final years of her life when she was suffering from breast cancer. She died in 1847, a few weeks before her 48th birthday. In her lifetime, museums proudly displayed her finds without crediting her at all. Today, museums all over the globe benefit from her discoveries, and now they all acknowledge the name of Mary Anning.

Opposite Erosion along the Dorset coastline has exposed rocks dating back 180 million years, revealing a wide range of fossils.

[sketch]

scale one inch to each foote

Sir

I have endeavoured in a rough sketch to give you some idea of what it is like. Sir you understood me right in thinking that I said it was the supposed plesiosaurus, but its remarkable long neck and small head shows that it does not in the least verifie their conjecturs; in its analogy to the Ichthyosaurus it is large and heavy but one thing I may venture to assure you it is the first and only one discovered in Europe, Colonel Birch offered one hundred guineas for it unseen, but your letter came one days post before but I consider your claim to an answer prior to his. Should you like it the price I ask for it is one hundred and ten pounds. One hundred guineas was my intended price, but if [I] take the same sum as Col B is offering he would think I had used him ill in not taking his money. Sir I am gratefully obliged to both you & Dr Bunbry for condescending to think of my favourite. He returned to Lyme at midnight quite well. I [am] also greatly obliged for your kind present of the game.

Your most humble servant
Mary Anning

Lyme, December 26 1823

P.S. Sir since I wrote the above I have received an order from the Duke of Buckingham if not sold to send him the specimen on his account. I hope you will not think me impertinent in requesting an answer by return of post I had forgot the Ichthyosaurus it is about four feete long although Not equal to C[aptain] Warrings it is not a bad specimen. The price is five pounds.

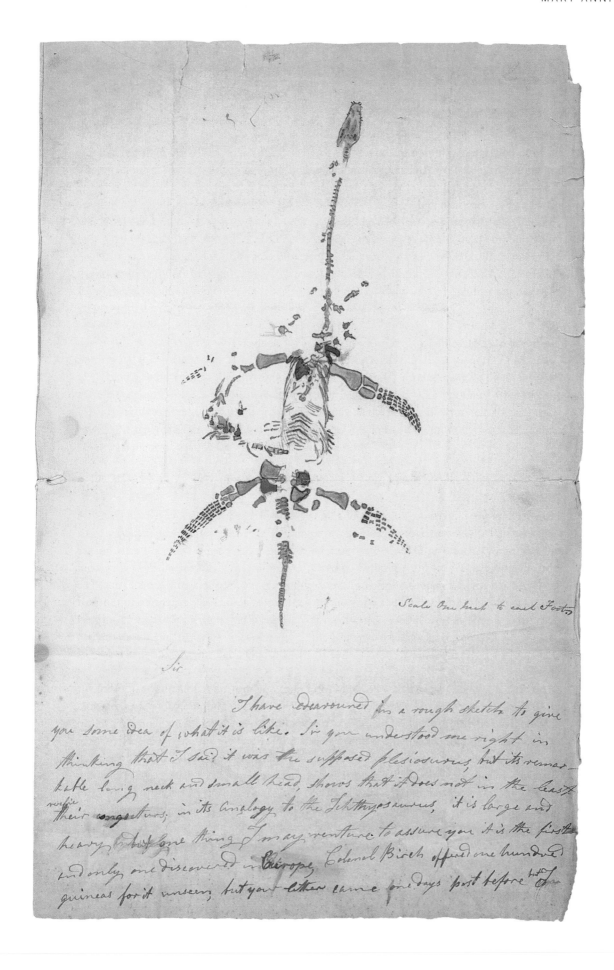

Scale One Inch to each Foot

Sir

I have endeavoured for a rough sketch to give you some idea of what it is like. Sir you understood me right in thinking that I said it was the supposed plesiosaurus, but its remarkable long neck and small head, shows that it does not in the least verifie their conjectures, in its analogy to the Ichthyosaurus, it is large and heavy, but one thing I may venture to assure you it is the first and only one discovered in Europe, Colonel Birch offered one hundred guineas for it unseen, but your letter came five days post before

MANUELA SÁENZ

Revolutionary, 1797–1856
To Simón Bolívar, 16 June 1824

Manuela Sáenz de Vergara y Aizpuru was born in Quito, Ecuador, which was then part of the Spanish Empire. Her father was a Spanish nobleman and her mother was his young mistress. Manuela grew up to live an unconventional life as a revolutionary, with her marriage to a wealthy English merchant being the only socially acceptable aspect of it.

Manuela's marriage in 1817 was a strategic one. It was socially advantageous, giving her access to many influential and politically engaged men who shared military secrets about the ongoing revolution against the Spanish. She was already radicalised and living outside social norms, having left her husband to travel back to Quito, when she met Simón Bolívar, who in 1819 had taken part in the successful liberation of New Granada.

The attraction between the two was instant and powerful, as evidenced in the letters they almost immediately began to exchange, many of which were preserved by Manuela herself, who became an archivist for the revolution. It is worth noting that, as with all translated texts, something is lost in translation. Although the erudition and erotic charge of the words is evident, what is lost is the deliberate use of both the formal and the intimate second-person pronouns, which allows for both Manuela's physical passion for her 'darling Simón' and for her admiration and respect for 'His Excellency, My Dear Sir'. In this letter, she plays with the notion that Bolívar the lover might have a rival in her 'love of independence'.

Bolívar and Sáenz were often separated – hence the many letters – but she was always on his side, and on more than one occasion she saved his life, earning her title 'Liberator of the Liberator'. She fought and won her own battles and quelled a mutiny in Quito, wearing military uniform for the first time – a colonel's uniform, in public and on the battlefield. She also went to war to win men's minds, fighting for women's rights through a series of polemical pamphlets.

Manuela's role in the wars of independence was honoured with the Order of the Sun, and she initially remained politically active after Bolívar's death in 1830. However, Bolívar's star was waning, and she was exiled to Jamaica from the newly established republic of New Granada by President Santander, a former ally of Bolívar turned bitter rival. On attempting to return to Ecuador in 1835, her papers were revoked, so she took refuge in Peru, in the coastal town of Paita, where the whale hunters would anchor and where *Moby Dick* author Hermann Melville sought her out in 1841.

Manuela Sáenz died in poverty in 1856, in a house where the termite-ridden stairs had collapsed and disabled her. She was buried in a pauper's grave. Her name was resurrected in 1989 by Gabriel García Márquez's novel *The General in His Labyrinth*. In 2010, some of the earth from the pauper's grave was taken to Venezuela, where it was interred alongside Bolívar in the National Pantheon in Caracas.

Opposite Top A Venezuelan military cadet carries the symbolic remains of Manuela Sáenz during her ceremonial reinterment in Caracas in 2010.

Huamachuco, 16 June, 1824
To His Excellency the Liberator Simón Bolívar

My darling Simón,

My love:

The adverse conditions that will appear on the road in the campaign that you intend to wage, they do not intimidate me as a woman. Quite the reverse, I defy them! What must you think of me! You have always told me that I have more trousers than any of your officers. Is that not so? I tell you from my heart: you will not have a more loyal comrade than me and not a single complaint will pass my lips to make you regret your decision to take me on.

Will you take me with you? Well here I come. This is not a reckless state, but one made from courage and from the love of independence (don't be jealous).

Yours always,

Manuela Sáenz

Will send down to the S… before tomorrow evening, Brookes's formulae & also the Reports of the Royal Society on your machine. I suppose you can get it easily, and I particularly want to see it, before I see you on Wed [nesday] mor[ning].

It appears to me that I am working up the notes with much success; and that even if the book be delayed in its publication, a week or two, in consequence, it would be worth Mr Taylor's while to wait. I will have it well & fully done; or not at all.

I want to put in something about Bernoulli's numbers, in one of my notes, as an example of how an implicit function may be worked out by the engine, without having been worked out by human head and hands first. Give me the necessary data and formulae.

Yours …
A.A.L

ADA LOVELACE

Mathematician and pioneer of computing , 1815–1852
To Charles Babbage, 2 May 1842

Augusta Ada Byron was the daughter of Lady Annabela Byron (née Milbanke) and the poet Lord Byron. Her parents separated when Ada was a few weeks old, and her estranged father died when she was eight. Lady Byron was a keen mathematician, so she employed the mathematician Mary Fairfax Somerville to tutor her daughter.

In June of 1833, when Ada was 17 years old, she attended a party in London, at which Mary Fairfax Somerville introduced her to fellow mathematician, and inventor, Charles Babbage. He was a fellow of the Royal Society and working at the time on what he called his 'Difference Engine', which has become known today as the very first design for a mechanical computer. Soon, Babbage was asking Ada to work with him on two of his ideas for calculating machines: the Difference Engine and the Analytical Engine, a fully programmable computer. This more ambitious machine was to inspire the work for which Ada Lovelace is most famous today.

In 1835, Ada married William King (the first Earl of Lovelace), and her work was necessarily interrupted by the births of their three children (between 1836 and 1839). When she returned to her work, Ada continued to expand on Babbage's research. Babbage had recently given a demonstration of his work in Turin, Italy, after which the scientist Luigi Meabrea had published a paper about Babbage's Analytical Engine. In the early 1840s, Ada translated Luigi Menabrea's work into English, working with Babbage and from her own knowledge to expand on the subject. Her paper, which included the very first published algorithm, appeared in Taylor's *Scientific Memoirs* in August of 1843. The author was identified only as 'A.A.L.'.

Babbage was determined that Ada should not be barred from further education because of her sex. In 1843, he wrote to the scientist Michael Faraday that Ada had 'thrown her magical spell around the most abstract of Sciences and has grasped it with a force which few masculine intellects (in our own country at least) could have exerted over it'. Although British women were not yet permitted a tertiary education, Babbage arranged for Ada to be taught by Augustus De Morgan (father of the designer William De Morgan) at the University of London. In 1844, De Morgan wrote to Lady Byron that Ada possessed a 'power of thinking ... utterly out of the common way for any beginner, man or woman'.

Ada understood mathematics and its wider implications in a way that few people of her era did. She predicted that, in the future, machines inspired by Babbage's engines would have applications in the wider world, not only in mathematics. Ada understood that computers could be programmed to follow instructions – she foresaw the computer age and created the concept of what today is known as software.

Although her work was forgotten for decades, in the mid-twentieth century her contribution to computing finally started to be recognised. In the 1980s, the US government named a new computer language 'Ada' in her honour. In 2009, Ada Lovelace Day (the second Tuesday in October) was founded as an annual celebration honouring women in STEM.

GEORGE ELIOT

Author, 1819–1880

To Mary Sibree, 10 May 1847

Mary Ann Evans was born in Nuneaton, Warwickshire, and sent to boarding school at the age of five. Although she loved reading and fell in love with the study of history, the young Mary Ann, who was very religious, did not agree with reading novels. Ironically, in later life she would join the ranks of Britain's most well-respected novelists.

Mary Ann left school at the age of 16 when her mother died. She became her father's housekeeper and they moved to Foleshill, near Coventry. It was while living in Foleshill that wrote this letter to her friend Mary Sibree. In her new life, Mary Ann began to meet and make friends with freethinkers, and she began to question her religious faith. This loss of faith – something she mourned and analysed frequently in her novels – led her father to threaten to turn her out of the house. She agreed to keep attending church with him even though she no longer believed.

When her father died, Mary Ann was 30 years old. Suddenly liberated, she travelled to Switzerland with friends, and decided to stay for several months. On returning to England, in 1850, she moved to London, where she lived with the publisher John Chapman and his wife, working as an editor for Chapman. Through this new circle of friends, she met and fell in love with the literary critic George Henry Lewes, who was separated from his wife. They set up home together. While living in Warwickshire, Mary Ann had written several religion-themed books, but in her new life in London, she was inspired to write fiction, and Lewes encouraged this ambition.

Fearing her private life would be made public if she published under her own name, Mary Ann chose the male pseudonym of George Eliot. In 1858, she published her first fictional book, *Scenes of Clerical Life*, a collection of short stories she had previously published in *Blackwood's Magazine*. Charles Dickens wrote 'George Eliot' a fan letter, in which he expressed not only his admiration but his belief that the author was a woman. In his capacity as magazine editor, Dickens spent several years unsuccessfully trying to persuade her to let him to serialise one of her novels.

George Eliot's first novel, *Adam Bede*, was published in 1859. She published seven novels between 1859 and 1876, including *The Mill on the Floss*, *Middlemarch* and *Daniel Deronda*. She also wrote poetry. By the end of her life, George Eliot was considered one of Britain's greatest living novelists. Her realist works portrayed psychologically complex characters, combining detailed observation with sharp social commentary.

In 1880, two years after the death of George Henry Lewes, Mary Ann married the banker John Cross. Instead of conferring respectability on a woman who had previously lived 'in sin' with her lover, this marriage was also considered scandalous, as John Cross was 21 years younger than Mary Ann. Just seven months after their wedding, at the age of 61, Mary Ann Cross died from kidney disease. Despite her great fame, she was not buried at Poets' Corner in Westminster Abbey because her love life was deemed too scandalous – though this was not something that had prevented male writers from being buried there. Instead, Mary Ann Cross was buried in Highgate Cemetery in North London. On the centenary of her death, in 1980, 'George Eliot/Mary Ann Evans' was finally given a memorial stone in Poets' Corner.

Foleshill, Thursday

My dear Mary,

     I obtained your direction from Mrs. Sibree this morning that I might express my regret to you for having failed in sending 'Past and Present'. I did really get the book on the very day I promised to do so, but the next day my amazing faculty of forgetting together with a bad headache made me quite oblivious of the whole affair. This is no excuse, but it is something to be penitent – "Who with repentance is not satisfied is not of heaven, nor earth". So says Shakespeare, & as I am very sure that you are composed of some of the earth's best mould, I am not afraid that you will withhold your forgiveness. I am so sorry that Mr. Sibree has missed the opportunity of having that thrilling book, while he is at leisure & (I am sorry to hear) an invalid. Pray tell him that it is still at his service when he comes home.

     Clifton must look lovely under these smiling skies. I hope you are drinking in all kinds of profit & pleasure, & will remember everything to tell me when we are tête à tête. You are missing nothing good except Mr. Macdonald's lectures. He gave one last evening on Self-educated men, & there is to be a second this evening on the State of society. This is no caviare however, but very simple food, and I dare say you are getting much better where you are. Farewell until you come like a rosy beam of morning to smile on me in my study. In a hurry as usual,

                                Thine,

                                 Mary Ann Evans

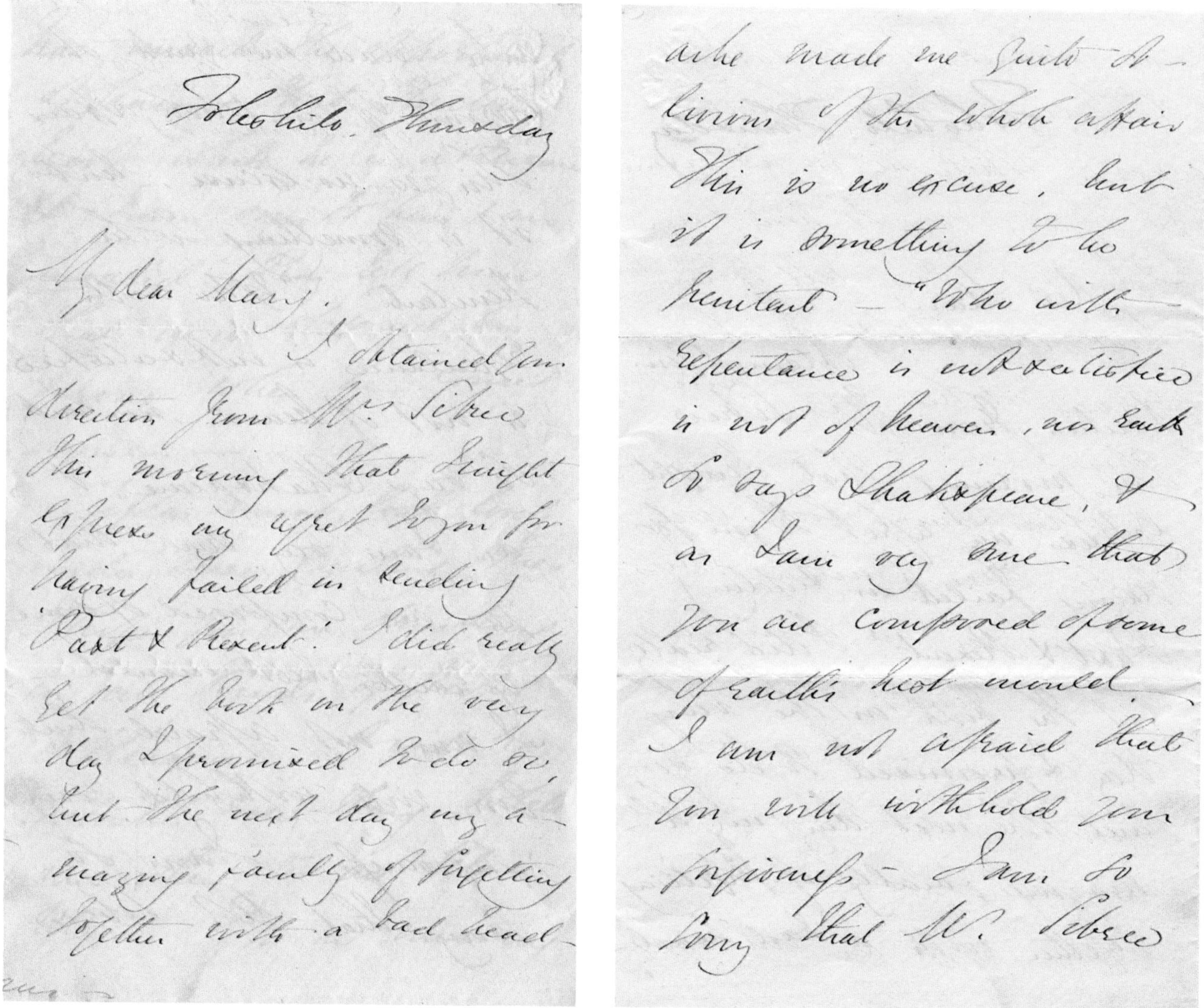

Foleshill. Thursday

My dear Mary,

I obtained your direction from Mrs Pears this morning that I might express my regret to you for having failed in sending 'Past & Present'. I did really get the book on the very day I promised to do so, but the next day my amazing faculty of forgetting together with a bad head-ache made me quite oblivious of the whole affair. This is no excuse, but it is something to be penitent — "Who with repentance is not satisfied is not of heaven, nor earth" so says Shakespeare, & as I am very sure that you are composed of some of earth's best mould. I am not afraid that you will withhold your forgiveness — I am so sorry that Mr. Pears

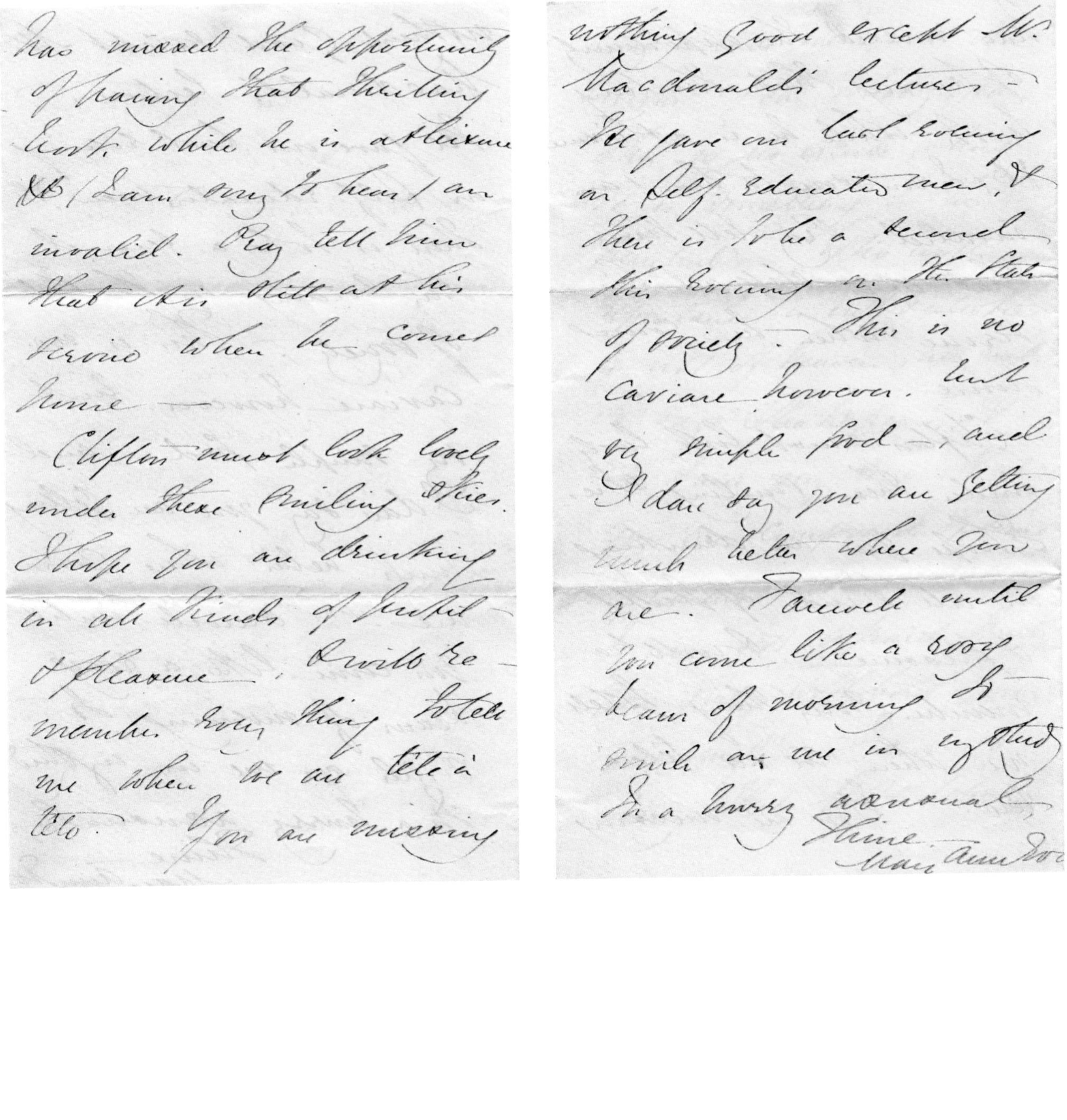

has missed the opportunity
of hearing that thrilling
cost. While he is at leisure
&c. I am sorry to hear I am
invalid. Pray tell him
that it is still at his
service when he comes
home —

Clifton must look lovely
under these smiling skies.
I hope you are drinking
in all kinds of useful
& pleasure. I will re-
member everything to tell
me when we are tête à
tête. You are missing

nothing good except Mr.
Macdonald's lectures —
He gave one last evening
on Self-Educated men, &
there is to be a second
this evening on the State
of Society. This is no
Caviare, however, but
very simple food — and
I dare say you are getting
much better where you
are. Farewell until
you come like a rosy
beam of morning to
smile on me in my study
In a hurry as usual,
thine,
Marian Evans

CHARLOTTE BRONTË

Author, 1816–1855
Letter to W.S. Williams, 25 December 1848

Charlotte Brontë was the third of six children born to the Reverend Patrick Brontë and his wife Maria. The Brontë children grew up in Haworth, a town on the Yorkshire Moors, where their father was the vicar. The family was haunted by tragedy from the time their mother died of cancer. Charlotte was aged just five when she lost her mother. The youngest sibling, Anne, was barely one year old.

In 1824, the four oldest Brontë girls were sent to school at Cowan Bridge in Lancashire, at the Clergy Daughters' School. Charlotte was only eight years old at the time, and she was desperately homesick. The school's pupils lived in poor, insanitary and harsh conditions, and the girls were removed from the school a year later, but by that time both Maria and Elizabeth Brontë, the two eldest siblings, had become very ill. Shortly after the girls returned to their home in Haworth, both of Charlotte's older sisters died of consumption (tuberculosis). The girls' experiences at Cowan Bridge School were to have a profound influence on Charlotte's writing, and it is believed to be the model for Lowood School in her 1846 novel *Jane Eyre*.

Charlotte and her younger sisters Emily and Anne created fantastic imaginary worlds, peopling them with extraordinary characters. In childhood, their brother Branwell was also a part of this creative coterie. He later became an artist, but he struggled with addictions to alcohol and drugs and never achieved his sisters' fame. Their experiences with Branwell's addiction helped the sisters to create some of their troubled fictional characters.

As a young woman, Charlotte worked as a teacher and a governess. She travelled to Brussels, where she studied French, taught at a boarding school, and fell unrequitedly in love with the headmaster of the school. When she returned to Haworth, she concentrated on writing, which she had always felt to be her vocation.

The three sisters adopted the masculine pseudonyms of Currer, Ellis and Acton Bell. In 1846, they published a joint volume of poetry. The following year, Charlotte's first novel, *Jane Eyre*, was published under the name of 'Currer Bell'. (In the same year, Emily published *Wuthering Heights* and Anne published *Agnes Grey*.) *Jane Eyre* was an instant success and as a result, when Charlotte published *Shirley* in 1849, she did so under her own name. *Vilette* was published in 1853.

The brilliant Brontë family left no descendants. Branwell died on 24 September 1848 and Emily died just a few weeks later on 19 December. On Christmas Day of that year, Charlotte wrote this heartbreaking letter about Emily's death and how worried she was about her father's and Anne's health. Anne died just a few months later, in May 1849. Following the deaths of her three siblings in less than a year, Charlotte remained with her father at the parsonage. In 1854, she married the curate Arthur Bell Nichols, but she died just nine months after the wedding. She was newly pregnant at the time of her death. Charlotte Brontë's final novel, *The Professor*, was published posthumously in 1857.

Opposite A portrait of the Brontë sisters painted by their brother Branwell in 1834. From left to right are Anne, Emily and Charlotte. Branwell painted himself out of the picture.

My dear sir

I will write to you more at length when my heart can find a little rest – now I can only thank you very briefly for your letter which seemed to me eloquent in its sincerity.

Emily is nowhere here now, her wasted remains are taken out of the house. We have laid her cherished head under the church aisle beside my mother's, my two sisters' – dead long ago – and my poor, hapless brother's. But a small remnant of the race is left – so my poor father thinks.

Well – the loss is ours, not hers, and some sad comfort I take, as I hear the wind blow and feel the cutting keenness of the frost, in knowing that the elements bring her no more suffering; their severity cannot reach her grave; her fever is quieted, her restlessness soothed, her deep, hollow cough is hushed for ever; we do not hear it in the night nor listen for it in the morning; we have not the conflict of the strangely strong spirit and the fragile frame before us – relentless conflict – once seen, never to be forgotten. A dreary calm reigns round us, in the midst of which we seek resignation.

My father and my sister Anne are far from well. As for me, God has hitherto most graciously sustained me; so far I have felt adequate to bear my own burden and even to offer a little help to others. I am not ill – I can get through daily duties, and do something towards keeping hope and energy alive in our morning household. My father says to me almost hourly, "Charlotte, you must bear up, I shall sink if you fail me"; these words, you can conceive, are a stimulus to nature. The sight, too, of my sister Anne's very still but deep sorrow wakens in me such fear for her that I dare not falter. Somebody <u>must</u> cheer the rest.

So I will not now ask why Emily was torn from us in the fullness of our attachment, rooted in the prime of her own days, in the promise of her powers; why her existence now lies like a field of green corn trodden down, like a tree in full bearing struck at the root. I will only say, sweet is rest after labour and calm after tempest, and repeat again and again that Emily knows that now.

Yours sincerely,
C. Brontë

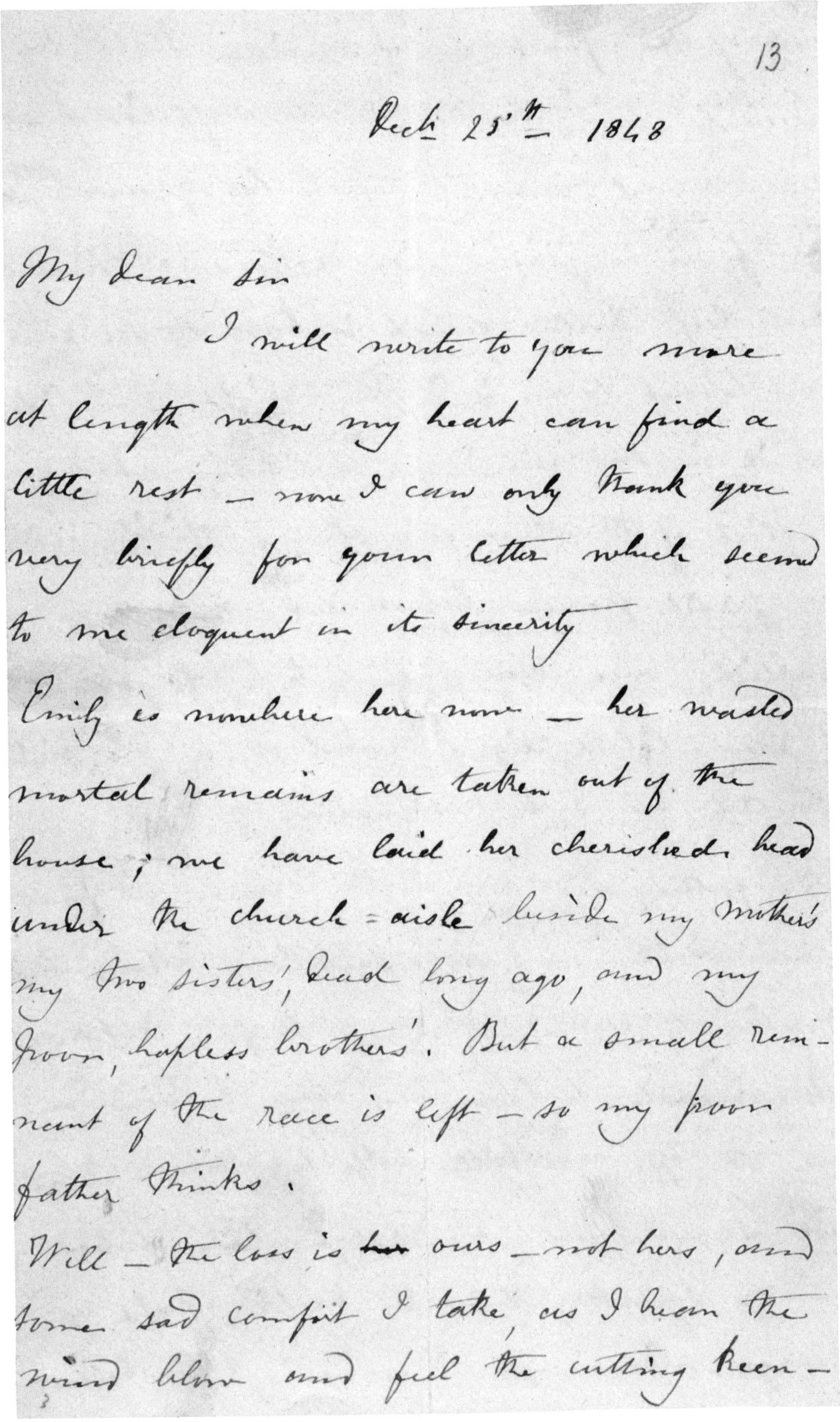

13

Dec^{br} 25th — 1848

My dear Sir

I will write to you more
at length when my heart can find a
little rest — now I can only thank you
very briefly for your letter which seemed
to me eloquent in its sincerity

Emily is nowhere here now — her wasted
mortal remains are taken out of the
house ; we have laid her cherished head
under the church = aisle beside my mother's
my two sisters' dead long ago, and my
poor, hapless brother's. But a small remnant of the race is left — so my poor
father thinks .

Will — the loss is ~~her~~ ours — not hers, and
some sad comfort I take, as I hear the
wind blow and feel the cutting keen —

ness of the frost, in knowing that the
elements bring her no more suffering –
their severity cannot reach her grave –
her fever is quieted, her restlessness soothed
her deep, hollow cough is hushed for ever
we do not hear it in the night nor listen
for it in the morning: we have not the
conflict of the strangely strong spirit in
the fragile frame before us – relentless
conflict – once seen, never to be forgotten
A dreary calm reigns round us, in the midst
of which we seek resignation

My father and my sister Anne are far
from well – as to me, God has hitherto most
graciously sustained me – so far I have
felt adequate to bear my own burden and
even to offer a little help to others – I am
not ill – I can get through daily duties
and do something towards keeping hope and
energy alive in our mourning household.

14

Father says to me almost hourly
Charlotte, you must bear up — I shall
sink if you fail me!" These words —
you can conceive are a stimulus to
nature. The sight too of my Sister Anne's
very still but deep sorrow wakens in me
such fear for her that I dare not falter.
Somebody must *cheer* the rest.

I will not now ask why Emily was
torn from us in the fullness of our attachment, rooted up in the prime of her own days
in the promise of her powers — why her existence now lies like a field of green corn
trodden down — like a tree in full bearing —
struck at the root; I will only say, sweet
is rest after labour and calm after tempest
and repeat again and again that Emily
knows that now.

Yours sincerely
Brontë

FLORENCE NIGHTINGALE

Nurse and medical pioneer, 1820–1910
To Dr William Farr, 14 March 1858

This letter was written two years after the end of the Crimean War, a bloody conflict that not only revealed the harsh realities of warfare to all those who read the newspapers, but also made the name of Florence Nightingale, 'the Lady with the Lamp', who became famous throughout the British Empire. Over 100 years after her death, her name remains synonymous with nursing and medical care.

Florence Nightingale was born in Florence, Italy, after which she was named, into a wealthy and well-connected English family. The family returned to England when Florence was an infant. Her parents were horrified when she announced her desire to become a nurse, something considered lower-class and definitely not a respectable profession. After years of arguments, her parents finally permitted her to travel to Germany to study nursing for three months. On her return from Düsseldorf, she was employed as the superintendent at a hospital for 'gentlewomen' in London's prestigious Harley Street. This was all the nursing experience Florence had when, in 1854, she decided travel to Scutari in Turkey to run a hospital for soldiers fighting in the Crimean War. Using her family's connections, she was able to persuade the War Office to allow her to take a group of 38 nurses to Turkey.

Nightingale was not alone in her desire to bring about change in this masculine-dominated world of helping those wounded in war. One of her peers was the half-Jamaican, half-Scottish nurse Mary Seacole (1805–1881), who travelled from her home in Jamaica to the War Office in London to ask for assistance in setting up a hospital in the Crimea. The War Office gave her no help, a decision seemingly based solely on the colour of her skin. When Mary arrived in the Crimea, having funded the journey herself,

Florence promised her any assistance she could provide. For many decades, Mary Seacole's name had been forgotten, but today she is finally gaining her rightful importance alongside Florence Nightingale.

After Nightingale returned from the Crimea, she contacted Dr Farr, a pioneer of medical statistics, asking for help with the data she had collated. Their work revealed the appalling mortality rates during the war. In 1859, a year after writing this letter to Farr, Florence Nightingale published her seminal book, *Notes on Nursing*. A year later, she established the first professional training school for nurses, the Nightingale School, at which her book became the standard text. For the rest of her life, even when she became incapacitated and needed to spend much of her time in bed, Florence campaigned ceaselessly for improvements in hygiene and health standards. She used her fame to further her aims, writing thousands of letters to influential people, including Queen Victoria, and often directing her volunteers from her sickroom. She was also influential in ensuring trained nurses were available to help everyone, notably insisting that people in workhouses should have the same access to trained nurses as those in private hospitals.

In 1883 Florence Nightingale was awarded the Royal Red Cross medal, and in 1907 she received the Order of Merit, becoming the first woman to do so. She died three years later, at the age of 90. It was suggested to her family that she be buried at Westminster Abbey in London, but the family chose to have her buried in their local church in Hampshire. Two years after her death, the Red Cross began awarding their Florence Nightingale Medal for nurses who have given outstanding service.

Opposite A nineteenth-century lithograph showing Florence Nightingale on duty at on a ward at Scutari Hospital in Turkey during the Crimean War. The hospital was established in a converted army barracks.

30 Old Burlington Street
W

March 14/58

My dear Dr. Farr,

There were three letters in the Lancet yesterday against our Army Medical School. They are easily answered. But Mr. Herbert has also received remonstrances from Lord Hass and Lefroy, M.P. for Dublin. And we want to have the Lancet on our side.

Would you ask the Editor not to commit himself till he has heard our side of the question.

You will find Sutherland here tomorrow at 6 o'clock. And we will draw up a statement which we depend upon you to father upon the Lancet, and make them give a leading article in our favour.

Yours most sincerely,

F. Nightingale

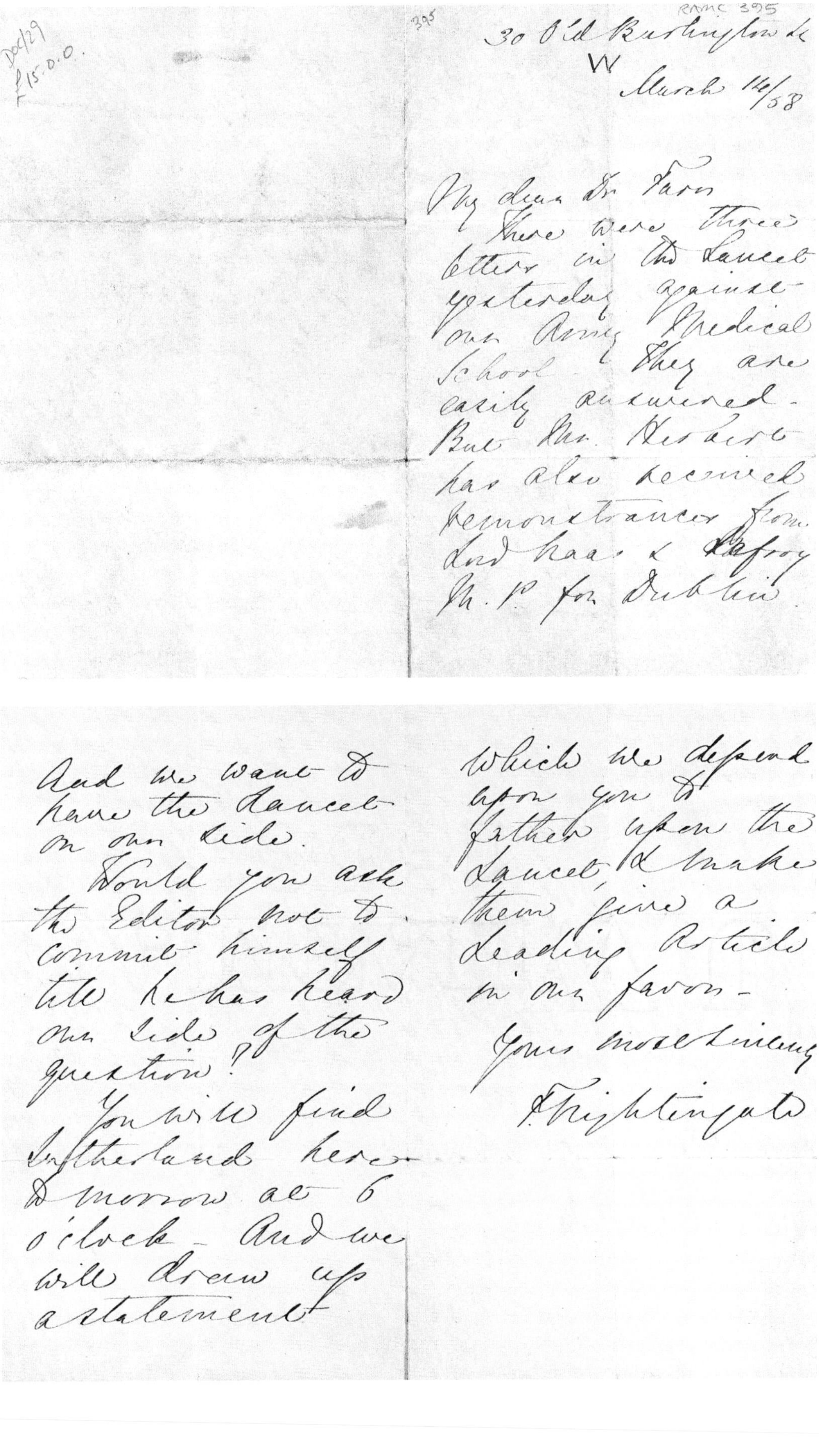

Oct/29
£15.0.0.

RAMC 395

395

30 Old Burlington St
W
March 14/58

My dear Dr Faris

There were three
letters in the Lancet
yesterday against
our Army & Medical
School — They are
easily answered.
But Mr. Herbert
has also received
Remonstrances from
Lord Raea & Lefroy
M.P. for Dublin

And we want to
have the Lancet
on our side.

Would you ask
the Editor not to
commit himself
till he has heard
our side of the
question?

You will find
Sutherland here
to morrow at 6
o'clock — And we
will draw up
a statement

Which we depend
upon you to
father upon the
Lancet, & make
them give a
Leading Article
in our favour —

Yours most sincerely

F Nightingale

ELIZABETH BARRETT BROWNING

Poet, 1806–1861
To Henry F. Chorley, 1859

Elizabeth Barrett Browning was amongst the few female poets in Victorian Britain who attained fame through their work. Her epic poem *Aurora Leigh* (1856), often described as a novel in poetic form, was criticised heavily by reviewers but adored by the public, and it made her a household name.

Elizabeth Barrett grew up near Ledbury in Herefordshire, the oldest of 12 children in a wealthy family, and immersed herself in books at every opportunity. Her first published poem was an epic narrative about the Battle of Marathon (fought between the ancient Greeks and Persians). The poem was published privately when she was just 14. As a teenager, she became dangerously ill and suffered from a painful spinal disease, a condition that made her dependent for the rest of her life on the drug laudanum, and made her family think she would be unlikely to find a husband.

When Elizabeth was in her early 30s, the Barrett family moved to London, where they lived on Wimpole Street in a fashionable area near Regent's Park. One of Elizabeth's cousins was the poet John Kenyon, and through his connections Elizabeth was introduced to some of Britain's foremost poets. In 1845, Elizabeth began a romance with the poet Robert Browning, initially through poetry and letters. She wrote to him of her enjoyment of his poems – many of which had been treated very harshly by critics – and he responded with thanks, expressing admiration for her writing. This epistolary courtship led to clandestine meetings and an engagement, of which her father disapproved,

as he believed that Robert Browning was interested only in his daughter's fortune.

On 12 September 1846, while her family was away from home, Elizabeth Barrett and Robert Browning met at Marylebone Parish Church, very close to her home, and were married in secret. A few days later, they left to live in Italy, making their home in Florence. In 1847, they moved into the Casa Guidi, a fifteenth-century palazzo originally built for the aristocratic Ridolfi family. Two years later, Elizabeth gave birth to their only child, Robert Wiedeman Barrett Browning, who was known as 'Pen'. He grew up to become a professional artist. When Pen was a year old, Elizabeth published what would become her best-known work, *Sonnets from the Portuguese*, a collection of love poems. These were highly personal poems, documenting her relationship with her husband, whose pet name for her was 'my little Portuguese'.

By 1859, the date on which this letter was sent, Elizabeth had become one of the most famous residents of Florence. It was written to Elizabeth's friend, the journalist and music critic Henry Chorley, who worked for *The Athenaeum* magazine, in which Elizabeth's poem, 'A Tale from Villa Franca' had been published. It reflects her interest in politics, which inspired her 1860 collection *Poems Before Congress*, including her anti-slavery poem 'A Curse for a Nation' (written in 1854). Two years after sending this letter, Elizabeth Barrett Browning died at the age of 55. She is buried in what has become known as 'the English Cemetery' in Florence.

Siena - Sunday;

I thank you my dear Dr. Horley - I submit gracefully, to being overcharged for my politics - In return I will read to your private ear an additional stanza which should interpose as the real seventh but was left out. I did not send it to you the day after my note; though sorely tempted to do so, because it seemed to me likely to annul any small chance of Athenæum = tolerance which might fall to me - Would it have done so, do you think?

"A great Deed in this world of ours!
        Unheard of the pretence is.
It plainly threatens the great Powers,
        Is fatal in all senses.
A just Deed in the world! Call out
        the rifles! — be not slack about
        the national Defences — "

Thank you, my dear Mr. Chorley, I submit gratefully to being snubbed for my politics. In return I will send to your private ear an additional stanza which should interpose as the real seventh but was left out. I did not send it to you the day after my note, though sorely tempted to do so, because it seemed to me likely to annul any small chance of 'Athenæum' tolerance which might fall to me. Would it have done so, do you think?

'A great deed in this world of ours! Unheard of the pretence is. It plainly threatens the Great Powers; Is fatal in all senses. A just deed in the world! Call out The rifles! ... be not slack about The National Defences.'

Certainly if I don't guess 'the Sphinx' right, some of your English guessers in the 'Times' and elsewhere fail also, as events prove. The clever 'Prince-Napoleon-for-Central-Italy' guess, for instance, has just fallen through, by declaration of the 'Moniteur.' Most absurd it was always. At one time the Prince might have taken the crown by acclamation. He was almost rude about it when he was in Tuscany. And even after the peace, members of the present Government were not averse, were much the contrary indeed. At that time the autonomy was still dear, we had not made up our minds to the fusion. Now, è altra cosa, and to imagine that a man like the French Emperor would have waited till now, producing, by the opportunities he has given, the present complication, in order to impose the Prince, is absurd on the very face of it.

While standers-by guess, the comfort is that circumstances ripen. We are in spirits about our Italy. The dignity, the constancy, the calm, are admirable, as the unanimity of the people is wonderful. Even the contadini have rallied to the Government, and the cry of enthusiasm to which the cross of Savoy was uncovered in the market place of Siena yesterday was a thrilling thing. Also we will fight, be it understood, whenever fighting shall be necessary. At present, the right arm of Austria is broken; she cannot hold the sword since Solferino, at least in central Italy. Let those who doubt our debt to France remember where we were last year, and see what our political life is now – real, vivid, unhindered! Our moral qualities are our own, but our practical opportunities come from another; we could not have made them by force of moral qualities, great as those are allowed to be. And how striking the growth of this people since 1848. Massimo d'Azeglio said to Robert and me, 'It is '48 over again with matured actors.' But it is even more than that: it is '48 over again with regenerated actors. All internal jealousies at an end, all suspicions quenched, all selfish policies dissolved. Florence forgets herself for Italy. This is grand. Would that England, that pattern of moral nations, would forget herself for the sake of something or someone beyond. That would be grand.

I wish you were here, my dear Mr. Chorley, since I am wishing in vain, though we are almost at the close of our stay in this pretty country. We have a villa with beautiful sights from all the windows; and there, on the hill opposite, live Mr. and Mrs. Story, and within a stone's throw, in a villino, lives the poor old lion Landor, who, being sorely buffeted by his family at Fiesole, far beyond 'kissing with tears' (though Robert did what he could), took refuge with us at Casa Guidi one day, broken-hearted and in wrath. He stays here while we stay, and then goes with us to Florence, where Robert has received the authorisation of his English friends to settle him in comfort in an apartment of his own, with my late maid, Wilson (who married our Italian man-servant), to take care of him; and meanwhile the quiet of this place has so restored his health and peace of mind that he is able to write awful Latin alcaics, to say nothing of hexameters and pentameters, on the wickedness of Louis Napoleon. Yes, dear Mr. Chorley, poems which might appear in the 'Athenæum' without disclaimer, and without injury to the reputation of that journal.

Am I not spiteful? I assure you I couldn't be spiteful a short time ago, so very ill I have been. Now it is different, and every day the strength returns. What remains, however, is a certain necessity of not facing the Florence wind this winter, and of going again to Rome, in spite of probable revolutions there. We talk of going in the early part of November. Why won't you come to Rome and give us meeting? Foolish speech, when I know you won't. We shall be in Florence probably at the end of the present week, to stay there until the journey further south begins. I shall regret this silence. And little Penini too will have his regrets, for he has been very happy here, made friends with the contadini, has helped to keep the sheep, to run after straggling cows, to play at 'nocini' (did you ever hear of that game?) and to pick the grapes at the vintage – driving in the grape-carts (exactly of the shape of the Greek chariots), with the grapes heaped up round him; and then riding on his own pony, which Robert is going to buy for him (though Robert never spoils him; no, not he, it is only I who do that!), galloping through the lanes on this pony the colour of his curls. I was looking over his journal (Pen keeps a journal), and fell on the following memorial which I copy for you – I must.

'This is the happiest day of my hole [sic] life, for now dearest Vittorio Emanuele is really nostro re.'

Pen's weak point does not lie in his politics, Mr. Chorley, but in his spelling. When his contadini have done their day's work he takes it on him to read aloud to them the poems of the revolutionary Venetian poet Dall' Ongaro, to their great applause. Then I must tell you of his music. He is strong in music for ten years old – and plays a sonata of Beethoven already (in E flat – opera 7) and the first four books of Stephen Heller; to say nothing of various pieces by modern German composers in which there is need of considerable execution. Robert is the maestro, and sits by him two hours every day, with an amount of patience and persistence really extraordinary. Also for two months back, since I have been thrown out of work, Robert has heard the child all his other lessons. Isn't it very, very good of him?

Do write to us and tell me how your sister is, and also how you are in spirits and towards the things of the world? Give her my love – will you?

I had a letter some time ago from poor Jessie Mario, from Bologna. Respect her. She hindered her husband from fighting with Garibaldi for his country, because Garibaldi fought under L.N., which was so highly improper. Her letter was not unkind to me, but altogether and insanely wrong as I considered. (Not more wrong though, and much less wicked, than the 'Times.') I was too ill at the time to answer it, and afterwards Robert would not let me, but I should have liked to do it; it's such a comfort to a woman (and a man?) to sfogarsi, as we say here. Also, I was really uneasy at what might be doing at Bologna; so, in spite of friendship, it was a relief to me to hear of the police taking charge of all overt possibilities in that direction.

Is it really true that 'Adam Bede' is the work of Miss Evans? The woman (as I have heard of her) and the author (as I read her) do not hold together. May God bless you, my dear friend! Robert shall say so for himself.

Ever affectionately yours,

Elizabeth Barrett Brow

My dear Mr. Chorley, – Reading over what I have written I find that I have been s ungrateful as not to say the thing I would when I would thank you. Your Dedi will b accepted with a true sense of kindness and honor together; I shall be proud perhaps you have changed your mind in the course of this long sile

And now where's room for Rober

HARRIET TUBMAN

Abolitionist, *c.*1822–1913
To John G. Whittier, 21 January 1862

Known as 'Grandma Moses', Harriet Tubman was an escaped slave who devoted her life to helping others do the same and bringing about the end of slavery in the United States. She was the fifth of nine children born to enslaved parents in Maryland. At birth, her name was Araminta Ross. Her birth date is unknown, but is believed to have been in 1822 (years on official documents vary between 1815 and 1825). Her mother Harriet Green and her father Ben Ross were owned by two different slave-owning families, meaning the family was forcibly separated when Araminta was young. Her mother was sold to another family, as were two of Araminta's older sisters. Araminta's working life began when she was five years old, and her childhood was marked by violence and abuse. When she tried to prevent a slaveowner from hurting an enslaved man, she was beaten in the head, which left her physically disabled and with permanent headaches.

When Araminta was 24 she married a freeborn man named John Tubman. At this time, she also changed her first name to Harriet, perhaps to honour her mother. In September 1849, she and her brothers made their escape from slavery, running away in the night. They were free for a couple of weeks until her brothers insisted they all return – her brothers had left behind wives and children and were fearful of what might be happening to them as punishment. The following month, Harriet escaped again, although her husband refused to leave with her. She worked in a variety of jobs, including as a lumberjack – a trade she had learned from her father – until she was safely in Philadelphia. In Philadelphia, she worked as a cook, a trade learned from her mother, and began to form connections in the abolitionist movement.

Soon, Harriet had become a conductor on the Underground Railroad, an intricate escape system by which 'conductors' helped enslaved people escape, provided them with clothes to wear so they didn't look like runaway slaves, and led them to safety. Harriet made multiple 'railroad' journeys on which she helped dozens of slaves escape from the South to relative safety in the North. In 1896, Harriet Tubman proudly commented, 'I was the conductor of the Underground Railroad for eight years, and I can say what most conductors can't say – I never ran my train off the track and I never lost a passenger.' Her Underground Railroad activity helped prepare her for the American Civil War, during which she offered her services to the Union Army as a nurse, a cook, an armed scout and a spy. Harriet was never taught to read or write, which meant that her letters and life story were dictated to friends. This letter was dictated to Lydia M. Childs, a white abolitionist and friend of Harriet's.

In the late 1860s, John Tubman (who had married a second time) was murdered by a white man, who was acquitted of the killing. After John's death, Harriet married again. Her second husband, Nelson Davis, was a soldier who is believed also to have escaped slavery. Together they adopted a daughter, Gertie, making their home in Auburn, New York State. Although Davis was about 20 years younger than his wife, she outlived him by several decades. Harriet Tubman died of pneumonia in her early nineties.

Opposite Harriet Tubman pictured with her second husband Nelson Davis and their adopted daughter Gertie in 1887.

[The North] may send the flower of their young men down South, to die of the fever in the summer, and of the ague in the winter. They may send them one year, two year, three year, till they tired of sending, or till they use up all the young men. All no use!

God won't let Master Lincoln beat the South until he does right thing. Master Lincoln, he's a great man, and I'm a poor Negro but this Negro can tell Master Lincoln how to save money and young men. He can do it by setting the Negroes free. Suppose there was an awful big snake down there on the floor. He bites you. Folks all scared, because you may die. You send for doctor to cut the bite; but the snake rolled up there, and while doctor is doing it, he bites you again. The doctor cuts out that bite; but while he's doing it, the snake springs up and bites you again, and so he keeps doing it, till you kill him. That's what Master Lincoln ought to know.

Source: Letter from Lydia Maria Child to John G. Whittier, 21 January 1862

Opposite Harriet Tubman
pictured in 1868 or 1869.

EMILY DICKINSON

Poet, 1830–1886
To Thomas Wentworth Higginson, 15 April 1862

It was only after her death, at the age of 55, that the world – and her own family – began to learn the full extent of Emily Dickinson's poetry. This letter was sent when Emily was in her early thirties. She had read an article entitled 'Letter to a Young Contributor' in *The Atlantic*, written by Thomas Wentworth Higginson, an author, abolitionist and women's rights campaigner. The article prompted Emily to contact Higginson and ask for his opinion on four of her poems. This initial letter led to a lifetime of correspondence, as Higginson proved an invaluable mentor to the younger poet.

Emily Dickinson grew up in a strict Calvinist household in Amherst, Massachusetts. Her family was influential in society. She was born in the house her grandfather had built and attended the prestigious school Amherst Academy (which later became known as Amherst College), which he had founded. Her teachers were impressed by her writing skills, but her family were almost entirely unaware of her writing. Both of the Dickinson parents were interested in science and the natural world, and this was reflected in the curriculum at Amherst Academy. This early scientific education, especially her interest in botany, can be discerned in much of Emily's writing.

After graduating from Amherst, Dickinson enrolled at the Mount Holyoke Female Seminary, which was a religiously oriented institution. The students were divided into three groups: those who professed their faith; those who hoped to profess their faith; and those who were 'without hope'. Emily was placed in the last category. She spent only one year at the seminary before returning home. Around this time, in 1849, Emily's father gave her a dog, a brown Newfoundland named Carlo. He became her trusted confidante and companion on her many long walks.

When Emily Dickinson was in her twenties, her parents bought the Homestead – the large house, formerly her grandparents' home, in which Emily had been born. Her brother Austin and his family lived next door and Emily lived in a tight social circle, which included her friend Mary Loomis Todd. Emily, however, was often melancholy, a mood exacerbated by a chronic eye condition. She was devastated when Carlo died, at the age of 17, in 1866. Towards the end of her life, Emily became increasingly reclusive, concentrating on her writing and gardening.

It is now known that Emily Dickinson wrote around 1,800 poems, but only 10 were published in her lifetime, all anonymously. Scholars still dispute whether Emily was aware of even this limited exposure, or whether the poems were submitted for publication by friends to whom she had sent them. It was only after Emily's death that her younger sister Lavinia discovered the wealth of her literary output. Lavinia talked to Mary Loomis Todd, who contacted Thomas Wentworth Higginson, and the two of them worked on editing and collecting Emily's poetry and letters.

The first collected volume of her poems was published in 1890, four years after the poet's death. The next two volumes were published in 1891 and 1896. In 1894, two volumes of her letters were published. These books placed Emily Dickinson firmly in the canon of America's finest poets.

Mr Higginson,

      Are you too deeply occupied to say if my Verse is alive? The Mind is so near itself – it cannot see, distinctly – and I have none to ask.

Should you think it breathed – and had you the leisure to tell me, I should feel quick gratitude.

If I make the mistake – that you dared to tell me – would give me sincerer honor – toward you.

I enclose my name – asking you, if you please – Sir – to tell me what is true?

That you will not betray me – it is needless to ask – since Honor is it's [sic] own pawn –.

I'll tell you how the sun rose –
A ribbon at a time –
The Steeples swam in Amethyst –
The news, like Squirrels, ran –
The Hills untied their Bonnets –
The Bobolinks – begun –
Then I said softly to myself –
"That must have been the Sun"!
But how he set – I know not –
There seemed a purple stile
Which little Yellow boys and girls
Were climbing all the while –
Till when they reached the other side –
A Dominie in Gray –
Put gently up the evening Bars –
And led the flock away –

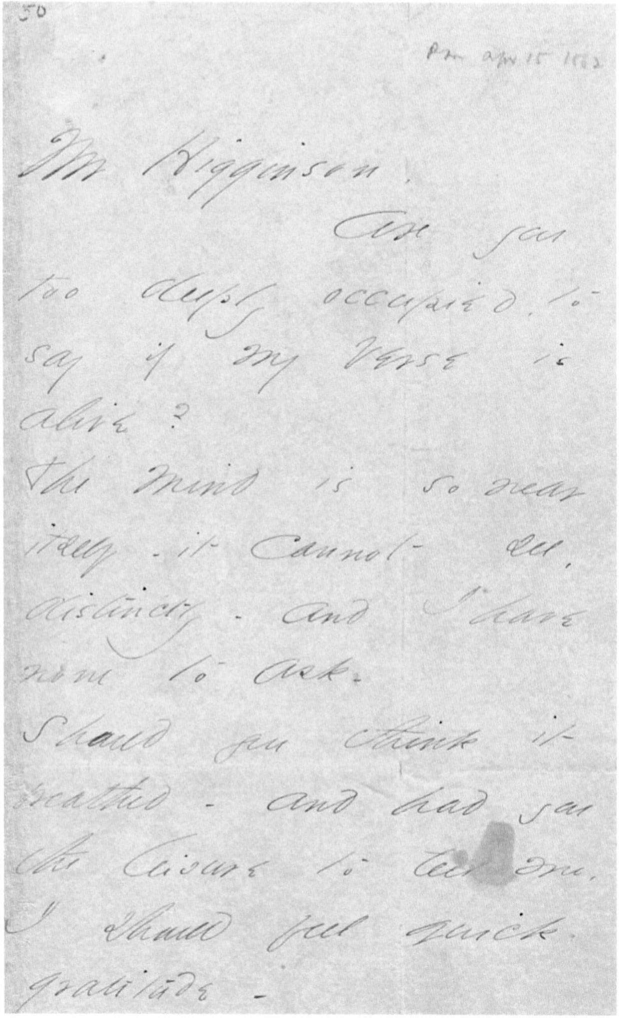

50

Pm apr 15 1862

Mr Higginson,

Are you
too deeply occupied to
say if my Verse is
alive?

The Mind is so near
itself - it cannot see,
distinctly - and I have
none to ask.

Should you think it
breathed - and had you
the leisure to tell me,
I should feel quick
gratitude -

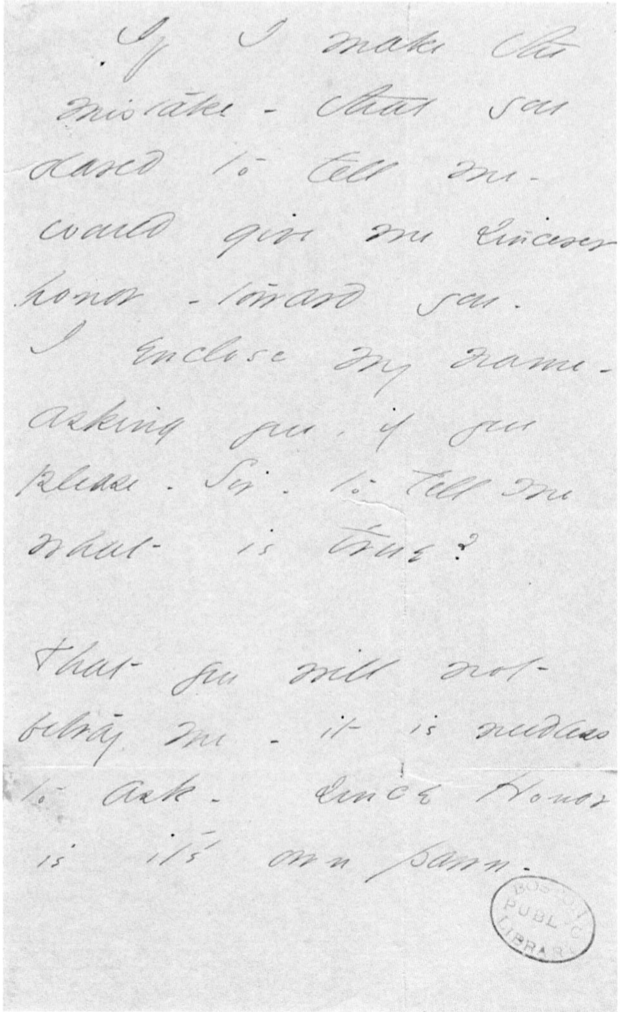

If I make the
mistake - that you
dared to tell me -
would give me sincerer
honor - toward you.

I enclose my name -
asking you, if you
please - Sir - to tell me
what is true?

That you will not
betray me - it is needless
to ask - since Honor
is it's own pawn -

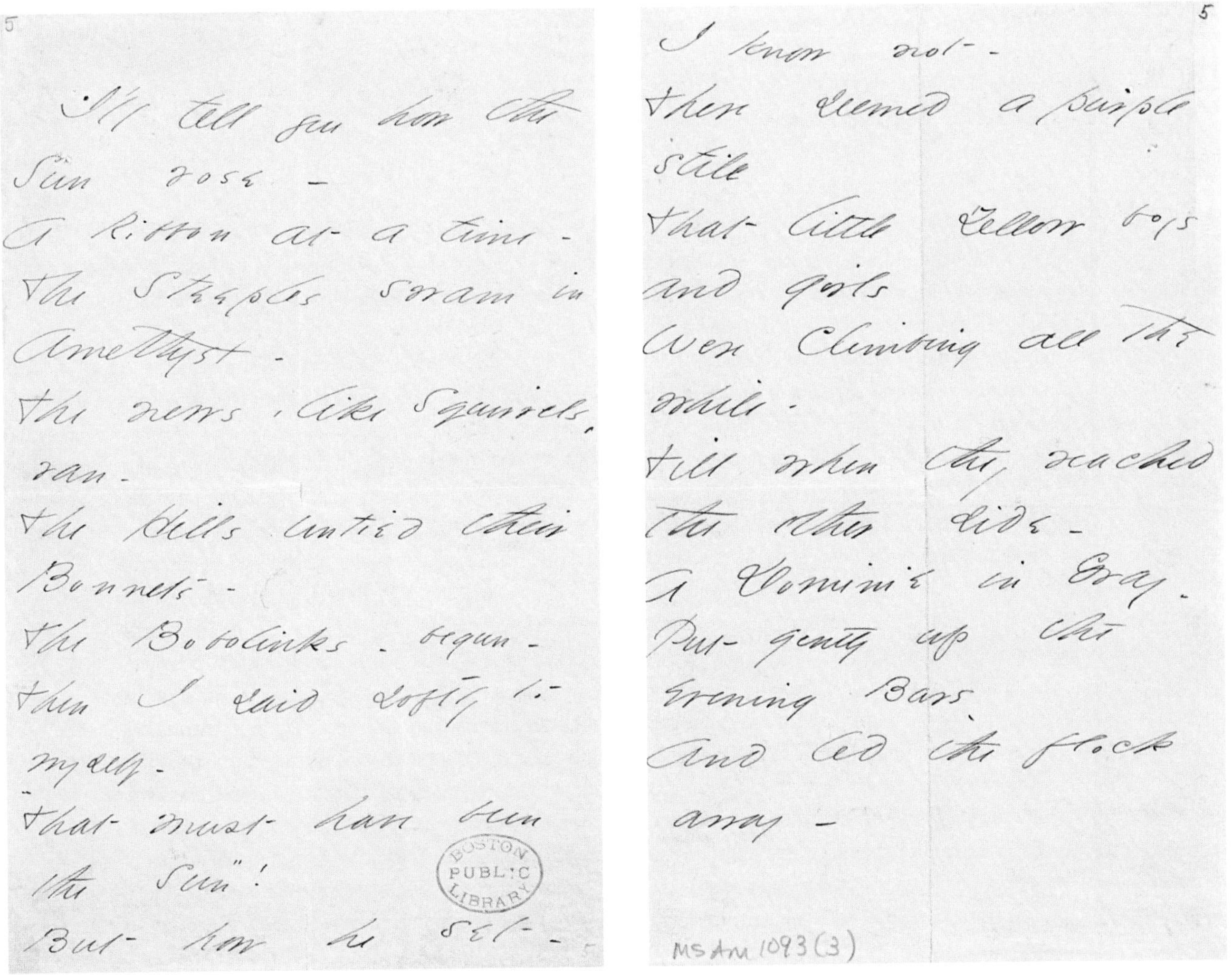

I'll tell you how the
Sun rose -
A Ribbon at a time -
The Steeples swam in
Amethyst -
The news, like Squirrels,
ran -
The Hills untied their
Bonnets -
The Bobolinks - begun -
Then I said softly to
myself -
"That must have been
the Sun"!
But how he set -

I know not -
There seemed a purple
stile
That little Yellow boys
and girls
Were climbing all the
while -
Till when they reached
the other side -
A Dominie in Gray -
Put gently up the
evening Bars -
And led the flock
away -

MS Am 1093 (3)

RACHEL HENNING

Pioneer and writer, 1826–1914
To Etta Boyce, 4 March 1864

In 1861, 35-year-old Rachel Henning set sail on Isambard Kingdom Brunel's steam ship, the SS *Great Britain*. The voyage would change her life forever, as she was leaving her home in Britain and emigrating to Australia. Today, her extensive diaries and letters form an essential social history of life in Australia in the mid-nineteenth century.

Rachel was born in Bristol in 1826, the eldest child of the Reverend Charles and Mrs Rachel Lydia Henning. By the time Rachel was 19, both her parents and two of her younger siblings had died. Rachel became responsible for looking after her three younger sisters, Annie, Amy and Etta, and their brother, Biddulph, who had also almost died of scarlet fever and was in delicate health. Four of the five surviving Henning children were destined to end up in Australia; only Etta, who married a clergyman, stayed behind in England.

In 1853, Biddulph and Annie set sail for Sydney, from where Biddulph took on the lease of a farm in New South Wales. The following year, Rachel and Amy travelled to Australia to join them, but after two years, Rachel returned to England, having been overwhelmed by homesickness and disliking the classless society of Australia. They were a wealthy family and she was used to an upper-class existence. After she returned home, however, she realised that she did not want to remain in England while three of her siblings were living in Australia. It was after she had taken the decision to join them that she undertook her journey on the SS *Great Britain*, resolving, as she wrote in her diary, to 'make a

do of it'. This diary, in which she wrote faithfully throughout the journey, is now housed in the Brunel Institute in Bristol. It has become a vitally important document of social and maritime history, recording such incidents as the discovery of a stowaway and the birth of a baby who was given the extraordinary shipboard names of John Gray Morland Hocking Great Britain Magazine (as Rachel noted, he was named after the captain, the ship's doctor and the onboard newsletter). Of equal historic importance are the letters she wrote home, such as those sent to her sister Etta, many of which contained Rachel's sketches of Australian life.

As this letter to Etta shows, Rachel became an enthusiastic pioneer woman, embracing life on her brother's farm (or 'station') in Queensland, writing about and sketching the wildlife and plants. She became intrigued and fascinated by her new country, and her attitudes to life changed dramatically after settling in Australia. In 1866, two years after writing this letter, Rachel married one of her brother's colleagues, Deighton Taylor. After his death in 1900, Rachel and her widowed sister Annie set up home together. Rachel died in Sydney, at Biddulph's home, in 1914.

Although Rachel Henning herself probably assumed that nobody except the recipients would see her letters, her name became famous several decades after her death. In the 1950s, the letters were published in the magazine *The Bulletin*. In 1963, their status in the canon of Australian literature was secured when they were turned into a book, with accompanying illustrations by the artist Norman Lindsay.

My Dearest Etta,

We have a regular mail now, but we have hardly felt the benefit of it yet, for owing to the floods the roads have been impassable, and even the steamer was stopped at Rockhampton for three weeks. The Fitzroy was a mile wide, and coming down such a torrent that no vessel could go down the current for fear of being swept on shore or against sandbanks.

Such a wet season as this was never known within the memory of the oldest inhabitant; that is to say, for about five years. I suppose it is the counterbalance to the drought of last year. Besides various thunderstorms and minor rains about three weeks ago, it poured incessantly for three nights and two days, real tropical rain, and accompanied on the second day by a perfect hurricane of wind.

The "Station Creek", which is generally a small stream, came down a roaring river; such a torrent that it carried away and swept down with it the whole of the paddock fence which crossed its bed, though it was built in that part of entire trunks of trees, large thick ones, too. What we call the "Little Creek", which runs into the other, overflowed the whole of the flat at the bottom of the hill and formed a lake. Both the creeks have plenty of rocks in them, and the roar of water all round us was something fine, especially when we were quite safe from them; for nothing but an unusual deluge would reach us at the top of this hill.

A few old sheep, about twenty-five, I think, died from the continual cold and wet. Some iron was blown off the roof of the store, and the drays were stopped for three weeks on the bank of the Bowen; and that is all the harm we took by the rain. Exmoor is a capital run for sheep, as besides the rich plains where they can feed in dry weather there are plenty of dry stony ridges where they flourish when it is wet.

But on some of the low-lying runs in the Broad Sound country the losses have been frightful. At Fort Cooper, seventy miles from here, 2,000 sheep were washed away by the sudden rise of a creek, and most of the other stations to the southward have lost great numbers. At Mr Palmer's station on the other side of the Broken River he had left two men to take care of the place while he went to Sydney; and these unfortunates were short of provisions when the flood came, and there they had to stay for a fortnight, hemmed in between the Broken River and the Dart, with nothing to eat except meat. They were obliged to kill the calves, as it is a cattle station, and eat as much as they could while it was fresh; for they had no salt.

The moment the current was a little abated they contrived to swim the river, and get over here, one of them very ill with scurvy. He soon recovered under the influence of the kitchen physic, but the Irish family we have as servants were so alarmed at the idea of getting scurvy also, though there is no earthly reason why they should, that the two little girls for some time devoted their leisure to picking "pigweed", rather a nasty wild plant, but supposed to be exceedingly wholesome, either chopped up with vinegar or boiled. John, the cook, used to boil a large milk-bucket full of it every day and administer it to the kitchen in general by way of vegetable.

There are generally twelve or fourteen people who have their meals in the kitchen, and I wonder the said John does not go distracted. Our Irish family number six, and there are two shepherds, a bullock-driver and two or three blackboys besides. The blacks are not allowed to dine with the white aristocracy. They "takes their meals in the wash-'ouse", or, in other words, on a bench outside the kitchen door.

To the north, the floods have done great mischief. The Burdekin River overflowed the country for miles, and there are reports of herds of cattle being carried away, but they are probably exaggerated, as cattle have more sense than sheep, and can generally take care of themselves. It is certain, however, that the township on the Burdekin to which the steamer runs (for the river is navigable some way up) was nearly all washed away. The steamer had just brought up supplies for the squatters about there; and these, being left on the quay, were all lost. So there is every probability of a scarcity of provisions in those regions.

There were two small vessels anchored in the Burdekin when the flood came on. One of these was washed from her moorings and carried away into the bush, where she now lies high and dry among the gum-trees. A man on board jumped into the water to try and save her, and was taken down and killed by an alligator. Only one tent was left standing in Port Denison. A great part of the population there dwelt in tents; and very desirable abodes they must have been in that wind and rain.

All this rain has still further delayed our visit to Sydney by delaying Biddulph's journey to the Flinders. He talks of starting next week if there is no more rain. I suppose he would be home about the end of April, and in that case we might start from here about the middle of May; but it is impossible to reckon on very long beforehand. On a station so many things turn up which require immediate attention.

It is just as well that we were not going in February, for unless we liked to swim the Bowen on horseback or to cross in a bark canoe we could never have got to Port Denison. Biddulph crossed the Bowen in a canoe last week-end, and he said he took off his boots before starting, fully expecting to have to swim for it, such was the leaky state of the boat. By the same token, he left his spurs in the canoe and lost them.

Biddulph is just the same careless mortal as to small properties that he used to be. The country round must, I think, be supplied by the knives he loses. A shepherd brought in two silk handkerchiefs the other day which he said the master had used on two different occasions to tie up hurdles with, and left behind him; and the disappearance of whips, saddle-straps, saddle-cloths, hobbles and all minor articles of saddlery is something marvellous. But that, I believe, is always the case on a station. Everybody takes what is good in his own eyes, saddle-straps especially.

We got the mail a few days ago after a month's delay. All the English papers came, but as I said before, no English letters. We have written to Sydney, and asked them to forward the February and March letters. We have come to the end of the summer, and though it has been a wet one it has been a very cool one and nobody seems any the worse for it, though it is said that people feel the second summer more than the first in a tropical climate.

I do not suppose we have had what you would call much rain in England. We often have none for a fortnight or three weeks, but when it does come it is in such torrents that it floods the rivers and makes the roads impassable. We have not been riding much lately, the roads have been so heavy; but the lambs and I have been walking every evening, and very beautiful the evenings are now. I often go a short way in the bush before breakfast, too; and the early mornings are, if possible, better than the evenings.

All the gum-trees are in blossom now. Such masses of white flowers; and when the dew is on them they smell like honeysuckle. I go and sit under a flowering gum-tree and watch the lambs feed and they come up in their turns to be petted and have their noses rubbed! "Beauty", one of my last year's pet "lambs", is now grown a very handsome sheep; and she yesterday presented us with a lamb of her own. Such a pretty little creature.

I often think I would much rather stay here than go down. I know I shall often wish I was feeding the lambs in the beautiful bush when I am grinding about the Sydney streets shopping, or trying to keep Amy's children quiet at Bathurst.

I wish I had some letters from you to answer, but we cannot hear for a fortnight, and that only provided the river does not rise again. How I wish I could see you all, instead of hearing from you only! Now I must say good-bye, dearest Etta. My kind love to Mr Boyce, and Constance, and Leighton – but they cannot have the slightest remembrance of me – and with very much love to yourself, believe me, my dear Etta,

Ever your most affectionate sister,

RACHEL HENNING

P.S. March 5th. I finished my letter rather in a hurry yesterday, expecting the postman to come; but he did not arrive; and as it poured all last night, he is not very likely to make his appearance today. It is a beautiful morning after the rainy night, and I have been paddling about in very old goloshes ever since breakfast to enjoy it. This hill is so gravelly and stony that it never remains wet, but the long grass is just damp enough to be cheerful.

I have taken the lambs out to feed, and left them enjoying the short grass on a dry ridge while I went down to survey the creek, which rose about five feet last night, and looks very fine this morning tumbling over the rocks and sweeping round the sandy points, much wider than the river at Bathpool. In the last flood it hollowed out a hole in its channel about eight feet deep, which is a source of great rejoicing to all the inhabitants of Exmoor, as they go there to bathe. I often wish we could bathe, too.

There are some beautiful flowers out by the creek this morning, almost like a wild holly border, large pure white blossoms with a crimson eye; but they die off in an hour or two. The different kinds of convolvulus are most beautiful of a damp morning like this. It is to be hoped the postman will come today or you may have more "last words" inflicted on you. Good-bye once more, my dearest Etta.

CLARA BARTON

Nurse, 1821–1912
To the Office of Correspondence with the Friends of the
Missing Men of the U.S. Army, 8 December 1865

Clarissa (known as Clara) Harlowe Barton was born in Oxford, Massachusetts, the youngest of five children in a farming family. During her childhood, her brother David was seriously injured, and Clara learned how to nurse him, a skill that she returned to in later life. As a teenager, she trained to become a teacher and started working in a local school. Her older brother also asked her for help with his business, so she undertook the bookkeeping and clerking for his company. At the age of 24, she founded her first school. She continued teaching for several years, before leaving the teaching profession in her early thirties, an act of frustration at not being paid the same salary as her male colleagues.

Clara moved to Washington, DC, in 1854, taking a job at the US Patent Office. Some of her male colleagues made her working life extremely challenging, resenting the fact that they were working alongside a woman. Clara persevered despite their hostility and became well respected in her job – only to lose her position following the election of James Buchanan as president. Buchanan was in favour of slavery, and Clara was known to hold strong abolitionist views. She returned briefly to Massachusetts, but was accepted back at the Patent Office after Abraham Lincoln was elected.

When the American Civil War began, Clara became increasingly concerned about how many people would suffer and die, and she began working as a volunteer nurse for wounded soldiers. Soon she began to realise how crucial it was to start collecting medicines and other much-needed items for the troops, as well as how difficult it was to get these supplies to the places where they were needed. Clara solved the problem by taking the supplies directly to the soldiers, risking her life in order to nurse their wounds and cook for the injured men. She became known as the 'Angel of the Battlefield'. This letter, written to an organisation that helped families discover what had happened to their missing loved ones, details Clara's personal knowledge of what life was like in the middle of a battle.

After the end of the Civil War, Clara travelled to Europe, where she learned about a new humanitarian charity, the Red Cross, which had been founded in Geneva, Switzerland, in 1863. She became determined to take its work to the United States. In 1881, at the age of 59, Clara founded the American Red Cross, remaining its president for the next 23 years. She retired from Red Cross service at the age of 83, in 1904.

Three years later, she published her autobiography, *The Story of My Childhood*, inspired, as explained in its preface, by letters she had received from schoolchildren telling her that they were studying her life in their history classes. In 1912, Clara Barton died at Glen Echo, her home in Maryland. The house is now a National Historic Site.

Opposite In her later years, Barton became a well-known public figure. Here, she is seen ceremonially planting a tree in a hospital garden.

December 8th

Dear friends

A letter of Dec 4 asking information of your "Son," D.H. Windham, last heard of at Fort Wagner is before me. Ordinarily I should reply to your inquiry by saying that I would place the name upon my rolls of Missing Men, and search as best I could. I will do so – But your letter draws upon my recollections for a few words more. Not that I remember your son, I wish I did, but I remember the charge on Wagner that terrible night at the 18th of July 1863 – Only those whose eyes took in that scene will ever realize it. – During four long hours preceding that charge, I watched those doomed men marching and countermarching, or fixed in a solid phalanx waiting that charge of death. Then four other hours of carnage such as God grant you may never realize, where the rolling valleys of destruction alone lit up the misty blackness of the night, then they bore the wounded back along the wave washed beach, and the surging ocean sang its solemn requiem for the dead.

They lay by hundreds, wounded and bleeding, in the wet salt sands about my little tent, and and [sic] God in his goodness gave me speed to my feet and strength to my arms through the hours of that fearful night that I might nourish the fainting, slake the thirst of the dying, and strive to staunch the life stream as it ebbes away. It seemed as if day light would never come, but when at length its welcome beams broke over us, we were no longer swept by shot, but the field of palid upturned faces and eyes forever still, showed only too plainly how broad a wing the Death Angel had flapped above us, and they told us of a six hundred that lay dead in the Fort, whereon no comrade ere might look, whereof no mother know.

I will not ask your pardon my dear friends for having recalled here events to you – they will neither appease nor distress you, your son was a soldier, his regiment well known to me and you who have suffered so much will be still strong enough to listen while I who stood among, and saw, and knew them all, relate the scenes which to him I fear were the last of earth – true he may have been captured and a prisoner after this – this I will endeavour by all means in my power to ascertain for you. And I will write to his surgeon, who is my friend, and one of the noblest men in the world, for any clue which he may give me, and if I can get a trace however small I will send it at once to you …
Pardon my long letter, …

Truly your friend,
Clara Barton

Office of Correspondence with the Friends of the

Missing Men of the United States Army,

Washington, D. C., Dec. 8th , 1865.

Dear friends

A letter of Dec 4 asking information
of your "Son" D.H. Windham. last heard of at Fort Wagner
is before me.   Ordinarily I should reply to your inquiry
by saying that I would place the name upon my rolls of
Missing Men, and search as best I could. — I will do so —
But your letter draws upon my recollections for a few
words more. Not that I remember your son. I wish I
did; but I remember the charge on Wagner — that
terrible night of the 18th of July 1863 — Only those whose
eyes took in that scene will ever realize it; — During
four long hours preceeding that charge. I watched
those doomed men marching and countermarching, or
fixed in solid phalanx awaiting that charge of
death. then four other hours of carnage such
as God grant you may never realize, where the
rolling volleys of destruction alone lit up the
misty blackness of the night; then they bore the
wounded back along the wave washed beach, and the
surging ocean sang its solemn requiem for the dead;
They lay by hundreds, wounded and bleeding

Office of Correspondence with the Friends of the
Missing Men of the United States Army,

Washington, D. C., _____ , 1865.

in the wet salt sands about my little tent. and
and God in his goodness gave speed to my feet and
strength to my arms. through the hours of that fearful
night. that I might nourish the fainting. slake the
thirst of the dying, and strive to staunch the life
stream as it ebbed away, It seemed as if day
light would never come. but when at length its welcome
beams broke over us, we were no longer swept by
shot, but the field of palid upturned faces and eyes
forever still, showed only too plainly how broad a
wing the Death Angel had flapped above us. and
they told us of Six hundred that lay dead in the
Fort. whereon, no comrade eye might look whereof
no mother know.

I will not ask your pardon my dear
friends for having recalled these events to you
— they will neither appall nor dishers you. your
son was a soldier, his regiment well known to me
and you who have suffered so much will be
still strong enough to listen while I who stood
among, and saw, and knew them all, relate the

Office of Correspondence with the Friends of the
Missing Men of the United States Army,

Washington, D. C., _____ *, 1865.*

scenes which to him I fear, were the last of
earth – true he may have been captured
and a prisoner after this – this I will
endeavor by all means in my power to
ascertain for you – And I will write to
his surgeon, who is my friend, and one of the
noblest men in the world, for any clue which
he may give me, and if I can get a trace
however small, I will send it at once to
you – Pardon my long letter, & believe me

Truly your friend
Clara Barton

Rev. C. R. Townsend
Chillicothe
Livingston Co
Missouri

Missing J. H. Windham
Co H. 100 N Y vols
last heard of at Wagner – on 18th July 1862 –

JULIA MARGARET CAMERON

Photographer, 1815–1879
To Henry Cole, 21 February 1866

Julia Margaret Cameron received her first camera when she was 48 years old. She had recently moved to a house at Freshwater on the Isle of Wight, an island off the south coast of England. Although she loved her new home, she found life there rather lonely and isolating. Her husband was working in Ceylon (present-day Sri Lanka) and her sons were away at school. The camera was a present from her daughter Julia, who had recently married and moved away from home. She and her husband sent it to her mother in December 1863 with a note saying, 'It may amuse you … to try to photograph your solitude at Freshwater.'

Julia Margaret Pattle was born in Calcutta (present-day Kolkata). She was one of the legendary Pattle sisters, who grew up in India before moving to London and entering fashionable bohemian society. Julia was friends with many of the foremost artists and writers of her time, and through her photography she captured images of many of the most famous Victorians. Ever since the royal family had built a home on the Isle of Wight, it had become an increasingly fashionable location, and one of Julia's neighbours was the Poet Laureate, Alfred Lord Tennyson. Their homes became renowned for the brilliant people who visited, and Julia frequently used them as her models. In addition to her famous friends, she also paid models, predominantly women, to help create her ideal of the perfect artistic photograph.

This letter was sent to Henry Cole, the first director of the South Kensington Museum, now known as the Victoria & Albert Museum (V&A), less than three years after she had first started taking photographs. Her progress was extraordinarily rapid considering that she later recorded that she 'began with no knowledge of the art', explaining 'I did not know where to place my dark box, how to focus my sitter', but she persevered and created an entirely new style of photography. She was firmly of the belief that she didn't need to stick to the rules that were already being created for early photographers, famously saying that she often chose to focus the lens only to the point that she considered the most beautiful, not necessarily ensuring that the subject was in sharp focus. This, and the fact that she was a woman, ensured that she was roundly criticised by male photographers and critics, but she continued undaunted and confident in her abilities. A year before she sent this letter, her first museum exhibition had been held at the South Kensington Museum. The museum also bought many of her works for its collection.

Often known as the 'Pre-Raphaelite photographer', Cameron was considered an integral part of the art world. She was one of the very first women in the world to become a professional photographer and has remained influential ever since the 1860s.

In the mid-1870s, Julia returned to Asia. She and her husband, Charles Hay Cameron, owned several plantations in Ceylon. Their son Henry was living in the mountains in Ceylon, and in 1879, Julia became ill while visiting him. She died of a bronchial condition, something from which she had often suffered, at the age of 63. Julia Margaret Cameron is buried at the Glencairn Cemetery in Kandy, Sri Lanka.

Opposite In this photograph from 1872, Alice Liddell posed as Pomona, the Roman goddess of fruit trees. Aged 20 in this image, Liddell had been the inspiration for the title character in Lewis Carroll's *Alice's Adventures in Wonderland.*

Fresh Water Bay
Isle of Wight

Feb 21st [1866]

My Dear Mr Cole

I write to ask you if you will be having any Photographic Soirée or meeting soon at which I may send to the Science & Art Dept. for you to exhibit at the South Kensington Museum a set of Prints of my late series of Photographs that I intend should electrify you with delight & startle the world. I hope it is no vain imagination of mine to say that the like have never been produced & never can be surpassed! I am waxing mad in my own conceit you will say -

All I beg is that you show this assertion to our dear Annie Thackeray & sister Minnie & ask them if they take my assurance upon trust! Seeing is believing & you shall see & the world shall see if you can create for me a great occasion! Because these wonderful Photographs should come out all at once & take the world by surprise! They are quite ready – A new series of 12 & if you watch my opport[unities] for me & acquaint me I will answer at once by sending you the supply. Mr Thurston Thompson I hope will be delighted this time.

Won't the South Kensington Museum give me a crown! Not of diamond stones but those better diamond laurel leaves – or a Medal or honorable [sic] mention if this series of Photographs of mine surpasses all others – Talk of roundness I have it in perfect perfection!

Yet these great successes have come like meteors out of anxious troubled times–! I have been for 8 weeks nursing poor Philip Worsley on his dying bed – & I have been with him a great part of every day & also a great part of the night. The heart of man cannot conceive a sight more pitiful than the outward evidence of the breaking up of his whole being but he has had a sister to nurse him whose devotion has surpassed in power & sustained energy anything I have ever seen. For 8 weeks she has never been to bed! She won't sleep whilst I take my turn but only gets snatches of rest by his side in her chair. Please tell my old friend Mr Bruce also yr. son Allan what I say of my 12 new pictures & show Lord Elcho this note of triumph if you see him – for I have been too anxious with this case to learn if they are in Town –

Yours Ever

Julia Margaret Cameron

Fresh Water Bay
Isle of Wight
IW 21766

P.S. You will give my love to your Wife I hope I still have in a parcel awaiting an oppt. the set of prints frm my former Photos that I reserved for your Wife – and please tell me if you have heard of the arrival of your married son & his Wife I hope she likes India better than she expected to do –

Above *Annie*, described by Cameron as 'My very first success in
Photography', a portrait of ten-year-old Annie Philpot taken in 1964.

ELIZABETH GARRETT ANDERSON

Doctor, 1836–1917

To her sister, Millicent Garrett Fawcett, 1867

Elizabeth Garrett was born in Whitechapel, London, but grew up in Suffolk. As a teenager, she met Elizabeth Blackwell, a Briton who had become the first woman to qualify as a doctor in the USA after medical schools in the UK had refused to accept her. From that moment on, Elizabeth Garrett fought to become a doctor and, in doing so, paved the way for all female medics to come.

After she was denied the right to go to medical school in Britain, Elizabeth enrolled to train as a nurse and began studying on her own to become a doctor. Initially, she joined medical students' classes, but when the male medical students complained, she was banned from attending on the grounds of her sex. The establishment did not think, however, to extend this ban to prevent her from sitting for medical exams, and in 1865, she passed the Society of Apothecaries' exams. As a result, the Society of Apothecaries changed the legislation to prevent other women following her example. In the same year, she and a group of friends formed the Kensington Society, which fought for female suffrage.

Elizabeth refused to be cowed by the patriarchal medical world. In 1866, she opened the St Mary's Dispensary for Women in Central London. Determined to become a fully qualified doctor, and barred from doing so in Britain, she moved to Paris. There she completed her degree and, in 1870, qualified as a doctor. On returning home, she was appointed visiting physician to the East London Hospital. The following year she married James Anderson, a businessman with whom she had two daughters and a son. Their eldest daughter, Luisa, would also become a pioneering doctor.

In 1872, Elizabeth set up the New Hospital for Women in London, moving to purpose-built facilities in 1890. This was the first hospital in Britain to be staffed entirely by female medical staff. In 1918, the year after its founder's death, its name was changed to the Elizabeth Garrett Anderson Hospital.

In 1876, thanks largely to Elizabeth Garrett Anderson's tireless campaigning, British law was changed, and women were finally permitted to enter the medical profession. Seven years later, Elizabeth was appointed Dean of the London School of Medicine for Women, and in 1892 she became the first female member of the British Medical Association (BMA).

Elizabeth had benefitted from being born into a remarkable family of siblings, whose parents believed in their daughters' as well as their sons' abilities. One of Elizabeth's sisters, Millicent Garrett Fawcett, was the leader of the National Union of Women's Suffrage Societies (NUWSS). Another sister, Agnes Garrett, together with their cousin Rhoda Garrett, set up the very first female-run interior design company in Britain. This letter, written to Millicent in 1867, demonstrates Elizabeth's support for her sister's campaigning. Elizabeth's reluctance to publicly endorse women's suffrage at the time shows how precarious she felt her new medical practice to be.

In her seventies, Elizabeth Garrett Anderson made history again. She had retired from medicine in 1902 and returned to live in her childhood hometown of Aldeburgh, in Suffolk. There, in 1908, she became the first woman in Britain to be elected mayor.

Opposite Top A ward at the New Hospital for Women, pictured in 1899.
Opposite Bottom Female students at work in the Physiology Department at the London School of Medicine, to which women were first admitted in 1874.

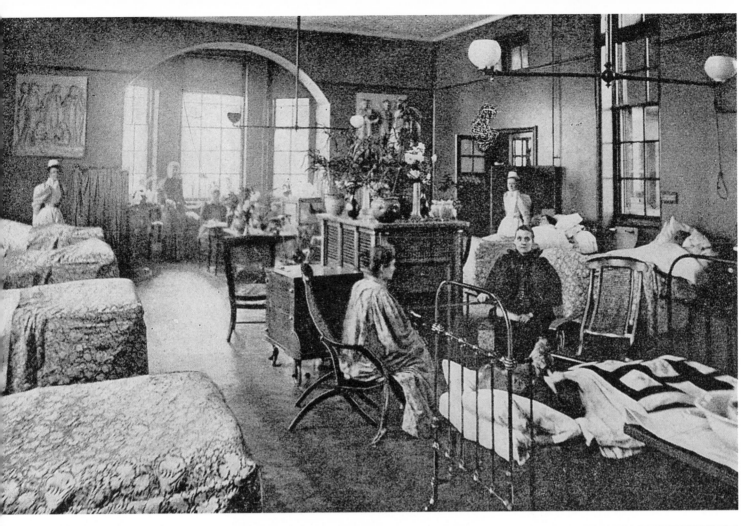

June 1867

Dearest Milly

I shall be very glad to subscribe £1.1/. a year to the Franchise Society but I wd. rather not have my name advertised on the Gen Committee.

I think it is wiser as a medical woman to keep somewhat in the background as regards other movements. I do not mind my name appearing in any list for private circulation but I particularly wish it not to appear in public advertisements.

Will you please tell Mrs. P.A. Taylor this, & beg her to put a mark against my name that my request may not by any inadvertence be forgotten.

I was very glad you went to the Volunteer Ball & enjoyed it. I wish it were safe for you to come here and tell me about it. I am getting very irritable with inactivity & silence. However it is two thirds over now, I am glad to say.

We are very much shocked by the news of Mrs ——'s sudden death. They live close by here.

Ever yours lovingly
Elizabeth

Opposite The New Hospital for Women moved to this purpose-built facility on the Euston Road, London, in 1890.

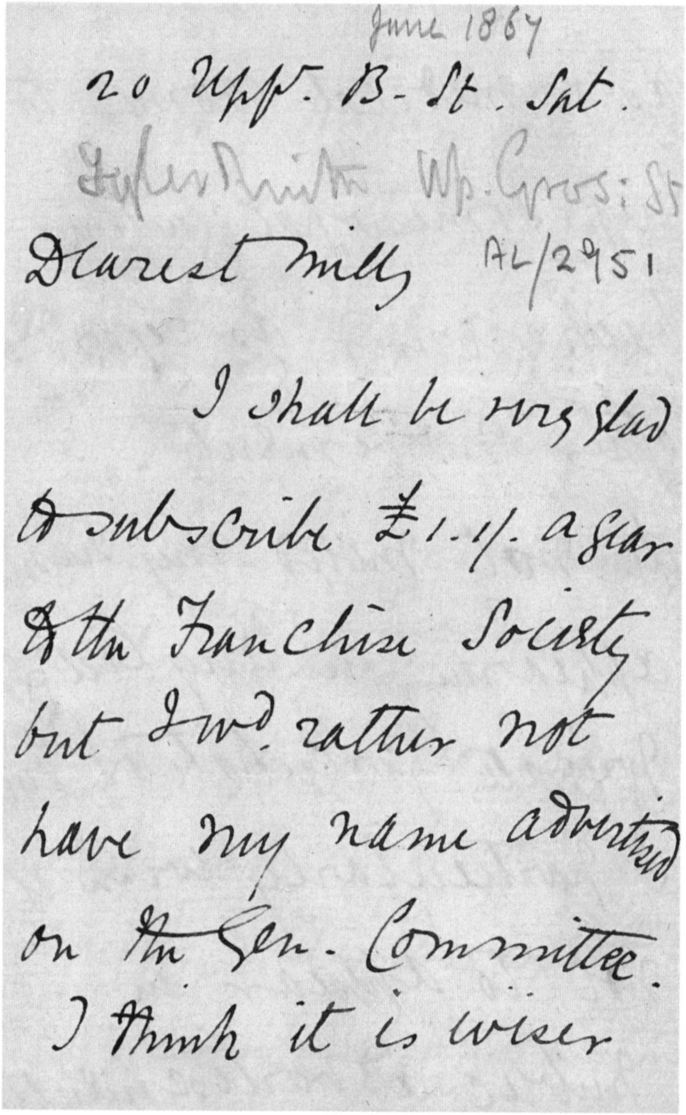

June 1867

20 Upp. B. St. Sat.

Tyler Smith Up. Gros: St

Dearest Milly   AL/2951

I shall be very glad
to subscribe £1.1/. a Year
to the Franchise Society
but I wd. rather not
have my name advertised
on the Gen. Committee.
I think it is wiser

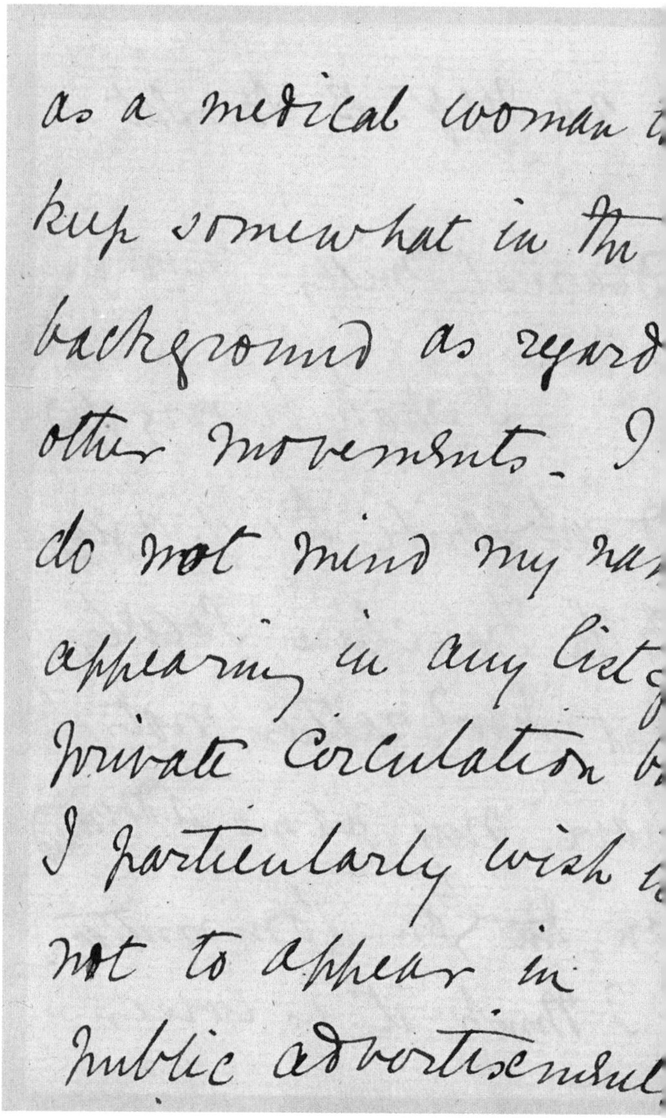

as a medical woman to
keep somewhat in the
background as regards
other movements. I
do not mind my name
appearing in any list for
private circulation but
I particularly wish it
not to appear in
public advertisement

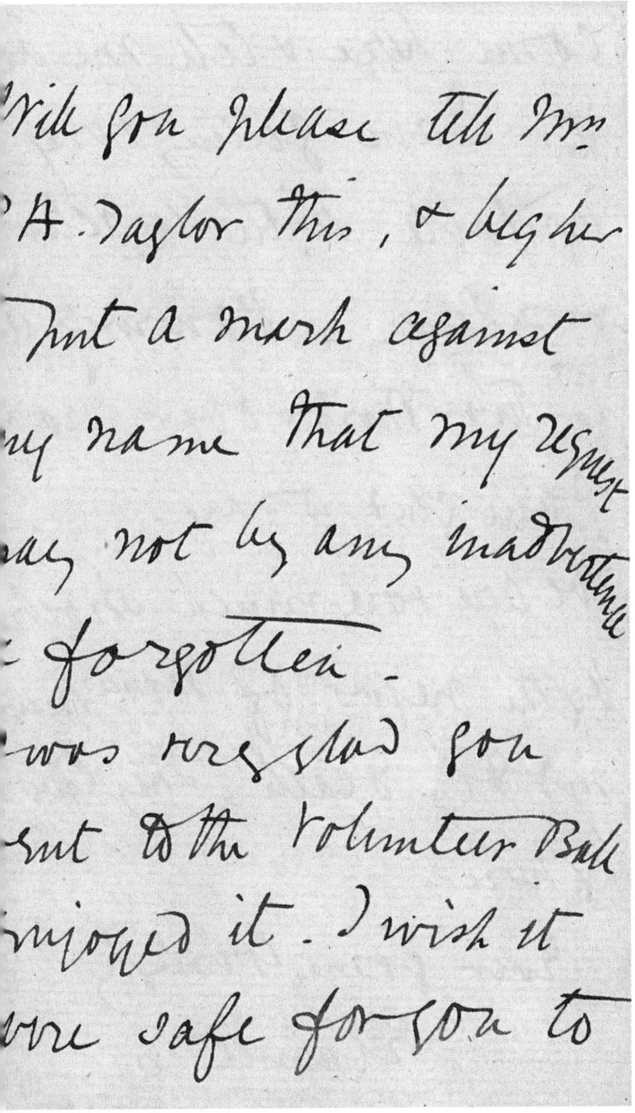

Will you please tell Mrs
A. Taylor this, & beg her
Put a mark against
my name that my request
may not by any inadvertence
be forgotten.

was very glad you
went to the Volunteer Ball
enjoyed it. I wish it
were safe for you to

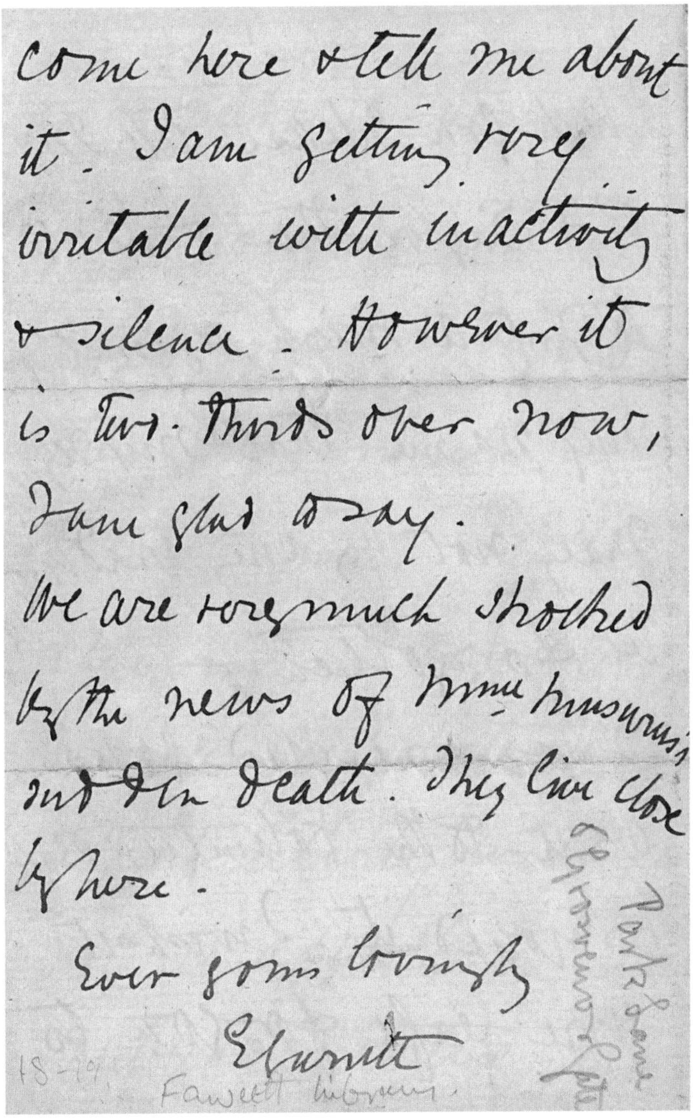

come here & tell me about
it. I am getting very
irritable with inactivity
& silence. However it
is Two-thirds over now,
I am glad to say.
We are very much shocked
by the news of Mrs. Husum's
sudden death. They live close
by here.

Ever yours lovingly

Elizabeth

EDMONIA LEWIS

Artist, 1844–1907
To Maria Weston Chapman, 3 May 1868

American artist Edmonia Lewis sent this letter from the former studio of Italian neoclassical sculptor Antonio Canovo in Rome. She was working there as part of a group that American author Henry James described as 'that strange sisterhood of American "lady sculptors"'. In a condescending article, James refers to Lewis as 'a negress, whose colour picturesquely contrasting with that of her plastic material [white marble], was the pleading agent of her fame'. He sneeringly suggests that Lewis's success was due to the novelty of a black female sculptor: a woman working with physically demanding materials in the neoclassical style, patronised by and pandering to liberal Americans. Ironically, Edmonia herself was well aware that her anomalous position could be used to her advantage as a marketing device, and she often embroidered the rich raw material of her life, taking advantage of the market for images of the 'noble savage' to overcome the barriers to her success. In the process, she became the first woman of colour to be recognised as a major artistic presence in America and Europe.

Playing to the stereotypes, Mary Edmonia Lewis claimed to have been 'born in a wigwam' and spent her childhood in the forest with her mother's people. Her mother was of Native American Ojibwe and African-American descent, while her father was African-American. But she was actually born in Albany, upstate New York, in 1844. After her parents died, she moved to Niagara Falls to live with her aunts, who sold Ojibwe baskets and embroidered blouses to tourists. In later life, she would be drawn to the poetry of Henry Wadsworth Longfellow, and she created a series of sculptures based on his work *The Song of Hiawatha* (1855), about the Ojibwe warrior. Longfellow visited Lewis's studio in Rome in 1869, and the bust she made of him was acquired for Harvard University.

Supported by her brother Samuel, who had made money in the Gold Rush, Edmonia was accepted to study art at Oberlin College, Ohio. Racism reared its head there when she was accused of poisoning two fellow students. She was subsequently savagely beaten by unknown assailants and accused of theft. As a result of these incidents, Edmonia felt forced to leave college before graduating. She moved to Boston to train as a sculptor, and had her first solo exhibition in 1864. Her initial sales were plaster and clay medallions of abolitionists and war heroes. Her bust of Colonel Robert Gould Shaw, commander of an African-American regiment, was purchased by his family, and she subsequently sold 100 plaster-cast reproductions of it for $15 each. This money allowed her to move to Rome, where she joined that 'sisterhood of lady sculptors' and met Maria Weston Chapman, to whom this letter is addressed.

Forever Free, mentioned in the letter, takes its title from the Emancipation Proclamation of 1863. Lewis shipped it, unsolicited, to Samuel Sewell, a Boston-based abolitionist lawyer, along with an $800 invoice. Sewell eventually found a buyer, and the statue is now housed in Howard University, Washington, DC. Her largest and most powerful piece, *The Death of Cleopatra*, was accepted for the Centennial Exhibition of 1876 in Philadelphia, but it did not sell and for many years was placed alongside a racetrack in a Chicago suburb. The statue eventually found its way to the Smithsonian, where much conservation work has been undertaken.

Edmonia Lewis's fame and fortune faded in the final decades of her life as her neoclassical style went out of fashion, and her exact movements in her later life remain unknown. It is known that she moved in 1901 to London, England, where she died of kidney disease in 1907.

Opposite Edmonia Lewis's sculpture *Forever Free*, created in 1867.

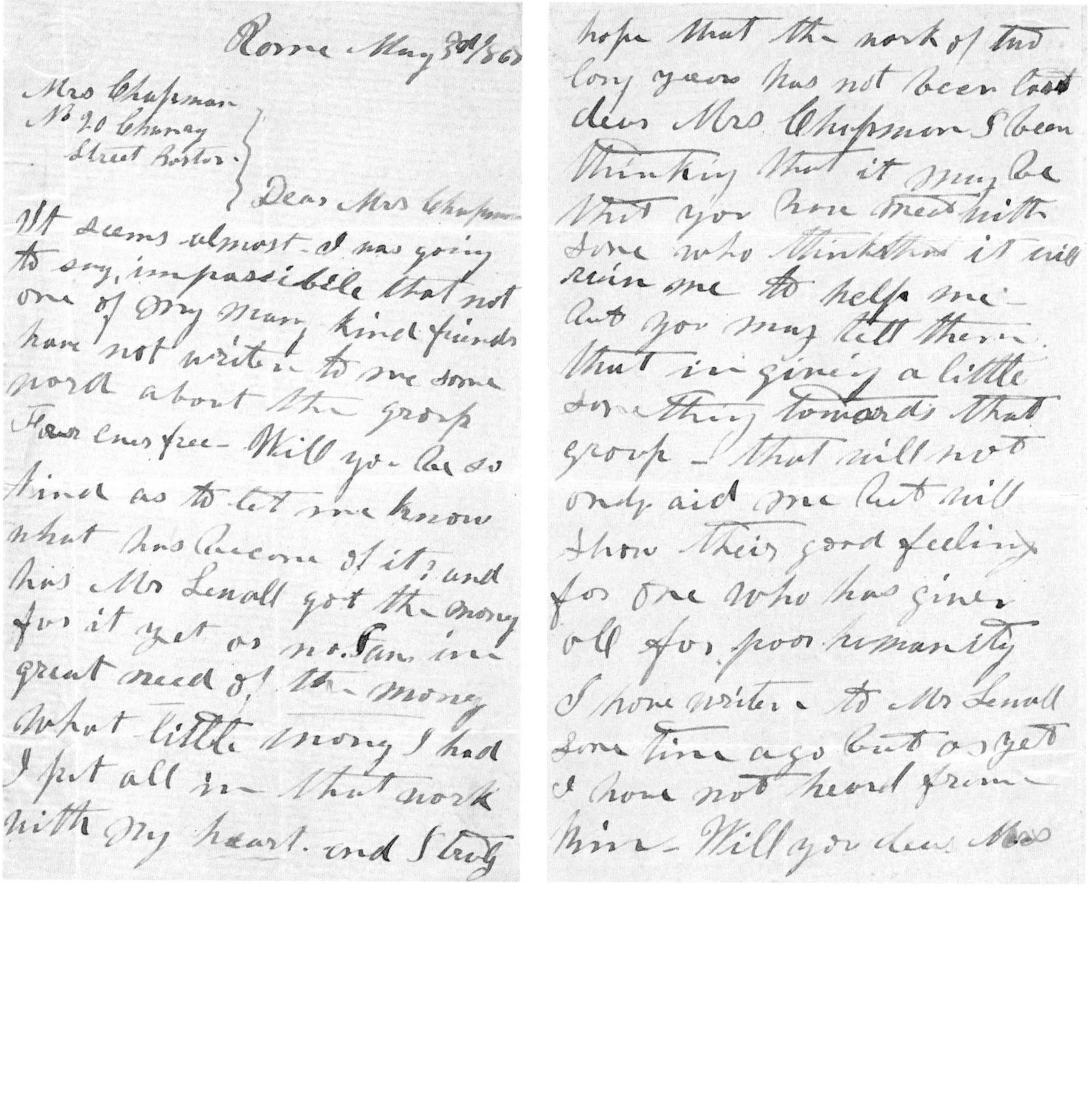

Rome May 3d/66

Mrs Chapman
No 20 Chauncy
  Street Boston

    Dear Mrs Chapman
It seems almost I was going
to say, impossible that not
one of my many kind friends
have not written to me some
word about the group
Forever free – Will you be so
kind as to let me know
what has become of it, and
has Mr Lenox got the money
for it yet or no. I am in
great need of the money
What little money I had
I put all in that work
with my heart. and I truly

hope that the work of two
long years has not been lost
dear Mrs Chapman I been
thinking that it may be
that you have met with
some who thinks that it will
ruin me to help me
But you may tell them
that in giving a little
something towards that
group – that will not
only aid me but will
show their good feeling
for one who has given
all for poor humanity
I have written to Mr Lenox
some time ago but as yet
I have not heard from
him – Will you dear Mrs

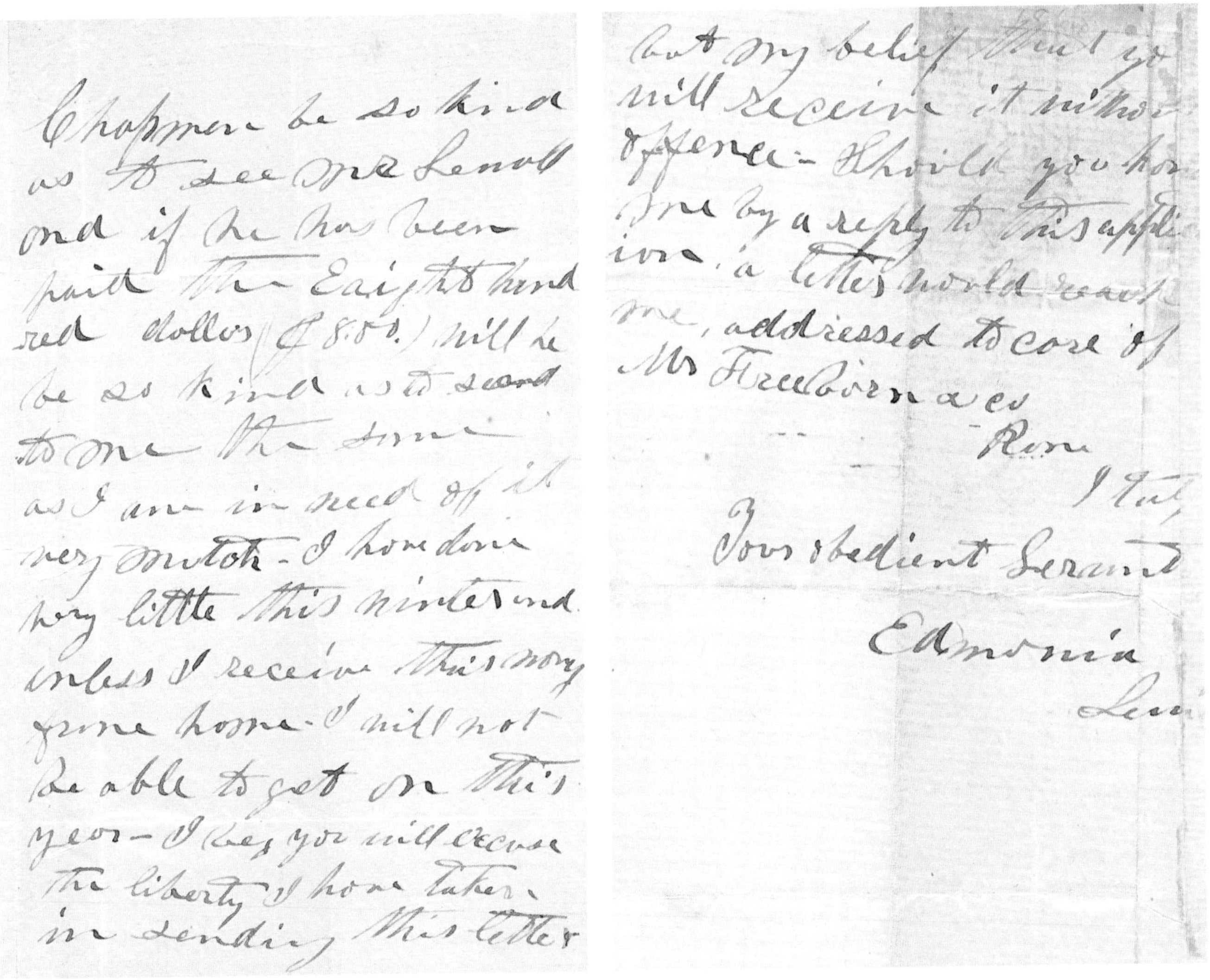

Chapman be so kind
as to see Mr Lenox
and if he has been
paid the Eaight hund
red dollars ($800.) will he
be so kind as to send
to me the same
as I am in need of it
very mutch - I have done
very little this winter and
unless I receive this money
from home I will not
be able to get on this
year - I beg you will excuse
the liberty I have taken
in sending this letter

but my belief that it
will receive it without
offence - Should you hon
our me by a reply to this applic
ion, a letter would reach
me, addressed to care of
Mr Freeborn & es
Rome
I'et,
Your obedient Servant
Edmonia
Lew

Rome May 3rd 1868

Mrs Chapman
No 20 Chauncy Street, Boston

Dear Mrs Chapman

It seems almost I was going to say, impossible that not one of my kind friends have not writen to me some word about the group For ever free – Will you be so kind as to let me know what has become of it? And has Mr Sewall got the money for it yet or not. I am in great need of the money. What little money I had I put all in that work with my heart. And I truly hope that the work of two long years has not been lost. Dear Mrs Chapman I been thinking that it may be that you have meat with some who think that it will ruin me to help me – but you may tell them that in giving a little something towards that group – that will not only aid me but will show their good feeling for one who has given all for poor humanity. I have written to Mr Sewall some time ago but as yet I have not heard from him – Will you dear Mrs Chapman be so kind as to see Mr Sewall and if he has been paid the Eight hundred dollars ($800.) will he be so kind as to send to me the same as I am in need of it very mutch – I have done very little this winter and unless I receive this money from home – I will not be able to get on this year – I beg you will excuse the liberty I have taken in sending this letter but my belief that you will receive it without offence – Should you honor me by a reply to this application, a letter would reach me, addressed to care of Mr Freeborn & Co

Rome
Italy

Your obedient Servant
Edmonia Lewis

Opposite Edmonia Lewis's work *The Death of Cleopatra*, created in 1876, won her great acclaim, but went unsold at the Centennial Exhibition.

Dear Miss Nightingale,

     I hope you have ere now received the official receipt of our treasurer Mr. Sheen for your kind donation to the fund for the little orphans. – But I must write myself & thank you for it individually. – Each among the large number who know her must feel that they held their own special place with the noble friend who is gone from among them, how deeply I felt this few if any can ever know, that magnificent grasp of the noblest spirit in wh life can be conceived, or action planned; that sympathy with utter unselfishness; that sweetness that never failed; generosity that knew no bound are not so much lost for their memory remains to us for ever, but the response to the best imaginations we cd reach. The never exhausted tenderness. The voice we never may hear, the works that never may strengthen us again, the love, the trust, that may not alter themselves any more in mortal voice so dear and so familiar leave a gap, a blank, a desolateness wh may not be filled here. – One can only hope to be better by all memories of the eternal things & to know that all that is eternal – all that is good – is safe for us somewhere when we shall have past through the waves of this troubled life.

     I had not known you knew her so well.

I am Yours truly
Octavia Hill

14 Nottingham Place W.
Nov 29th/77

OCTAVIA HILL

Social activist and campaigner, 1838–1912
To Florence Nightingale, 29 November 1877

Octavia Hill was born into an upper-middle-class family that lived under constant threat of poverty. This unusual background gave her both influential friends and a genuine understanding of what it was like to live not knowing how the bills were going to be paid. Her father was James Hill, a corn merchant, and her mother was Caroline Southwood Smith, daughter of Dr Thomas Southwood Smith, an influential campaigner and social reformer who had helped to revolutionise early-Victorian philanthropy. When James's business failed, his father-in-law gave the family financial aid, but life became very difficult for the Hill children as their father struggled with depression.

Octavia was greatly influenced by her mother, who took on employment to support the family – something highly unusual in their social class – and began working with various social campaigns. By then, the family had left their home in idyllic Wisbech in Cambridgeshire and moved to London, where Octavia was shocked to see the extent of poverty all around the city. After reading the work of social campaigner Henry Mayhew, she was inspired to follow a similar course.

A kind, generous and likeable woman, Octavia Hill used her charm and connections to fund and bring about social reform. This letter, about fundraising to help orphans, was written to the nurse and campaigner Florence Nightingale in 1877. Hill was very aware of the importance of making alliances with influential people.

Octavia was involved in many good causes, but her main work centred around housing reform, which was desperately needed in Victorian Britain. She was aided by the influential – and wealthy – art critic and philanthropist John Ruskin. By the mid-1870s, Hill was spearheading 15 different housing schemes, and these increased over the following decades, improving the lives of thousands of Londoners. In 1884, she was invited to become one of the commissioners on the Royal Commission on Housing – an invitation which was rescinded over fury that a woman had been asked to join. The housing charity she founded, now called simply Octavia, is still going today.

Another of Octavia Hill's passions was preventing beautiful landscapes from being bought by developers. To this end, she worked with her sister Miranda, who had founded the philanthropic Society for the Diffusion of Beauty (later renamed the Kyrle Society), whose aim was 'to bring beauty home to the people'. In the 1880s, she took on a challenge to save a garden under threat in south-east London. Her work on this project would lead to the foundation of one of Britain's most important historical charities, the National Trust.

The death of Octavia Hill in 1912 prompted widespread mourning among her wide circle of friends and colleagues. A wreath sent by the artist Princess Louise (daughter of Queen Victoria) carried the words, 'In deepest admiration and esteem for one who devoted her whole life and energy to the advancement and welfare of her fellow-countrymen.' It was a fitting epitaph for a woman who had improved so many lives, and whose legacy would continue to do so for generations to come.

Opposite Top This engraving from 1871 shows a vaccination programme in London's East End, where Octavia Hill did much work to highlight child poverty.

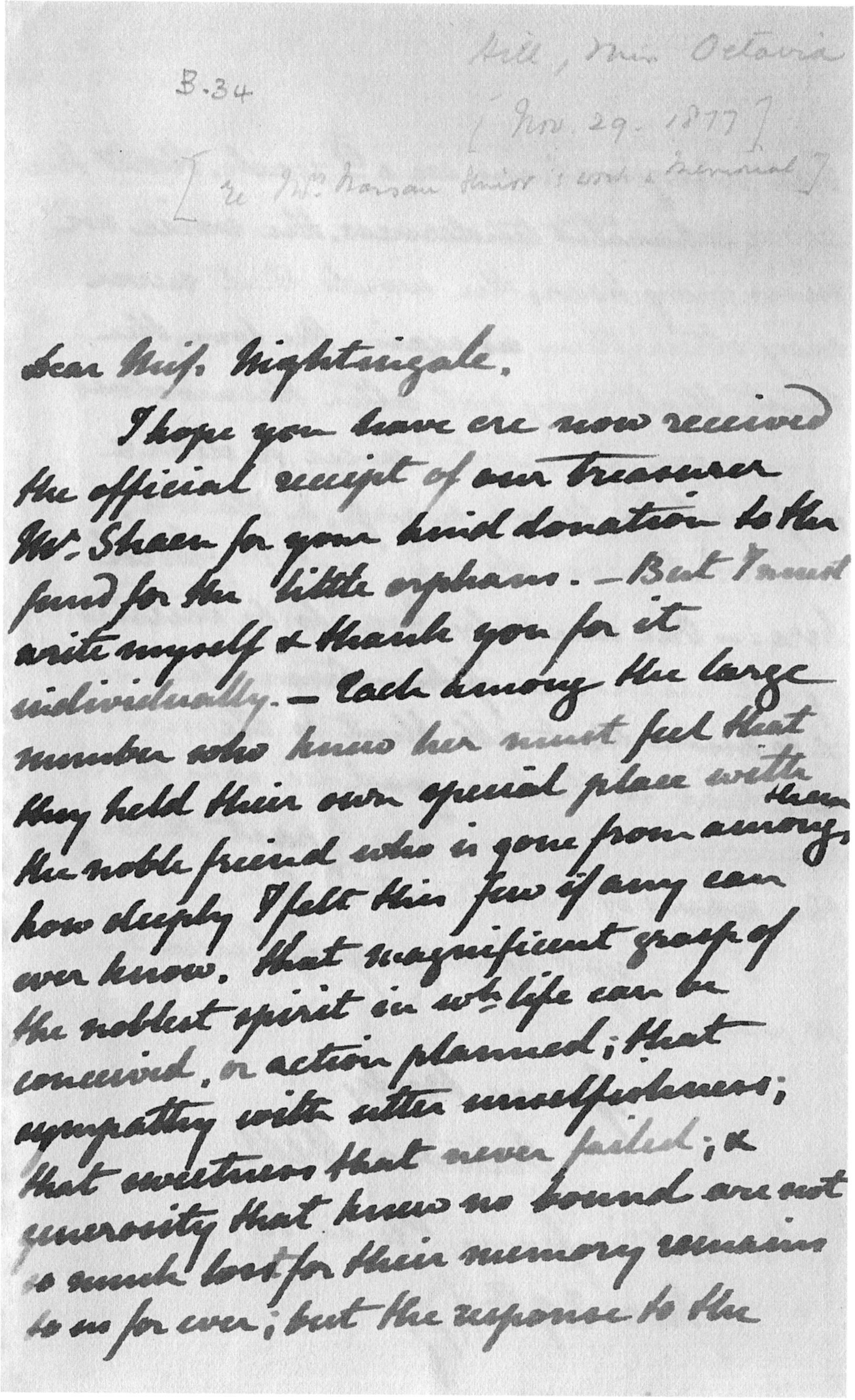

B.34

Hill, Miss Octavia

[Nov. 29. 1877]

[re Mrs Nassau Senior's work & memorial]

Dear Miss Nightingale,

I hope you have ere now received the official receipt of our treasurer Mr Sheen for your kind donation to the fund for the "little orphans. — But I must write myself & thank you for it individually. — Each among the large number who knew her must feel that they held their own special place with the noble friend who is gone from among them, how deeply I felt this few if any can ever know. That magnificent grasp of the noblest spirit in wh life can be conceived, or action planned; that sympathy with utter unselfishness; that sweetness that never failed; & generosity that knew no bound are not so much lost for their memory remains to us for ever; but the response to the best imaginations we cd reach, that the never exhausted tenderness, the voice we never may hear, the words that never may strengthen us again, the love, the trust, that may not alter themselves any more in mortal voice so dear & so familiar leave a gap, a blank, a desolateness wh may not be filled here. — One can only hope to be bettered by all memories of ~~the eternal things~~ & to know that all that is eternal — all that is that is good ~~is~~ safe for us somewhere where we shall have past through the waves of this troubled life. —

I had not known you knew her so well. — I am

Yours truly
Octavia Hill

14 Nottingham Place W.

Nov 29th/77.

SOPHIA JEX-BLAKE

Doctor, 1840–1912
To the editor of *The Scottish News*, 8 March 1886

Born into a middle-class family in Hastings, England, Sophia Jex-Blake fought against her parents' wishes and the prevailing social norms in order to study maths, to become a teacher and, later, to be allowed to study medicine. As a teenager, she attended Queen's College in London, a pioneering school that trained women to become teachers; while she was studying, Sophia began working as a mathematics tutor. Her father was against her working for a living, so he only permitted her to work as a teacher if she refused to accept a salary.

In her early twenties, Sophia had not yet thought about entering the medical profession. To further her teaching career, she took a position in Mannheim, Germany. After a year in Germany, she returned home, before setting sail for America, where she had been given an introduction to Dr Lucy Sewell in Boston. Sophia travelled around America visiting educational establishments, after which she wrote a book about her experiences. On returning to Boston, she started volunteering at the New England Hospital for Women and Children, and this inspired her to become a doctor.

Initially, Sophia travelled to New York to study with Elizabeth Blackwell, a British doctor who had become the first woman to complete a medical degree in the United States, graduating in 1849. Sophia's stay in New York was cut short when she learned that her father was gravely ill and returned to England. Back home, she hoped to become a medical student at the University of Cambridge but was denied entry. As a result of this rejection, she and six other female students began studying at the University of Edinburgh. When they were refused the chance to earn their degrees because of their sex, Sophia tried taking the university to court. Although her court case failed to achieve her aim of being allowed into the medical school, it succeeded in making her cause far more widely known, and it created a movement within the university faculty to bring about change. For years, the 'Edinburgh Seven' continued to lobby the government, and it was largely due to their persistence that the law finally changed in 1889, when an Act of Parliament finally sanctioned women being allowed to receive degrees. This letter to *The Scottish News* was sent at the height of their campaign, three years before the Act of Parliament was passed.

In the mid-1870s, exhausted by the battle in Edinburgh, Sophia moved to Berne, Switzerland, where she qualified as a doctor. While working as a doctor, she helped to found two medical training schools, one in Scotland and one in England: the Edinburgh School of Medicine for Women, and the London School of Medicine for Women. She also founded a women's hospital in Edinburgh, having realised that male doctors had scant knowledge of gynaecological medicine. She later joined the fight for women's suffrage, speaking at public meetings and sharing her own journey of fighting against the establishment.

In the 1890s, Sophia began a relationship with the writer Margaret Todd. They lived together as 'companions' until Sophia died in 1912. Five years later, Margaret published a biography of Sophia Jex-Blake, in which she referred to their partnership only as a 'romantic friendship'.

<u>Medical Education of Women</u>
Bruntsfield Lodge, Edinburgh March 8th 1886

Sir,

I think it cannot be too widely known that the Scottish Colleges of Physicians & Surgeons (of Edinburgh & Glasgow) have just decided a division to throw open their conjoint examinations to women, and to grant them their "triple qualification" in Medicine, Surgery and Midwifery.

Diplomas have long been open to women both in England and Ireland, and a special Medical School has existed in London since 1872 while last year the Irish College of Surgeons threw open not only all its examinations & diplomas but also all its classes to women, separate arrangements being made in Practical Anatomy only.

Now that the Scottish Colleges have decided on action of the same wise and liberal character, we believe that there will be no difficulty in re-opening medical classes for women also in Scotland, and I shall be glad to hear from all ladies who desire to join such classes in the summer or winter session.

I am sir,
Your obeds [obedient servant]
Sophia Jex Blake M.D.

[To] The Editor of
The Scottish News

Medical Education of Women

Bruntsfield Lodge, Edinburgh
March 8th 1886

Sir, I think it cannot be too widely known that the Scottish College of Physicians & Surgeons (of Edinburgh & Glasgow) have just decided within a division to throw open their ~~conjoint qualify~~ examinations to women, & to grant them their "triple qualification" in Medicine, Surgery, & Midwifery —

Diplomas ~~are already~~ have long been open to women both in England & Ireland, & a special Medical School has ~~been opened~~ existed in London since 18__ while last year the Irish College of Surgeons threw open not only all its examinations & diplomas but also all its classes to women, separate arrangements being made in Practical Anatomy only —

Now that the Scottish Colleges
have decided on the action of the
Senate wise a liberal character,
we believe that there will be no
difficulty in re-opening medical
classes for women also in Scotland,
& I shall be glad to hear from
all ladies who desire to join
such classes in the ensuing
Winter Session —

I am Sir

Y.r obed.t
Sophia Jex Blake M.D. —

The Editor of
The Scottish News —

MARY CHURCH TERRELL

Activist, 1863–1954
To Mrs Stuyvesant Fish, 17 February 1901

Mary Eliza Church was born in Memphis, Tennessee, in the middle of the American Civil War. Both of her parents had been born into slavery, but by the time Mary and her younger brother Robert were born, the family was well on its way to prosperity. After gaining his freedom, Mary's father, Robert Reed Church, had become a successful businessman and banker; he was one of the first African Americans to become a millionaire. Mary's mother Louisa (née Ayres) owned a hair salon. Although Louisa and Robert divorced when their children were young, both parents were united in their desire to ensure that their children were well educated.

After finishing school, Mary attended university, at a time when very few women in North America, especially African American women, were educated to tertiary level. After gaining a Bachelor's degree, Mary taught at Wilberforce University and at a high school in Washington, DC. She achieved a Master's degree, then embarked on a two-year tour of Europe from 1888 to 1890. Her diaries from this time demonstrate her linguistic skills, containing entries written in both German and French. After returning to the US, she went back to work at the high school, marrying one of her colleagues, Robert Heberton Terrell, in 1891. They had four children, of whom only one baby, a daughter, survived. Later they adopted a second daughter.

One year after their wedding, one of the Terrells' friends, Thomas Moss, a grocer from Memphis, was murdered by a lynch mob of white supremacists. This outrage marked the start of Mary's activism. She helped to found the National Association of Colored Women, and became its president, guiding the association to focus on the importance of training women for the workplace, fighting for equal pay and setting up good childcare. Mary fought for the improved education of all African-American children, helping to found the National Association for the Advancement of Colored People. This letter, requesting money to establish more kindergartens for black children, was sent to the wealthy socialite Mamie Stuyvesant Fish in 1901. It demonstrates how aware Mary was of the need to foster relations between the white and black communities, and her desire to make the welfare of the poor the responsibility of the rich.

Mary joined the women's suffrage campaign and founded an alumnae club for African American women who had attended university. She continually challenged racial stereotyping and spoke out against all forms of prejudice. In her later years, she published an autobiography, *A Colored Woman in a White World* (1940), and raised repeated legal challenges to discrimination. Even into her eighties, she continued to fight against the US policy of racial segregation. Mary Church Terrell's tireless campaigning helped to lay the foundations for the Civil Rights movement that would finally bring about an end to segregation in the United States, although she died a decade before the passing of the pivotal Civil Rights Act of 1964.

Opposite Mary Church Terrell (centre, in the fur shawl) pictured in 1947 with fellow members of the National Association of Colored Women.

Washington D.C, Feb – 17 1901

Mrs Stuyvesant Fish,

      Dear Madam:

      The colored women of the country are trying to do something to improve the condition of our people. We feel that by reaching our children at an early age, we shall be able to do the most good. We are trying therefore to establish kindergarten for them especially in the South. A few such schools have already been founded and great good has been accomplished. We are sorely in need of funds to carry out our work and I take the liberty of appealing to you for aid. I have read of your genuine interest in all good works and I entertain the hope that this may enlist your sympathy – if you establish a kindergarten in a southern city, we shall name it for you, if you will permit us to do so. The cost will not be great and it will do untold good to the poor little barbarians who need it most …

little barbarians who need it most.

      Hoping for a favorable reply,

      I am very truly yours,

      Mary Church Terrell

MARY CHURCH TERRELL, PRES.,
326 T ST., N. W., WASHINGTON, D. C.

MARY A. LYNCH, COR. SEC.,
LIVINGSTON COLLEGE, SALISBURY, N. C.

CONNIE E. CURL, REC. SEC.,
2935 ARMOUR AVE., CHICAGO, ILL.

CARRIE W. CLIFFORD, REC. SEC.,
88 BURT ST., CLEVELAND, OHIO.

S. LILLIAN COLEMAN, REC SEC.,
2824 DOUGLASS ST., OMAHA, NEB.

JOSEPHINE S YATES, TREAS.,
2122 TRACY AVE., KANSAS CITY, MO.

JOSEPHINE B. BRUCE,
1ST VICE PRES.,
TUSKEGEE, ALA.

LUCY E. PHILLIPS,
2D VICE PRES.,
JACKSON, TENN.

MRS. BOOKER T. WASHINGTON,
CHAIRMAN EXECUTIVE COMMITTEE,
TUSKEGEE, ALA.

MRS. JEROME JEFFREY,
NATIONAL ORGANIZER,
15 JAMES ST., ROCHESTER, N. Y.

National Association of Colored Women.

ORGANIZED 1896.

Office of the President.

326 T Street, Northwest.

Washington, D. C., Feb- 17 1901

Mrs. Stuyvesant Fish,

Dear Madam;

The colored women of the country are trying to do something to improve the condition of our people. We feel that by reaching our children at an early age, we shall be able to do the most good. We are trying therefore to establish kindergartens for them especially in the South. A few such school have already been founded and great good has been accomplished - We are sorely in need of funds to carry on our work and I take the liberty of appealing to you for aid.

I have read of your generous interest in all good works and I entertain the hope that this may enlist your sympathy- If you establish a kindergarten in a southern city, we shall name it for you, if you will permit us to do so. The cost will not be great and it will do untold good to the poor little barbarians who need it most-

Hoping to receive a favorable reply, I am

little barbarians who need it most-

Hoping for a favorable reply,

I am very truly yours,

Mary Church Terrell-

GAIL LAUGHLIN

Lawyer and suffragist, 1868–1952
To Anne Fitzhugh Miller, 10 January 1902

In 1896, Gail Laughlin was one of only three women accepted to Cornell Law School. They were told that their applications would only be considered if there were not enough men to fill the student quota for the course. When she graduated and opened her own law business, Gail Laughlin became the very first female lawyer to come from the state of Maine. Her legal expertise became a valuable weapon in the fight for women's rights.

Abbie Hill Laughlin grew up in Portland, Maine. After leaving school with the highest grades in her year, she worked as a bookkeeper, working to save money so she could go to university. After four years, she had saved enough to study at Wellesley College, which was where she changed her name to Gail. At Wellesley she 'won laurels' for her studies of classics, mathematics, history and economics. After graduating in 1894, she went back to bookkeeping and earned extra money writing for newspapers and magazines, including the *American Economist*. Two years later, having saved up the fees, she applied to study Law at Cornell. There, she was elected president of the Dramatic Club and Speaker of the Cornell Congress, winning prizes for her debating skills.

Gail Laughlin became famous for her campaigns on behalf of the National American Woman Suffrage Association. This letter, written on New York State Women Suffrage Association paper, refers to her upcoming address at the Geneva (NY) Political Equality Club.

Before her speech, a local newspaper reported that she believed in 'equal rights for all and special privileges for none'.

Three years later, Gail gave a speech at the 37th Annual National American Convention for Suffrage, in which she criticised Teddy Roosevelt's so-called Square Deal, his plan for domestic government in which the president promised 'a square deal for every man', with no mention of women. In her speech, which referenced the fight against slavery, she stated, 'The exclusion of women from participation in governmental affairs means the going to waste of a vast force, which, if utilized, would be a great power in the advance of civilization. ... Now, as in 1860, "the nation cannot remain half slave and half free," and either women must be made free or men will lose the liberty which they enjoy.'

By this date, Laughlin was living openly with her lover, Dr Marguerite Sperry. When the two women moved to Marguerite's native California, Gail opened a law office in San Francisco, served as a judge in police courts and fought for equal rights in the state of California. In 1924, five years after Marguerite's death, Gail returned to live near her family in Portland, Maine, where she began working with her brother, continuing to raise awareness of women's legal needs, such as the need to raise the marriageable age of girls from 13 to 16. When she returned to Portland, she took Marguerite's ashes with her. When Gail Laughlin died at the age of 83, Marguerite's ashes were buried with her.

Opposite Women march through Washington, DC, in the Suffrage Parade of 1913. Organised by the National American Woman Suffrage Association, for which Gail Laughlin was an active campaigner, it was the first ever organised march on the capital for political purposes.
Overleaf Lawyer Inez Milholland Boissevian was one of the four mounted heralds at the Suffrage Parade.

45 Broadway N.Y. City
Jany 10, 1902

My dear Miss Miller:

    Your letter fixing upon Jany 27 as date for my address in Geneva was duly received. Date is satisfactory, as you already know. The subject of the address will be "A Question of Arithmetic"; the substance will be equal suffrage.

    It will give me great pleasure to accept your kind invitation to stay with you while in Geneva. I will write you later in reference to the exact time of my arrival.

Sincerely yours,
Gail Laughlin

45 Broadway N.Y. City
Jany 10, 1902

My dear Miss Miller:

Your letter fixing upon Jany 27 as date for my address in Geneva was duly received. Date is satisfactory, as you already know. The subject of the address will be "A Question of Arithmetic"; the substance will be equal suffrage.

It will give me great pleasure to accept your kind invitation to stay with you while in Geneva. I will write you later in reference to the exact time of my arrival.

Sincerely yours,
Gail Laughlin.

"PRO PATRIA"

She was glad to die for her Country!   *Her Spirit Endureth Ever!*

EDITH CAVELL

Nurse, 1865–1915
To her mother, Louisa Cavell, 26 July 1915

Edith Louisa Cavell was born in Swardeston, Suffolk, the eldest of Reverend Frederick Cavell and his wife Louisa's four children. Frederick was the vicar at Swardeston Church – a church that now poignantly bears a memorial to his daughter.

After leaving school, Edith began working as a governess. She was proficient in French and, in her mid-twenties, took a job in Brussels for five years. She had already travelled a little around Europe, where she had been impressed by a free hospital she had visited. This interest stayed with her when she returned to England to nurse her father back to health. This made it apparent that nursing was her vocation. In 1896, she moved to London and began her nursing training at the Royal London Hospital in Whitechapel, then one of the city's poorest areas. Edith had always helped her mother with charitable causes, and this compassion continued in her nursing. Over the next decade she worked in some of the most deprived areas of the country, including during a typhoid epidemic in Kent and at hospitals for the poor and destitute in London and Manchester.

In 1907, Cavell returned to Brussels to work for Dr Antoine Depage, Belgium's Royal Surgeon. He wanted her to train the nurses at his new institute in the modern British style of nursing. She returned to England regularly to visit her mother (who had been widowed in 1910), to whom, as this letter shows, she remained very close. She was with her mother, in Norfolk, when she heard the news of the German invasion of Belgium. Despite her family's protests, she insisted on returning to Brussels, stating that her nursing skills would be 'more needed than ever'.

During World War I, Edith Cavell worked for the Red Cross. She also became part of an underground network helping Allied soldiers and Belgian men escape the Germans. Edith kept her nurses unaware of her activities so that they could not be found complicit. She sheltered the men in the cellar and attic of her clinic, caring for them, feeding them and sometimes giving them her own money, before they were smuggled out of the country. The German secret police became suspicious of Edith and the clinic and she was arrested in August 1915.

On 11 October, the Reverend Stirling Gahan, chaplain of Christ Church in Brussels, visited Edith in prison, to give her holy communion before her death. At dawn on 12 October 1915, Edith, dressed in her nurse's uniform and a blindfold, was tied to a stake and executed by firing squad. Her execution caused outcry around the world. Her body was buried in Belgium, but in 1919, after the war was over, it was taken home to England. There she was given a memorial service at Westminster Abbey before being buried in Norwich Cathedral.

In a letter, Reverend Gahan wrote about his visit to the prison. The letter records Edith Cavell's now-famous words, 'I know now that patriotism is not enough; I must have no hatred and bitterness toward anyone.' These have become her epitaph, carved onto memorial statues as wide apart as London and Melbourne.

Opposite Edith Cavell's death in 1915 caused widespread outrage in Britain. This print, made the same year, shows her spirit rising in the form of an angel from her dead body.

My darling Mother

Just a few lines to tell you how glad I was to see your letter of June 24th and to know you were well & all the family after so long a silence. There are fewer & fewer opportunities of sending here – you may have assumed that – all goes on here as usual and that we are very well. Gracie is better again but I fear not permanently – will you let her father know I received the money he sent, it was handed over to me by the German bank; they will probably have send [sic] him a receipt – signed by me. About my pension fund. Will you pay it from now to Dec. from the £25 you have in hand & take your money as well. The pension falls due to me in Jan. I think. Will you ask them to pay it direct to you quarterly if they can – and use it yourself. I enclose a word for the Secretary Mr Dick. We are without news and very quiet and I can tell you nothing – after, when I return there will be much to relate.

We move into the new School at the end of this week or the beginning of next. It advances rapidly now & the nurses are nearly all there already. The patients will be moved at the last. The little garden in front is gay with flowers & the cleaning in progress. It is very dirty as you may imagine & will want going over many times before it is really nice as the workmen are still in and are not likely to finish for some time yet.

We have had much rain. I often think of W. Runton & and of how much we should have regretted such a wet July. Will you please reply to the address which will be enclosed with this letter. I shall get your answer surely tho' probably with some delay.

We have more patients just now and are glad we shall not have to move them far. When I can get a good photo of the new place I will try & send it to you. Jackie is well & sends a lick – he gets old & is not quite so frisky as he used to be – there are no longer any motor-cars to run after but he lays outside and keeps his street in order & is overjoyed at a walk.

My dearest love to you & to all the family. I am looking forward to a happy meeting later on.

Ever your affectionate daughter

Edith

26th July 1915

Opposite Edith Cavell with her dogs in her garden in Brussels shortly before the outbreak of war.

My darling Mother

Just a few lines to tell you how glad I was to get your letter on June 24th. And to know you were well & all the family after so long a silence. There are fewer & fewer opportunities of sending but you may rest assured that all goes on here as usual and that we are very well. Gracie is better again but I fear not permanently. Will you let her father know I received the money he sent, it was handed over to me by the German

bank, they will probably send him a receipt. Signed by me. About my pension fund. Will you pay it for now to Dec. from the to 25 you to in hand & take your money well. The pension falls due me in Jan. I think. Will you ask them to pay it direct you quarterly if they can use it yourself. I enclose a for the Secretary Mr Dick. We without news and very & And I can tell you nothing after when I return there he much to relate.

We move into the new school at the end of this week or the beginning of next. It advan rapidly now & the nurses are nearly all there already - the patients - will be moved at the last - The little garden in front is gay with flowers & the cleaning in progress - It is very dirty as you may imagine & will want going over many times before it is really nice as the workmen are still in and are not likely to finish for some time yet.

We have had much rain & often think of W. Wimlow & of how much we should have regretted such a wet July - will you please reply to the address which will be enclosed with this letter. I shall get your answer surely tho' probably with some delay -

We have more patients just now and are glad we shall not have to move them far. When I can get a good photo of the new place I will try & send it to you. Jackie is well & sends a lick - he gets old & is not quite so frisky as he used to be - there are no longer any motor cars to run after but he lays outside and keeps his street in order & is over joyed at a walk -

My dearest love to you, & all the family - I am looking forward to a happy meeting later on - Ever your affectionate daughter

Edith

28th July 1915

GERTRUDE BELL

Explorer and cartographer, 1868–1926
To her stepmother, Dame Florence Bell, 9 March 1916

Gertrude Bell was born into a privileged, wealthy family in County Durham. Her early childhood was marred by the death of her mother in 1871, the year in which Gertrude turned three. She grew very close to her father, and after he remarried and had more children, Gertrude became the eldest of five siblings. She also developed a close relationship her stepmother, Florence Bell, to whom this letter was sent. As the letter shows, Gertrude wrote to her stepmother with the salutation 'Dearest Mother'.

Gertrude's early education was with a governess, at the family home, before she was sent to Queen's College school in London. After school, she was accepted to study at Lady Margaret Hall in Oxford, where she earned the equivalent of a first-class degree (at the time, women were denied the right to be awarded a degree). She also excelled at sports and was keen to indulge her other great passion – travel.

Although Gertrude had studied modern history, her great love was archaeology. As soon as she left Oxford, she set in motion plans to travel around Europe and the Middle East, where she explored the Arabian desert. In 1894, she published her first book of travel writing, *Safar Nameh: Persian Pictures*. In 1897, she set off on her first 'round the world' trip for a year, an adventure she repeated in 1902–1903. The year after her return, in 1904, she successfully scaled the Matterhorn, writing to her stepmother, 'It is a fine climb, not difficult under good conditions, as we had it, but nearly all of it interesting.' This was one of many climbing expeditions, on one of which she nearly died – something that did not diminish her love of mountaineering.

In 1907, Bell published an account of her travels in Turkey and Syria, *The Desert and the Sown*. Her other books include the 1911 publication *Amurath to Amurath*, about her travels around the Middle East, and her collection of poetry, *Poems from the Divan of Hafiz* (1897). Gertrude was passionate about studying the life and history of the Arab states. She learned several local languages and travelled extensively around the Middle East, getting to know the people and the archaeological sites. This knowledge and her friendship with several Arab tribes made her invaluable to the British Intelligence service, who recruited her to work for them during the First World War.

After the war, Bell remained in what was then called Mesopotamia, where she was deeply involved with politics. She helped to ensure that her chosen candidate, Faisal, was named king, when the new state of Iraq was founded in 1921. Bell remained an important figure in the political scene of Iraq, always concerned with the country's rich heritage, and was named Honorary Director of Antiquities. In this role, she founded the Iraq Museum in Baghdad.

By the early 1920s, Gertrude Bell's health was deteriorating. She had suffered several bouts of malaria, bronchitis and pleurisy, and may have kept a diagnosis of lung cancer secret. She died in Baghdad on 12 July 1926 from an overdose of barbiturates.

Opposite A photograph taken by Gertrude Bell at a well in Ba'ir fort, Saudi Arabia, in 1913. Bell extensively documented the everyday lives of the people she met on her travels around the Middle East.

Basrah. March 9

Dearest Mother.

I wish I ever knew how long I were going to stay in any place or what I were likely to do next. But that is just the kind of thing which one never can know when one is engaged in the indefinite sort of job which I am doing. There is however a great deal of work to be done here. I have already begun to classify the very valuable tribal material which I find in the files at the Intel. Dept. and I think there are pretty wide possibilities of adding to what has been collected already. It is extraordinarily interesting; my own previous knowledge, though there was little enough of it, comes in very handy in many ways – as a check upon, and a frame to the new stuff I am handling. And I can't tell you how wonderful it is to be in at the birth, so to speak, of a new administration, to watch the tidying up of old rubbish heaps and to be able to see at last what exactly they were composed of. As yet I can only guess at these things, but I shall learn more about them I hope in time. Everyone is being amazingly kind. I have found myself, or rather I have been given a lodging, next door to Headquarters in the big house on the river which Bellongs to Gray Mackenzie and Co. That is most convenient, for I have only to step across the bridge over a little creek to get to my work. Today I lunched with all the Generals – Sir Percy Lake, General Cawfer, General Offley Shaw and General Money, and as an immediate result they moved me and my maps and books onto a splendid great verandah with a cool room behind it where I may sit and work all day long. My companion here is Captain CampBell Thompson, ex-archaeologist – I knew him in his former incarnation – very pleasant and obliging and delighted to benefit with me by the change of workshop, for we were lodged by day in Col. Beach's bedroom (he is the head of the I.D.) a plan which was not very convenient either for us or for him. The whole of Basrah is packed full, as you may understand when it has had suddenly to expand into the base of a large army. Finally I have got an Arab boy as a servant; his name is Mikhail, he comes from Mosul and promises to be very satisfactory, so that I am now fully and completely established. Sir Percy Cox came back last night – he has been away at Bashire – and he also is going to help me to get all the information I want by sending on to me any Arabs whom he thinks will interest me. Therefore if I don't make something of it, it will be entirely my own fault.

Today came a mail with Father's letters of Jan 27 and Feb 2 which were a great joy. I'm thankful to think that M. [Maurice] won't be back in France at any rate till the end of April and I devoutly hope that it may be longer, bless him. The relief it is to know that he is not fighting – ! It's a dreadful story about George White's poor little boy, I do trust he is all right. And dear Henry James! it's happier that he should have died, but I'm so sorry. We are a dreadfully great distance apart, but when your letters come straight to me here I shall get them a little quicker. I don't know how much mine are censored and find the doubt a great impediment to my style. We are living in rather an electric atmosphere. A rumour that Enver has been wounded, or more, has reached us, as well as further suggestions that the Turks may be going to give in. For the moment this possibility obscures for us even the horrible tales of the Verdun actions; the situation might develop very rapidly here and there is a feeling of changing tide which is exciting and disturbing. My days are however very uneventful. I work at G.H.Q. from 8.30 to 12.30, come in to lunch, and go back there from 2 till near 6. Then, it being sunset, wonderfully cool and delicious, I walk for half of an hour or so through palm gardens – it's more like a steeple chase than a walk for the paths are continuously interrupted by irrigation channels, over some of which you jump while over the others you do tight rope dancing across a single palm trunk. I shall fall in some day, and though I shall not be drowned it will be disgustingly muddy. In about 2 months time we shall have blazing hot weather and it is quite possible that I may still be here therefore (I need not say!) I want you please to send me out some real hot weather clothes and I think I had better have the following, to be sent in small parcels by post – that's the secret way of getting them:

4 cotton voile gowns; these must be bought as I haven't got the sort of thing which is needed. They must be simply made so that they can wash easily, not too much trimming or elaborate fastenings. And they should be loose, no tight bands round the waist, for choice blue (not too light) or mauve, a plain colour or white with little stripes. If Moll is in London perhaps she would get them for me or Sylvia would certainly get them for me and she would be very clever about it. The Ladies Shirt Coy is where I generally go. They ought to cost about '4 a piece. Marie might slip them on – if they will fit her they will fit me. They must not be too long and I think she had better send me at the same time a couple of thinnish white petticoats just the length of the gowns and very simply made.

4 crepe de chine shirts, cream or pale pink, also quite simple, opening at the neck – Marie knows the kind of thing I like.

4 pairs of thin black thread stockings and 4 pairs of white ditto.

And if possible I should very much like a cream coloured lace gown to wear in the evening – not a low clingy[?] dress, but a sort of half and half thing that I can wear for dinner when it's very hot. It must be long, touching the ground all round. One can get absolutely nothing here of course. I can get from India the white gowns I've asked you to send for me to Mrs Shaw but it would be much better to have clothes that are loose at the waist – the heat in May is outrageous – and I think the present fashions admit of it, don't they? I mean they can be found. Hats don't matter as one can wear nothing but a sun helmet till it's too dark to signify what one wears.

2 yards of narrow black velvet ribbon such as I wear round my neck.

Some lace shirts Marie made me last summer – I think two of them are good enough to wear here in the evening. Would she make and send me a pair of tussore nickerbockers [sic]. And she might go to my staymaker and ask her to send me two pairs of very thin washing stays for hot weather – Mareyle is her name and she lives in Bond St.

Finally would you ask Callaghan to send me a pair of eyeglasses and a pair of spectacles slightly stronger than those I'm using. He had a prescription for two varieties, one a little stronger than the other of which I use now only the stronger – could he not make me some a little stronger still? I am forever doing fine map work which is very tiring to the eyes.

This sounds a terrible amount to ask for but suppose I want to stay on here it would be a great bore to add to the discomforts of heat by not having washing clothes and I should need them in Egypt if I did not need them here.

ALEXANDRA KOLLONTAI

Politician, 1872–1952
To Dora B. Montefiore, 13 September 1920

As a leading Russian revolutionary, Alexandra Kollontai fought tirelessly for the rights of women and children, calling upon all women to take their place as equals in Russian society. She was a close friend and ally of Lenin, who appointed her the first female minister in his Bolshevik government, making her the commissar of women's and social rights. Following the Russian Revolution, Alexandra became infuriated that women were still being expected to do all the childcare and housework, while working the same hours as men, despite the alleged equality of the new Soviet Russia.

Alexandra (née Domontovich) was born into an aristocratic Russian family; her father was a general in the Imperial Russian Army and her mother was an heiress and socialite. Her childhood was one of closeted wealth, being educated at home under the care of an English nanny. In 1893, against her parents' wishes, Alexandra married an engineer named Vladimir Kollontai, and had a son. She was becoming increasingly interested in politics and, within a few years, she left her husband, and travelled to Switzerland to become a student. On her return to Russia, she joined the Social Democratic Party and went on to become an active member of the International Socialist Women's Movement. When her activities brought her to the attention of the authorities, she travelled around Europe and Scandinavia to evade arrest, working as a teacher and disseminating Communist literature. In the early months of World War I, she travelled to the USA, where she gave over 100 speeches urging Americans not to enter the war.

During her time in Lenin's government, Alexandra Kollontai called for radical change in the laws that governed marriage, divorce and family life. She regularly interviewed female workers and became famous for her articles about the social problems encountered by women. As an advocate of free love, she argued that marriage left women at the mercy of men, demanded state childcare for everyone and tried to change social and legal attitudes towards 'illegitimate' children. She worked even when in very poor health, as this letter makes explicit, but her time as a prominent politician was to be short-lived. Following a public disagreement with Lenin at the 10th Communist Party Congress in 1921, she was forced out of the top stream of politics. She subsequently became a leader of the Workers' Opposition, a breakaway movement within the Communist Party.

When Lenin cut ties with his former close friend, Alexandra Kollontai became considered an embarrassment by the establishment. In 1923, to keep her out of politics at home, she was sent on a diplomatic posting to Norway, where she had been living before the revolution. A few years later she published a fictional book aimed at women, entitled *Love of Worker Bees*. She was kept away from Russia, in diplomatic roles, for the next two decades, including postings in Sweden, Finland and Mexico. She died in Moscow a couple of weeks before her 80th birthday, having somehow evaded the fate that had been meted out to her ex-husband, her lover and so many of her friends, all of whom were executed during the Stalinist regime.

Moscow,

13th Sept., 1920.

Dear Comrade Montefiore,

I was ever so glad to get your kind greeting. I could not answer it at once, as unfortunately I got very ill (typhus fever) at the time of the International Congress. We live in a new world where the beautiful hopes of the future real Communism are mixed up with so many remains of the old capitalistic world. It is a hard struggle to make of Russia a real Communistic state, but little by little the work goes on. If only the comrades in the rest of the world would give us more active support! One thing is achieved: there is actually no capital, no private property in Russia, and the psychology of the masses has changed so greatly, that it seems we have stepped forward many centuries from the time of the beginning of the imperialist war. Also, the place of the women in the state and family has changed: all women have to work, for 'who does not work does not eat' in Soviet Russia. We have less and less of those women who were but a burden to their husbands and family.

Oh, there is ever so much I would like to tell you about Soviet Russia. Come to us some day, dear friend! But remember always before you criticise us that we could not and have not yet achieved Communism; one country, one nation, alone, cannot do it! Communism must be the work of all proletarians of the world. And we have great hopes that our English comrades will soon show us that they can do more than Russia, who was oppressed by the Tsar; where we had no good mass organisations, where the economical conditions are much less prepared for Communism than in Great Britain.

Dear comrade, my love to you and my Communist greetings. I hope we shall meet soon.

Yours in Communism,

ALEXANDRA [Kollontay]."

SARAH BERNHARDT

Actress, 1844–1923
To Dr Emanuel Libman, 19 July 1922

Sarah Bernhardt was the illegitimate daughter of a Jewish Dutch courtesan. Her birthday is uncertain, as no birth certificate survives, and the identity of her father is unknown. She was educated at a convent before studying acting at the Conservatoire de Musique et Déclamation in Paris. After completing her studies, Sarah began working with the Comédie-Française, a very prestigious theatre company, with whom she made her stage debut on 31 August 1862, as the eponymous character Iphigénie in the tragedy by Jean Racine. Her performance was not considered a success and she made her situation even worse by becoming embroiled in a physical fight with another actress, which led to her dismissal from the company. Bernhardt left Paris and worked for a while in Brussels, where she met Henri Prince de Ligne, with whom she had a son, Maurice, in 1864.

After a few years playing small roles, in 1868, Sarah was cast in *Kean* by Alexandre Dumas and as Cordelia in *King Lear*. This heralded a rise to international stardom. By 1872, the Comédie-Française was begging her to work for them again. Over the ensuing decades, Sarah Bernhardt performed in more than 70 roles, playing both male and female characters, and appearing on stage all over the world. She toured Europe, North and South America, the Middle East and Australia. Although she always performed in French, often for an audience who did not understand the language, she was universally adored. She was applauded as the teenaged Joan of Arc, despite performing the role at the age of 46, and adored as Hamlet even when an elderly woman. After she injured herself in her 70s during a performance of *Tosca*, her right leg was amputated. This did not daunt her. She continued to act, playing both male and female roles of all ages, using a crutch in place of her missing leg or propelling herself across the stage in a wheelchair. In the final years of her life, Bernhardt appeared in several silent films, including a documentary about her life.

The year in which this telegram was sent is uncertain, but it seems likely to have been 1922, shortly before she died. Bernhardt relied heavily upon Dr Libman, a pioneering American doctor who became her friend as well as her physician. Libman's other patients included Albert Einstein, Thomas Mann, Fanny Brice and Gustav Mahler. Sarah Bernhardt died in March 1923, of kidney failure. She is buried in Père Lachaise Cemetery in Paris.

The enduring reputation of the actress lovingly known as 'the Divine Sarah' is aided by stories of her unhappy marriage, her numerous lovers, her ease at playing both male and female roles and her numerous eccentricities, such as her fascination with hot-air ballooning, her adherence to a mostly vegetarian diet, and the rumours of her sleeping in a coffin and possessing a letterbox made from a skull. Bernhardt was painted and written about constantly during her lifetime, and her legendary personality continues to captivate the creative imagination long after her death. In 1960, she was given a star on the Hollywood Walk of Fame. In 1980, Andy Warhol created a portrait of her. She has also inspired novels and plays, and a fascinating array of places and things have been named after her, including theatres, restaurants, an award-winning peony, a square in Paris and a crater on Venus.

Opposite A poster dating from 1896 by the Czech artist Alphonse Mucha. Paris-based Mucha produced a series of striking Art Nouveau posters for Bernhardt's productions throughout the 1890s.

July 19th 3.10 p.m.

Telegram from Sauzon, France
Telephoned over from Zurich by Dr Bircher

Dr Libman, Zurich

I know that you are resting from your great work and great devotion.

I am very ill and am in great need of your diagnosting. I will respect your rest if however chance would bring you in my neighborhood must I tell you the great joy it would be to have you as my guest.

With all my grateful heartthanks and thanks
Sarah Bernhardt

(The above telegram will be forwarded to Dr Libman, Grand Hotel, Paris, by mail)

Opposite Sarah Bernhardt as the eponymous Theodora, from a production of the play by Victorien Sardou in Paris in 1884.

QUEEN SĀLOTE III

Queen of Tonga, 1900–1965
To Rev. C. Moore, 12 December 1923

Queen Sālote Tupou III was the daughter of King George Tupou II and Queen Lavinia Veiongo of Tonga. Her parents' marriage caused anger in Tonga because Queen Lavinia was considered lower-class, and as a child Sālote's life was often felt to be under threat. When Sālote was only four years old, her mother died of tuberculosis. Her father remarried seven years later.

Sālote's early childhood was spent in the palace at the Tongan capital Nuku'alofa. Aged nine, she was sent to New Zealand to attend school. She lived with a local family and was a pupil at the Diocesan High School for Girls in Auckland. When her father died in 1918, Sālote was proclaimed Queen of Tonga. She was only 18 at her coronation. She was the third monarch to rule the country, after her father and great-grandfather. It was her great-grandfather who had converted the family to Christianity. This letter is to the Reverend Charles Moore, a British man who had migrated to Australia with his family and become a church minister. Moore spent several years in Tonga as a Methodist missionary.

In 1916, two years before she became Queen, Sālote married the high chieftain Viliami Tungi Mailefihi, known as Tungi. They had three sons, born between 1918 and 1922 (their middle son died in 1936). In 1923, Tungi was named Prime Minister of Tonga, a role he maintained until his death in 1941. Sālote retained links to New Zealand and owned property in Auckland. They were also regular visitors to Australia, where Tungi had studied as a young man.

In 1953, Queen Sālote put herself, and Tonga, on the front pages of international newspapers. At the coronation of Queen Elizabeth II in London, rainy weather encouraged most of the coronation procession to travel in covered carriages. Queen Sālote, however, refused to disappoint the people who had stayed out all night, and kept her carriage open. She won the hearts of Britain and the world by smiling and waving, dressed in her finery during the downpour. One British journalist penned a song which included the words 'Linger longer, Queen of Tonga, linger longer do'. Queen Sālote was a far more accomplished poet than the journalist. Many of her poems were set to music, and a collection of her poems and songs was translated into English and published some years after her death.

Queen Elizabeth II visited Tonga just a few months after her coronation, and photographs of the two women – the only female monarchs in the Commonwealth – were sent around the world. Standing 6 feet 3 inches tall, the Tongan queen towered over her European counterpart as they walked together.

Queen Sālote III reigned for 47 years. She worked hard to free Tonga from debt and to improve social conditions. She was also an accomplished diplomat, creating close ties with other world leaders. She encouraged the growth of Tongan arts and culture, while helping to maintain Tongan traditions. At the end of her life, she returned to New Zealand for medical treatment, dying of cancer at the Auckland City Hospital. The people of New Zealand mourned her almost as much as the people of Tonga. Her funeral in Tonga was attended by more than 50,000 people – two-thirds of the country's entire population.

Tau'akipulu
Lifuka
12th December 1923

To

      Rev. C. Moore
            Chair of the Wesleyan Church of the Ha'apai Division
            Lifuka

Sir,

You are well aware of the adjustments to the Free Church of these days. Furthermore it is apparent to me that there is a great opportunity to enable the union of the two churches, the Free Church of Tonga and the Wesleyan Church of Tonga, so they are one and would then be named as per His Majesty King George Tupou I had willed it to be, and as such is confirmed in the Constitution of the Wesleyan Church of Tonga but has not been published or used. As such I have written to the Chair of the Wesleyan Church in Tongatapu, and expressed what is in my heart that our two churches be united, and I defined in my letter the focus and the aims of my wishes as we aspire to carry out this very serious and important work.

I received a letter of reply from Rev. M Page on the 26th of October past. And that reply was of great comfort to me, even though it was only his words but it was akin to abundant encouragement to my soul that this be reinvigorated as the will of God to happen during my time so that there can be a complete and peaceful unification of His church here in the islands of Tonga. And so, I wrote back to him to express my ... of the Wesleyan Church that will be held in Tongatapu this month, and what they would like.

Therefore, I would like to ask you directly what your thoughts are on my wish that the two churches be unified; and I would be happy if you could propose this at your quarterly meeting that is anticipated to take place this month, so that they articulate to me what they want.

I do not want to propose things that I wish in my heart for the meeting as there are a myriad of things like matters pertaining to the law things that need to be witnessed, but the most important thing is the development and pressing forward of the spiritual lives of the people of God here in the Tongan islands and that peace and prosperity visit upon our people.

And should the quarterly meeting of the Wesleyan Church in Ha'apai be in agreement with it, I hope that you will lend your encouragement so that this very important work goes smoothly, with God's help.

            With the Greatest Love
            S Tupou

Tauʻakibulu
Lifuka
12ᵗ Tisema 1923.

Kiu

Rev. C. Moore,
Sea ʻae Jiaji Uesiliana ʻoe Vahaʻo Haʻapai
Lifuka.

Tagataʻeiki,
Ohage be koia kuoke meaʻi ʻae
meʻa koia ʻoku kau kihe fakatonutonu ʻoku
kau kihe jiaji Tauʻataina ihe gahi ahoni.
Bea ihe ʻene ha kiate au ʻoku iai ha fiu
faigamalie ʻe lava ai ke feiga ke fakataha
ʻae ogo jiaji, ʻae jiaji ʻo Toga Tauʻataina bea
moe jiaji Uesiliana i Toga, ke hoko koe
jiaji be taha ʻo ui ʻaki ʻae higoa koia naʻe
tomuʻa finagalo lelei kiai ʻehe ʻEne ʻAfio
ko Kigi Jiaosi Tubou I aia be ʻoku faka-
babau ʻehe Konisitutone ʻoe jiasi Tauʻataina
ka ʻoku teeki bulusi mo gaue ʻaki. Koia neu
tohi leva kihe Sea ʻoe jiaji Uesiliana i Toga
Tabu, ʻo fakahaha kiate ia ʻae ʻaga hoku loto
ke fakataha hotau ogo jiasi, beau fakamahino
foki ihe ʻeku tohi koia ʻae g. meʻa niihi aia
ʻoku tefito ai mo tuunga kiai ʻeku loto ke
fai ʻae gaue mamafa mo mahuiga koia.
Neu maʻu ha tohi tali meia
Rev. Mr. Page ihe aho 26 ʻo Okatoba kuo hili.
Bea koe tali koia ʻoku fiu fakafiemalie kiate
au, neogo ko ʻene tohi be ʻaana ia kae hage

105

'oku boubou lahi ki hoku loto 'eku tui koe
finagalo 'oe 'Eiki ke ui'i 'ae mea ni 'ihoku kuoga
ke lava hano fakakakato mo faka-melino
foki 'ahono jiasi ihe otu Toga. Bea kuou toe
tohi atu foki kiate ia kene fakaha atu hoku
_ _ _ _ _ _ Kuata 'oe jiasi Uesiliana oku
amanaki fai ihe mahina ni i Toga Sabu, ka
'eku fie miu honau loto.

Koia, oku ou fie fakaha totonu 'eau
kiate koe be koeha ha'o fkkaukau kiai kihe eku
loto ke fakataha hotau ogo jiasi; bea teu fiefia
foki kabau teke agalelei 'o fokotuu atu ia ki ho'o
mou fakataha faka-Kuata oku amanaki fai ihe
malina ni, ke nau fakaha mai kiate au honau
loto.

Oku ikai keu toe fie fohtiu heni 'ae
g. mea 'oku boubou aki hoku loto ke fai 'ae faka
taha he 'oku teke fili 'ohage ko Kao 'ae g.mea
kehekehe ke fakamioni aki, ka koe mea tebu
be, 'ae tubulekina mo laka ki muiu 'ae moni
fakalaumalie 'ae kakai lotu mae jiasi 'oe 'Eiki
ihe otu Togani, bea nofo loto melino mo monuia
ai 'ae kakai 'oe fonua.

Bea 'oka loto fiemalie kiai 'ae faka
taha faka-Kuata 'oe jiasi Uesiliana 'o Haafai ni
bea teu amanaki leva te mou tokoni mai
aki homou tukuigata ke lava vave mo fai –
gofua age hano faka-hoko 'oe fuu gaue kafa
kafani, ihano tokoni kitautolu 'ehe 'Eiki

Ofa atu fau.
S. Tubou

143

EMMY NOETHER

Mathematician, 1882–1935
To Albert Einstein, 7 January 1926

Following Amalie Emmy Noether's death in 1935, Albert Einstein wrote in the *New York Times*, 'In the judgement of the most competent living mathematicians, Fraulein Noether was the most significant creative mathematical genius thus far produced since the higher education of women began.'

Emmy (she used her middle name from a young age) might well have taken exception to this 'judgement' by a man she considered a peer and whose opinion she appears to question in this letter of 7 January 1926 'to his office'. Noether, whose eponymous theorem is fundamental in mathematical physics, is one of the most significant and influential mathematicians of any sex of all time. Noether's Theorem proves that the symmetries found in the laws of nature leads to the conservation of quantities such as energy. Her work provided a profound insight into the workings of the universe.

Noether is, of course, just one of a long line of brilliant women with an extraordinary facility for numbers from Hypatia (*c.* 350–370), through Ada Lovelace and Katherine Johnson, to the first female recipient in 2019 of the Abel Prize (the so-called Nobel Prize for Maths), Karen Uhlenbeck, whose plenary lecture at the 1990 International Congress of Mathematicians was the first by a woman since Emmy Noether's in 1932. Uhlenbeck was also the Noether Lecturer of the Association for Women in Mathematics in 1988, suggesting that – 53 years after her death – Noether was still being labelled a 'woman mathematician' and an anomaly, rather like Samuel Johnson's 'dog walking on its hind legs'.

Born in 1882 in Erlangen, Germany, Noether stood her ground in a male-dominated Jewish family, the only sister of three younger boys. Her father was a mathematician, while her brothers Arthur and Felix became highly accomplished academics. After qualifying in 1900 to teach French and English, she entered academic life at the University of Erlangen, where her father taught.

Her life from this point would prove to be unconventional and hampered, though not curtailed, by the prejudices against women in higher education – at Erlangen she was one of only two women in the midst of nearly 1,000 men, and she had to ask the permission of any (male) professors whose lectures she wished to attend. She graduated in July 1903 and went on to complete her dissertation 'On Complete Systems of Invariants for Ternary Biquadratic Forms' in 1907. She spent seven years working at the university without pay. Even when invited to work at the University of Göttingen, she was not given an official position, and was not paid for several years, despite being remembered as an inspirational teacher.

In the winter of 1928–29, Noether was invited to Moscow State University, where she expressed admiration for 'the Bolshevik project'. Ironically and tragically, her brother Felix, working in Tomsk, Russia, after leaving Nazi Germany, was executed by the Communist regime for 'anti-Soviet propaganda' in 1941.

Noether, too, was expelled by the Nazis in 1933, along with Einstein and many other Jewish academics. While Einstein took refuge in Princeton, New Jersey, where Noether often lectured, she went to the prestigious women's college Bryn Mawr in Pennsylvania. Following her sudden death, aged 53, in 1935, four days after the removal of an ovarian cyst, her ashes were interred under the cloisters of the college library.

Had she lived longer, there is no doubt that Emmy Noether would have been honoured as a mathematical genius in her own lifetime, alongside Albert Einstein. Her true abilities are at least now being recognised posthumously.

Opposite Emmy Noether in a picture taken some time before 1910.

Blaricum (North Holland), Villa Cornelia,
7 January 1926 (until 10 January 1926)

Dear Professor,

Currently I am writing to your office regarding the article by Zaycoff, which unfortunately is by no means suitable for the Math[ematische] Annalen.

First of all, it is not at all a clear restatement of the principal theorems of my "Invariante Variationsprobleme" (Gött[inger] Nachr[ichten], 1918 or 19), with a slight generalization – the invariance of the integral up to a divergence term – which can actually already be found in Bessel-Hagen (Math[ematische] Ann[alen], around 1922), in his work on the conservation laws of electrodynamics, which is related to the above-mentioned note.

In section 3, there is a reference to Bessel-Hagen's work (citing me there is an error); the obvious integration of the conservation laws is then carried out, and this is not in Bessel-Hagen.

In the subsequent paragraphs, using the calculus of variations, he establishes the field equations and their identities in the case of general relativity; first in the case where the electric field vanishes, then without that assumption, and finally in Weyl's case or in a still more general case; since there are only calculations and there is not a single word of explanation (except in the introduction), this is hard to understand. All the systematization with respect to earlier work – above all with respect to Klein – depends on the fact that the formulae are established for any action of function W and that the value of W is only specified in the final formulae. It would be impossible for someone who does not know the theory to understand the calculations.

Therefore, the article does not represent any significant progress because, in conclusion, nearly everyone at this point has worked with the variational principle. For me, what was the most important in the "Invariante Variationsprobleme" was to state in a rigorous fashion the significance of the principle and, above all, to state the converse, which does not appear here.

I cannot appreciate to what extent the integration of the conservation laws is interesting from the point of view of physics. If that is the case, it might be possible to induce a physics journal to accept this limited part, with a reference to Bessel-Hagen; it would also be possible to introduce in it a reference to the statement of my theorems in Courant–Hilbert (Yellow Collection), p. 216, one of the most recent volumes, with an explanatory text. But for this, I must leave it to the physicists to judge the value.

With my best wishes for 1926 and my best regards,
Your devoted,
Emmy Noether

Emmy Noether   Blaricum (Noordholland), Villa Cornelia
(bis 10.1.26);   7/1.26.

Sehr geehrter Herr Professor:

Gleichzeitig geht als Geschäftspapier an Ihr Institut die Arbeit Zaycoff zurück, die leider für die math. Annalen ganz und gar nicht paßt.

Es handelt sich zwar um eine nicht alltägliche durchsichtige ... der Ungenauigkeit meiner "invarianten Variations-probleme" (Gött. Nachr. 1918 u. 19), mit einer geringen ... — ... des Integrals ... die sich schon bei Bessel-Hagen findet (Math. Ann., etwa 1922) in ... an die obige dort anschließende Arbeit ist die ... der ...

In § 3 wird über diese Arbeit von Bessel-Hagen ... (daß er noch ... ist ...); es wird dann die ... Integration der ... durchgeführt die bei Bessel-Hagen fehlt.

In den nächsten Paragraphen wird nach der Variations-methode die Aufstellung der Feldgleichungen (im Fall der allgemeinen Relativität durchgeführt; ...

Sind ihre Achtungsvollen ...

A. Einstein Archive
24 - 172

unter Bezeichnung nach Bessel-Hagen — in einer geschichtlichen Fußschrift nachzuweisen; und es könnte dort auch unter Bezeichnung auf die Wiedergabe meiner Sätze bei Courant-Hilbert (Galte Sammlung), P. 216, einer der letzten Nummern mit erläuterndem Text vorgenommen werden. Aber hier muss ich die Darstellung des Ähnliches den Physiker überlassen.

Mit besten Wünschen für 1926 und mit besten Grüßen Ihre
sehr ergebene
Emmy Noether,

RADCLYFFE HALL

Writer, 1880–1943
To Lytton Strachey, 13 December 1928

Today, the author Radclyffe Hall is best known for her 1928 novel *The Well of Loneliness*. It was the first recognisably lesbian novel published in the English language, and became notorious for being banned almost as soon as it was published.

Marguerite Antonia Radclyffe Hall was born into a turbulent marriage. Her father was a very wealthy Englishman and her mother was an American, unhappy and angry with her life. Marguerite's relationship with her mother was perennially difficult. Her father had left when his daughter was still a toddler, and that rejection affected Marguerite throughout her life. Her father did not neglect them financially, and Marguerite grew up wealthy and financially independent – in an era when the vast majority of women had no choice but to be financially dependent on a man. As an adult, she stopped using her feminine first name and became known simply as Radclyffe Hall. Her friends called her John.

In 1907, Radclyffe Hall met the singer Mabel Batten, who was almost twice her age. Mabel was married, but after her husband died, the two women began living together. In 1915, Radclyffe Hall met Mabel's cousin, Una, Lady Troubridge, a sculptor and writer, who was also married. The two women fell in love. After Mabel died in 1916, Una and Radclyffe Hall set up home together. They remained together until Radclyffe Hall's death.

Radclyffe Hall became celebrated as a poet and author, writing seven novels. In 1926, she published the award-winning, *Adam's Breed*. The adulation she had received changed sharply when her fifth novel, *The Well of Loneliness*, was published. The main character of this book is a woman named Stephen Gordon, whom Radclyffe Hall described as 'inverted', her own preferred term for her sexuality. The book is not sexually explicit and some critics praised its literary style, but one critic was so incensed about its lesbianism that he began a furious campaign. On 18 August 1928, just a month after publication, James Douglas, editor of the *Sunday Express*, called for the novel to be banned 'immediately'. In his article he wrote, 'I would rather give a healthy boy or a healthy girl a phial of prussic acid than this novel.'

The Home Office responded rapidly, and on 24 August, the book's publisher, Jonathan Cape, announced that publication of *The Well of Loneliness* had been ceased. Radclyffe Hall's response was that 'two years of incessant work, following upon many years of deep study, [has] suffered at the hands of wilful ignorance and of prejudice amounting to persecution. ... [F]ar from encouraging depravity, my book is calculated to encourage mutual understanding between normal persons and the inverted, which can only be beneficial to both and to society at large.'

The letter shown here was written to her friend, the openly homosexual writer and critic Lytton Strachey, a member of the Bloomsbury Group. It demonstrates Radclyffe Hall's fury with the judicial process: a court in which the deciding jury had not even read her book had proclaimed it obscene for its depiction of 'unnatural practices between women'. By the time *The Well of Loneliness* was finally published in Britain, its author had been dead for six years.

Opposite Radclyffe Hall (standing) picutured with Lady Una Troubridge in 1927, the year before the publication of *The Well of Loneliness*.

37, Holland Street,
Church Street,
Kensington, W.8.

[Dec 18, 1928]

Dear Mr Strachey,

      As you were not present at London Sessions on Friday last, December 14th, to hear how the Attorney General found it necessary to open his case for the prosecution of the publishers of THE WELL OF LONELINESS by narrating the entire story of the book, and detailing the names, functions and sections of each separate character, to the bench of magistrates who presumedly should have read the book before sitting in judgement upon it. you may find the enclosed letter form [sic] the Public Prosecutor Sir Archibald Bodkin interesting as throwing light upon the Government's legal (?) procedure in connection with the preparation of their case.

Yours sincerely,

Radclyffe Hall

PS As you may know, the Chairman of the Court mentioned in Bodkin's letter is Sir Robert Wallace, whose judgement of my book you will have seen in the papers.

01   69

                                              37, Holland Street,
                                              Church Street,
                                              Kensington, W. 8.

                                                   [Dec. 18. 1928]

Dear Mrs Strachey -

        As you were not present at London Sessions on Friday last,
December 14th, to hear how the Attorney General found it necessary to open his case for the prosecution of the publishers of
THE WELL OF LONELINESS by narrating the entire story of the
book, and detailing the names, functions and actions of each
separate character, to the bench of magistrates who presumedly
should have read the book before sitting in judgement upon it.
you may find the enclosed letter form the Public Prosecutor
Sir Archibald Bodkin interesting as throwing light upon the
Government's legal (?) procedure in connection with the preparation of their case.

                        Yours sincerely,

                            Radclyffe Hall -

        PS As you may know, the Chairman of the
        Court mentioned in Bodkin's letter is Sir Robert
        Wallace, those judgement of my book you will
        have seen in the papers -

MARIE CURIE

Physicist, 1867–1934
To President Herbert Hoover, 3 November 1929

The name of Marie Curie has become famous around the world, but the name by which she was known as a child, Maria Sklodowska, has been all but forgotten. Maria Sklodowska grew up in Warsaw, Poland, where her parents were both schoolteachers. Maria was the youngest of five children, whose mother died when Maria was only 10 years old. As a result of their parents' profession, the Sklodowska children were given a good education, although there was very little money in the home.

Initially, Maria hoped to become a teacher like her parents, but her widowed father could not afford to pay for her to go to teacher training college, and women were banned from studying at the university in Warsaw. She took a job as a governess while studying secretly at what was known as the 'floating university', an illegal way for women to gain a university education. The money Maria earned as a governess helped her older sister Bronisława move to Paris and study medicine. In her early twenties, Maria moved to Paris to join her sibling, and she was accepted to study physics and mathematics at the Sorbonne. It was when she enrolled at the university that she registered her name as 'Marie'.

In 1894, Marie was introduced to Pierre Curie, a Parisian-born physicist. She was seeking a laboratory in which to carry out her research, and he employed her as his laboratory assistant. Within a year they had fallen in love, and they married in 1895, by which time Marie was working towards her PhD. They had two daughters, Irène (1897–1956) and Ève (1904–2007).

The Curies worked together at the School of Chemistry and Physics in Paris, experimenting with uranium and radioactivity. It was through this work that Marie made the great discovery for which she is famous: the existence of a new element she called radium. She isolated radium in 1902. It was extremely dangerous work, and both she and Pierre became ill as a consequence of their research. In 1903, Marie and Pierre Curie, together with physicist Henri Becquerel, were jointly awarded the Nobel Prize for Physics for their work on radioactivity.

Marie was widowed in 1906, when Pierre died in a road accident. After Pierre's death, Marie was asked to take his place as professor of general physics at the Sorbonne, where she continued her research. In 1911, Marie Curie received a Nobel Prize for Chemistry for her discovery of the elements radium and polonium. During World War I, she created portable X-ray units, which became known as 'Petits Curies'.

In this letter, Marie Curie thanks US president Herbert Hoover and his wife for their hospitality at the White House and for their support of her work. She had visited them at a very difficult time for America, at the start of the Great Depression.

Marie Curie's work has helped to save millions of people around the world – but it was at the cost of her own life. She died from exposure to radiation at the age of 66. Many institutions and a vital international cancer charity are named in her honour. Long after her death, her research continues to save lives.

Opposite Marie and Pierre Curie at work in their Paris laboratory in about 1903.

Institut du Radium
Laboratoire Curie
1, Rue Pierre-Curie, Paris (5e)

New York, le November 3, 1929

My dear Mr. President,

The first letter I have the opportunity to write during my sojourn in the United States, I wish to address to you. My visit to the White House I shall always remember as a great honor and a pleasure. I feel that it was very kind of you and Mrs Hoover to give time and thought to me in those particularly worried days.

I shall keep in memory your words at the Academy of Science and I am sure your address will be a precious document for the archives of the Radium Institute in Poland.

I beg you to believe that my good wishes shall follow you in your important work for piece [sic] and for the improvement of the world.

Sincerely and gratefully yours

Marie Curie

FACULTÉ DES SCIENCES DE PARIS

INSTITUT DU RADIUM

LABORATOIRE CURIE
1, Rue Pierre-Curie, Paris (5e)

TÉL. GOBELINS 14-69

Paris, le November 3, 1929
New York

My dear Mr. President,

The first letter I have the opportunity to write during my sojourn in the United States, I wish to address to you. My visit to the White House I shall always remember as a great honor and a pleasure. I feel that it was very kind of you and Mrs Hoover to give time and thought to me in those particularly worried days.

I shall keep in memory your words at the Academy of Science and I am sure your address will be a precious document for the archives of the Radium Institute in Poland.

I beg you to believe that my good wishes shall follow you in your important work for piece and for the improvement of the world.

Sincerely and gratefully yours

Marie Curie

ELEANOR ROOSEVELT

First Lady and humanitarian, 1884–1963
To Walter White, 19 March 1936

Eleanor Roosevelt turned the position of First Lady (the wife of the US president) into a career. Instead of staying behind the scenes, she became a political force in her own right, promoting the causes of equal rights (for people of all races and genders), the need for better housing for the poor and the furthering of women's careers. Her husband Franklin D. Roosevelt was US president for three terms between 1933 and 1945. This was a time when racial and gender inequality were rampant in the US, and when fascism was gaining power in many areas of the world.

Anna Eleanor Roosevelt was born into a wealthy and prestigious family – her uncle was President Theodore Roosevelt – but her childhood was often very unhappy. When Eleanor was eight, her mother Anna (née Hall) died of diphtheria, and her younger brother died a few months later. Eleanor's much adored but alcoholic father, Elliot Roosevelt, died in a sanatorium when she was just 10. After she was orphaned, her highly critical grandmother became Eleanor's guardian. Her life improved in 1889, when she was sent her to Europe to be educated. She attended Allenswood House in London, England, a school founded by a remarkable Frenchwoman, Marie Souvestre. Eleanor remained friends with Souvestre, who imbued her pupils with a sense of social conscience, until the end of the older woman's life.

At the age of 20, Eleanor married her fifth cousin Franklin Roosevelt. His mother had opposed the match for several years and, after their marriage, attempted to control their household and the raising of Eleanor and Franklin's six children. The marriage was not always easy, and both Eleanor and Franklin are rumoured to have had affairs. But they were well matched politically, and Eleanor became a vital force behind her husband's career. Just two days after her husband was elected for the first time, Eleanor Roosevelt became the first First Lady to hold a news conference. Every journalist invited was female. These press conferences became a regular event, with Eleanor seeking to further the women's careers, as well as getting her own ideas into the public domain. Eleanor was also the first First Lady to have a career as a broadcaster, with her own radio show and newspaper column.

Decades before segregation in the USA was brought to an end, Eleanor was pushing for a change in the laws. She famously talked of the 'stupidity' of not educating black children to the same level as white children, and was passionate about bringing to an end the vile practice of lynching. Unfortunately, her husband felt that, if he pursued his wife's cause, the controversy would lose him the next election. Eleanor sent this letter to Walter Francis White, the President of the NAACP (National Association for the Advancement of Colored People) explaining her husband's reasons for stalling, but in doing so, she openly showed her support for his work and encouraged him to keep talking to members of the Senate.

Eleanor was an essential part of Franklin Roosevelt's New Deal programme. In 1945, following the death of her husband, the new president, Harry S. Truman, appointed Eleanor Roosevelt as a delegate to the United Nations. She continued to campaign for causes she believed in until her death at the age of 78.

Opposite Eleanor Roosevelt
on the campaign trail in 1936.

PERSONAL AND CONFIDENTIAL

March 19, 1936

My dear Mr. White:

Before I received your letter today I had been in to the President, talking to him about your letter enclosing that of the Attorney General. I told him that it seemed rather terrible that one could get nothing done and that I did not blame you in the least for feeling there was no interest in this very serious question. I asked him if there were any possibility of getting even one step taken, and he said the difficulty is that it is unconstitutional apparently for the Federal Government to step in in a lynching situation. The Government has only been allowed to do anything about kidnapping because of its interstate aspect, and even that has not as yet been appealed so they are not sure that it will be declared constitutional.

The President feels that lynching is a question of education in the states, rallying good citizens, and creating public opinion so that the localities themselves will wipe it out. However, if it were done by a Northerner, it will have an antagonistic effect. I will talk to him again about the Van Nuys resolution and will try to talk also to Senator Byrnes and get his point of view. I am deeply troubled about the whole situation as it seems to be a terrible thing to stand by and let it continue and feel that one cannot speak out as to his feeling. I think your next step would be to talk to the more prominent members of the Senate.

Very sincerely yours,

Eleanor Roosevelt

PERSONAL AND CONFIDENTIAL.

THE WHITE HOUSE
WASHINGTON

March 19, 1936

W.W. 3-21-36

My dear Mr. White:

Before I received your letter today I
had been in to the President, talking to him about
your letter enclosing that of the Attorney General.
I told him that it seemed rather terrible that one
could get nothing done and that I did not blame you
in the least for feeling there was no interest in
this very serious question. I asked him if there
were any possibility of getting even one step taken,
and he said the difficulty is that it is unconstitutional apparently for the Federal Government to
step in in the lynching situation. The Government
has only been allowed to do anything about kidnapping because of its interstate aspect, and even that
has not as yet been appealed so they are not sure
that it will be declared constitutional.

The President feels that lynching is
a question of education in the states, rallying
good citizens, and creating public opinion so that
the localities themselves will wipe it out. However, if it were done by a Northerner, it will
have an antagonistic effect. I will talk to him
again about the Van Nuys resolution and will try
to talk also to Senator Byrnes and get his point
of view. I am deeply troubled about the whole
situation as it seems to be a terrible thing to
stand by and let it continue and feel that one cannot speak out as to his feeling. I think your next
step would be to talk to the more prominent members
of the Senate.

Very sincerely yours,

Eleanor Roosevelt

AMELIA EARHART

Aviation pioneer, 1897–1937
To President Roosevelt, 10 November 1936

Amelia Earhart's love of flying began in her early twenties, by which age she had already worked as a military nurse and as a social worker. She took her first flying lesson in January 1921 and immediately began saving for her first plane. It was a bright yellow Kinner Airster, which Amelia named 'The Canary'. Soon she had begun breaking records. In 1928, she became the first female passenger to fly across the Atlantic Ocean, together with two male aviators. Even though she wasn't flying the plane on this occasion, she wrote a very successful book, *2 Hrs., 40 Min.: Our Flight in the Friendship*, about the experience. In the book, Amelia wrote about women in aviation, commenting: 'Possibly the feature of aviation which may appeal most to thoughtful women is its potentiality for peace. The term is not merely an airy phrase. … I think aviation has a chance to increase intimacy, understanding, and far-flung friendships.'

The book was published by George Putnam, who had been one of the sponsors of the flight. When she met Putnam, Amelia was engaged to someone else and Putnam was married. Three years later, he was divorced, Amelia had ended her engagement, and they married – allegedly he proposed six times before being accepted.

In 1932, a year after their marriage, Amelia became the second person and the first woman to fly solo across the Atlantic. The only person who had managed to do so before her was Charles Lindbergh. Amelia made the flight in her single-engined Lockheed Vega, which was painted bright red. She took off from Newfoundland, intending to end her journey in Paris, but the weather conditions made navigation difficult and she landed her plane in Ballyarnot, in rural Northern Ireland – where the surprised landowners, the Gallagher family, welcomed her into their home and gave her a hot meal.

In 1935, Amelia became the first person to fly solo across the Pacific Ocean and the first person to fly solo from Mexico City to Newark. At this time she was, as this 1936 letter to President Roosevelt shows, making secret preparations to fly around the world. In 1937, Amelia and her navigator Fred Noonan began an attempt to circumnavigate the world in her customised Lockheed Electra plane. After an aborted first try, in which the plane became damaged and had to be repaired, they departed from Miami and flew – with frequent refuelling stops – to Lae, in Papua New Guinea. On 2 July 1837, they took off en route to Howland Island in the Pacific Ocean. They were never seen again. During the flight, Amelia transmitted their coordinates to the US coastguard on Howland Island. At 7:42 am, she reported, 'We must be on you, but we cannot see you. Fuel is running low. Been unable to reach you by radio. We are flying at 1,000 feet.' But her plane seemed unable to receive the answer. At 8:45 am, Earhart sent her last communication, 'We are running north and south.'

The fate of the plane and its two passengers remains unknown. In the 1940s, the skeleton of a woman was discovered on the Pacific Island of Nikumaroro. For decades, experts have tried to determine whether or not it is the remains of Amelia Earhart.

AMELIA EARHART   *Do what we can and contact Mr. Putnam*

2 West 45th Street,
New York City.

November 10, 1936.

Dear Mr. President:

        Some time ago I told you and Mrs.
Roosevelt a little about my confidential plans
for a world flight. As perhaps you know, through
the cooperation of Purdue University I now have a
magnificient twin-motor, all-metal plane,
especially equipped for long distance flying.

        For some months ~~we~~ *Mr. Putnam and I* have been pre-
paring for a flight which I hope to attempt probably in March. The route, compared with
previous flights, will be unique. It is east to
west, and approximates the equator. Roughly it
is from San Francisco to Honolulu; from Honolulu
to Tokio -- or Honolulu to Brisbane; the regular
Australia-England route as far west as Karachi;
from Karachi to Aden; Aden via Kartoon across
Central Africa to Dakar; Dakar to Natal, and
thence to New York on the regular Pan American
route.

        Special survey work and map
preparation is already under way on the less
familiar portion of the route as, for instance,
that in Africa.

        The chief problem is the jump west-
ward from Honolulu. The distance thence to Tokio
is 3900 miles. I want to reduce as much as possible
the hazard of the take-off at Honolulu with the
excessive over-load. With that in view, I am
discussing with the Navy a possible refueling in
the air over Midway Island. If this can be
arranged, I need to take much less gas from Honolulu,
and with the Midway refueling will have ample

AMELIA EARHART

-2-

gasoline to reach Tokio.   As mine is a land
plane, the seaplane facilities at Wake, Guam, etc.
are useless.

This matter has been discussed in
detail by Mr. Putnam with Admiral Cook, who was
most interested and friendly. Subsequently a
detailed description of the project, and request
for this assistance, was prepared. It is now on
the desk of Admiral Standley, by whom it is being
considered.

Some new seaplanes are being completed at San Diego for the Navy. They will be
ferried in January or February to Honolulu. It
is my desire to practise actual refueling
operations in the air over San Diego with one of
these planes. That plane subsequently from
Honolulu would be available for the Midway
operation. I gather from Admiral Cook that
technically there are no extraordinary difficulties.
It is primarily a matter of policy and precedent.

In the past the Navy has been so
progressive in its pioneering, and so broad-minded
in what we might call its "public relations",
that I think a project such as this (even involving
a mere woman!) may appeal to Navy personnel. Its
successful attainment might, I think, win for the
Service further popular friendship.

I should add the matter of international permissions etc. is being handled very
helpfully by the State Department. The flight,
by the way, has no commercial implications. The
operation of my "flying laboratory" is under the
auspices of Purdue University. Like previous
flights, I am undertaking this one solely because
I want to, and because I feel that women now and
then have to do things to show what women can do.

Forgive the great length of this
letter. I am just leaving for the west on a

AMELIA EARHART

-3-

lecture tour and wanted to place my problem
before you.

Knowing your own enthusiasm for
voyaging, and your affectionate interest in
Navy matters, I am asking you to help me secure
Navy cooperation -- that is, if you think well
of the project. If any information is wanted
as to purpose, plans, equipment, etc., Mr.
Putnam can meet anyone you designate any time
any where.

Very sincerely yours,

Hon. Franklin D. Roosevelt,
The White House,
Washington, D.C.

P.S.- My plans are for the
moment entirely confidential
-- no announcement has been
made.

2 West 45th Street,
New York City.

November 10, 1936.

Dear Mr. President:

Some time ago I told you and Mrs. Roosevelt a little about my confidential plans for a world flight. As perhaps you know, through the cooperation of Purdue University I now have a magnificent twin-motor, all-metal plane, especially equipped for long distance flying.

For some months Mr Putnam and I have been preparing for a flight which I hope to attempt probably in March. The route, compared with previous flights, will be unique. It is east to west, and approximates the equator. Roughly it is from San Francisco to Honolulu; from Honolulu to Tokio [sic.] – or Honolulu to Brisbane; the regular Australia-England route as far west as Karachi; from Karachi to Aden; Aden via Kartoon [sic.] across Central Africa to Dakar; Dakar to Natal, and thence to New York on the regular Pan American route.

Special survey work and map preparation is already under way on the less familiar portion of the route as, for instance, that in Africa.

The chief problem is the jump westward from Honolulu. The distance thence to Tokio [sic.] is 3900 miles. I want to reduce as much as possible the hazard of the take-off at Honoulu with the excessive over-load. With that in view, I am discussing with the Navy a possible refuelling in the air over Midway Island. If this can be arranged, I need to take much less gas from Honolulu, and with the Midway refuelling will have ample gasoline to reach Tokio [sic.]. As mine is a land plane, the seaplane facilities at Wake, Guam etc. are useless.

This matter has been discussed in detail by Mr. Putnam with Admiral Cook, who was most interested and friendly. Subsequently a detailed description of the project, and request for this assistance, was prepared. It is now on the desk of Admiral Standley, by whom it is being considered.

Some new seaplanes are being completed at San Diego for the Navy. They will be ferried in January or February to Honolulu. It is my desire to practise actual refuelling operations in the air over San Diego with one of these planes. That plane subsequently from Honolulu would be available for the Midway operation. I gather from Admiral Cook that technically there are no extraordinary difficulties. It is primarily a matter of policy and precedent.

In the past the Navy has been so progressive in its pioneering, and so broad-minded in what we might call its "public relations", that I think a project such as this (even involving a mere woman!) may appeal to Navy personnel. Its successful attainment might, I think, win for the Service further popular friendship.

I should add the matter of international permissions etc. is being handled very helpfully by the State Department. The flight, by the way, has no commercial implications. The operation of my "flying laboratory" is under the auspices of Purdue University. Like previous flights, I am undertaking this one solely because I want to, and because I feel that women now and then have to do things to show what women can do.

Forgive the great length of this letter. I am just leaving for the west on a lecture tour and wanted to place my problem before you.

Knowing your own enthusiasm for voyaging, and your affectionate interest in Navy matters, I am asking you to help me secure Navy cooperation – that is, if you think well of the project. If any information is wanted as to purpose, plans, equipment etc., Mr. Putnam can meet anyone you designate any time any where.

Very sincerely yours,

Amelia Earhart

Hon. Franklin D. Roosevelt,
The White House,
Washington, D.C.

P.S. – My plans are for the moment entirely confidential – no announcement has been made.

VIRGINIA WOOLF

Writer, 1882–1941
To George Bernard Shaw, 15 May 1940

Virginia Woolf was born into a bohemian world of privilege and education in London, but she was of the generation old enough to fight or lose loved ones in World War I, and then to have it happen all over again in the World War II. This poignant era in history explains much of why the seemingly frivolous Bloomsbury Group, of which Virginia Woolf was to become a pivotal member, suffered so much from depression. Virginia's depression began young, and was exacerbated by the deaths of her mother and half-sister when Virginia was a teenager, and her father and elder brother when she was in her twenties. It was also compounded by the sexual and emotional abuse she suffered from her half-brother George.

Virginia was the third of four children born to Leslie Stephen and his wife Julia (née Jackson). Both her parents had been married and widowed before, and both had older children: her father had a daughter and her mother had a daughter and two sons. Virginia was closest to her three full siblings, Vanessa (the artist Vanessa Bell), Adrian (a psychoanalyst) and Thoby (who died of typhoid aged 26). The artistic and literary Bloomsbury Group grew out of encounters with the university friends brought home by Thoby and Adrian.

In 1912, Virginia Stephen married Leonard Woolf, whom she had first met in 1900 when visiting Thoby at Cambridge. Together they set up the Hogarth Press in 1917. The company logo was a wolf, symbolic of their name. Their marriage was based on deep friendship, and survived both Virginia's depressions and her long-term love affair with a female friend, Vita Sackville-West.

Virginia Woolf's first novel, *The Voyage Out*, was published in 1915. She wrote and published eight further novels, including *Mrs Dalloway* (1925), written in the stream-of-consciousness style, and *Orlando* (1928). Her last novel was *Between the Acts*, published in 1941, the year of her death. She also wrote short stories, essays – including the extended essay *A Room of One's Own* (1929) – biographies, and the play *Freshwater*.

This witty letter, to the Irish playwright George Bernard Shaw, was written at the Woolfs' home, Monk's House, and demonstrates how integral Virginia was to the British literary scene. It was Monk's House, near the River Ouse in Sussex, that Virginia left on the morning of 28 March 1941. On that chilly Friday, Virginia Woolf wore a heavy coat and filled its pockets with stones, then she walked into the river. Her suicide note to her husband read: 'Dearest, I feel certain I am going mad again. I feel we can't go through another of those terrible times. And I shan't recover this time. … What I want to say is I owe all the happiness of my life to you.' The war had claimed the lives of several of her friends and she was worn down by the misery of the news headlines and the cruelty of humanity. She had attempted suicide on previous occasions, and had been undergoing therapy for her depression. Her body was not recovered until 18 April. She was cremated and her ashes were scattered at Monk's House.

                    Monk's House,
                    Rodmell,
                    near Lewes,   15th May 1940
                    Sussex.

Dear Mr Shaw,

          Your letter reduced me to two days
silence from sheer pleasure. You wont be
surprised to hear that I promptly lifted
some paragraphs and inserted them in my proofs.
You may take what action you like.
     As for the falling in love, it was not, let me
confess, one-sided. When I first met you at the
Webbs I was set against all great men, having been
liberally fed on them in my father's house.
I wanted only to meet business men and (say) racing
experts. But in a jiffy you made me re-consider all
that and had me at your feet. Indeed you have acted
a lover's part in my life for the past thirty years;
and though daresay its not much to boast of, I should
have been a worser woman without Bernard Shaw.
That is the reason---I mean the multiplicity of
your lovers and what you must suffer from them--
why Leonard and Virginia have never liked to
impose themselves upon you. But we have an *intermittent*
perch--37 Mecklenburgh Square-- in London;
and if ever Mr Shaw dropped his handkerchief--
to recur to the love theme-- we should ask nothing
better than to come and see you.
          As for the Roger Fry picture, I should accept it
gratefully. For that offer, and for your letter,
and for everything else that you have given me,
I am always yours humbly and gratefully,

                    Virginia Woolf

     Heartbreak House, by the way, is my
favourite of all your works.

Monk's House,
Rodmell,
Near Lewes,
Sussex.

15th May 1940

Dear Mr Shaw,

Your letter reduced me to two days silence from sheer pleasure. You wont be surprised to hear that I promptly lifted some paragraphs and inserted them in my proofs. You may take what action you like.

As for the falling in love, it was not, let me confess, one-sided. When I first met you at the Webbs I was set against all great men, having been liberally fed on them in my father's house. I wanted only to meet business men – and (say) racing experts. But in a jiffy you made me re-consider all that and had me at your feet. Indeed you may have acted a lover's part in my life for the past thirty years; and though daresay its not much to boast of, I should have been a worser woman without Bernard Shaw. That is the reason – I mean the multiplicity of your lovers and what you must suffer from them – why Leonard and Virginia have never liked to impose themselves upon you. But we have an intermittent perch – 37 Mecklenburgh Square – in London; and if ever Mr Shaw dropped his handkerchief – to recur to the love theme – we should ask nothing better than to come and see you.

As for the Roger Fry picture, I should accept it gratefully. For that offer, and for your letter, and for everything else that you have given me, I am always yours humbly and gratefully,

Virginia Woolf

Heartbreak House, by the way, is my favourite of all your works.

Opposite Virginia Woolf
pictured in 1927.

LEE MILLER

Photographer, journalist and model, 1907–1977
To Audrey Withers, around September 1944

Elizabeth 'Lee' Miller began her photographic career at the age of 19 as a model, working in her native New York. In her twenties, she travelled to Paris, where she became involved in the Surrealism art movement. She was a model and muse to her lover, the artist Man Ray. Miller lived in Paris for three years, setting up her own photography studio. When she returned to New York in 1932, it was as a successful photographer. Two years later, after marrying the engineer Aziz Aloui Bey, she moved to Cairo, dividing her time between Egypt and Europe. In 1937, she left her husband for the British Surrealist painter Roland Penrose.

Lee Miller maintained a long-term relationship with *Vogue* magazine. *Vogue* was initially sceptical about a former model working as a photographer, but Miller was given the chance to prove herself when many male photographers went away to war in 1939. Now based in London, she became the war correspondent for *Vogue*, initially documenting the Blitz. Her early work was crucial to the UK government's efforts to keep women informed and useful on the Home Front. In 1942, Miller was accredited as a war correspondent for the US Army. Her work over the next three years has become painfully iconic, remaining some of the most haunting of all photojournalism of the conflict.

In 1944, Miller was one of only four female official photographers working with the US military. This letter, to Audrey Withers, editor of British *Vogue*, was sent just after the Siege of St Malo. Lee's account of the siege – 'I thumbed a ride to the Siege of St Malo. I had bought my bed, I begged my board, and I was given a grandstand view of the fortress warfare reminiscent of Crusader times' – was published in British and American *Vogue*. She was the sole photojournalist present, and when the article revealed to the military that she had been there without authorisation, she was arrested and banned from the front line.

The most heartbreaking assignment of Lee Miller's career came in 1945, when she accompanied Allied troops as they liberated the concentration camps of Buchenwald and Dachau. Her photographs of the atrocities, and her knowledge of how cruel humanity could be, never left her. She barely ever spoke about what she saw, and destroyed some of the Dachau negatives, as she couldn't bear anyone else to witness them. Disillusioned, she wrote to Roland Penrose from Paris at the end of the war, 'Peace with a world of crooks who have no honour, no integrity and no shame is not what anyone fought for.'

Lee Miller married Roland Penrose in 1947, the same year in which their son Anthony was born. The family lived on a farm, Farleys House in Sussex in southern England. Despite this seeming idyll, the horrors of the war never left her and she struggled with depression and PTSD, as well as battling alcoholism, which she overcame. Lee Miller continued to work for *Vogue*, and took a series of photographic portraits of many of her famous friends, including the artists Pablo Picasso and Max Ernst. She died of cancer at her home in Sussex at the age of 70.

Opposite Lee Miller met up with Pablo Picasso in Paris in 1944, shortly after the city's liberation.

To Censor: Press Personal Message (Service Message) from Lee Miller, War Correspondent

Audrey Withers,
Vogue Magazine,
1 New Bond Street,
London, W.1.

I've been collecting some very exciting material and not a few adventures – which will get to you as soon as I catch my breath. I went to St. Malo and found that there was a siege on, and so stayed it out. The "press" had been to St. Malo already for the battle of the land part of the town and had left for greener pastures, so I had the sole coverage of a real old fashioned siege – like the battle of 'Acre' or something – and a grandstand view of air bombing and infantry attack – truces, exchange of wounded – refugees and the workings of Civil Affairs in a combat area. Also I contacted some charming French people who are very celebratedly connected with the Underground Movement – dined with them, played with them etc., and have photos of everything. I picked St. Malo, especially, as it was the twon [sic] from which I left nearly 5 years ago on the day of the war, for England – and because it is so well known to tourists etc. as a beauty spot – also I went over to Dinard immediately it fell – and took some pix of the well-known joints – Casinos, hotels, beaches etc. Just as the military part of the operation was over I got pulled out by the authorities as being too far into the "zone" for their taste – and have been hoisted back to Rennes. However, everything is alright and I'm going on the road to-morrow. It's too bad, as there were one or two details I wanted to clear up in my own mind. My adventures sound a little too much to believe if I wrote them down briefly now – so I'll wait and send the whole piece.

In the mean time I have sent a set of pictures thru' to London to John Morris of Life Magazine – as they are combat stuff, and must be offered to the Pool. I thot [sic] that he could handle it better than us – for the moment and he is supposed to keep the negs separate. Scherman and some news writers turned up in St. Malo for the "kill" – the surrender, and so I thot [sic] it best to connect my stuff with that of Life. A few hours after the taking of St. Malo (old city) I had a dark room working in the basement of a photographic shop which had been burned out on top – so my pix were already dev. before sending – and I have kept here for my writing the stuff which was of no interest to them. Get a set of prints made and hold on to them until I follow it up – save some space for me – but I'd rather that you didn't make a story up – just using the pix – as it's really part of a whole.

I'm still out of contact with my luggage since I left it in Valognes a week ago – but I've lived off the land and all my film even, is captured German stuff. Give my love to everyone – and Auntie Sylvia, Morton, and the boys. Tell Roland Penrose all love and everything O.K. – I've contacted Jean Pages also, here, who salutes you – he took the surrender of Cap Frehal [sic].

To Censor: Press Personal Message (Service Message) from **Lee Miller, War Correspondent**

Audrey Withers,
Vogue Magazine,
1 New Bond Street,
London, W.1.

I've been collecting some very exciting material and not a few adventures – which
will get to you as soon as I catch my breath. I went to St. Malo and found that
there was a siege on, and so stayed it out. The "press" had been to St. Malo
already for the battle of the land part of the town and had left for greener
pastures, so I had the sole coverage of a real old fashioned siege – like the
battle of 'Acre' or something – and a grandstand view of air bombing and infantry
attack – truces, exchange of wounded – refugees and the workings of Civil Affairs
in a combat area. Also I contacted some charming French people who are very
celebratedly connected with the Underground Movement – dined with them, played
with them etc., and have photos of everything. I picked St. Malo, especially,
as it was the twon from which I left nearly 5 years ago on the day of the war,
for England – and because it is so well known to tourists etc. as a beauty spot –
also I went over to Dinard immediately it fell – and took some pix of the well-
known joints – Casinos, hotels, beaches etc. Just as the military part of the
operation was over I got pulled out by the authorities as being too far into a
"zone" for their taste – and have been hoisted back to Rennes. However, everything
is alright and I'm going on the road to-morrow. It's too bad, as there were one
or two details I wanted to clear up in my own mind. My adventures sound a little
too much to believe if I wrote them down briefly now – so I'll wait and send the
whole piece.

In the mean time I have sent a set of pictures thru' to London to John
Morris of Life Magazine – as they are combat stuff, and must be offered to the
Pool. I thot that he could handle it better than us – for the moment and he is
supposed to keep the negs separate. Scherman and some news writers turned up
in St. Malo for the "kill" – the surrender, and so I thot it best to connect my
stuff with that of Life. A few hours after the taking of St. Malo (old City) I
had a dark room working in the basement of a photographic shop which had been
burned out on top – so my pix were already dev. before sending – and I have kept
here for my writing the stuff which was of no interest to them. Get a set of
prints made and hold on to them until I follow it up – save some space for me –
but I'd rather that you didn't make a story up – just using the pix – as it's
really part of a whole.

I'm still out of contact with my luggage since I left it in Valognes a
week ago – but I've lived off the land and all my film even, is captured German
stuff. Give my love to everyone – and Auntie Sylvia, Morton, and the boys. Tell
Roland Penrose all love and everything O.K. – I've contacted Jean Pages also, here,
who salutes you – he took the surrender of Cap Frehal.

RUBY PAYNE-SCOTT

Physicist, 1912–1981
To Sir Ian Clunies Ross, 20 February 1950

Ruby Payne-Scott was born in New South Wales, Australia, just before the outbreak of World War I. She grew up to become a pioneer of radio physics and was the first woman to work as a radio astronomer (studying naturally occurring radio waves from stars, planets and galaxies). She fought for equality throughout her career, recruiting other female scientists to her team and challenging workplace inequalities, but she was eventually forced out of the scientific arena at a time when married women were expected to give up working.

The young Ruby had excelled at school, and she entered Sydney University at the age of just 16. There she obtained a first-class honours degree in maths and physics, making her the university's third female graduate in physics. She began working in medical physics, obtaining her MSc and working at the Cancer Research Institute. The Institute closed down in 1938, and Ruby found it impossible to get another job in her field because of her gender.

Unable to find work, Ruby retrained as a teacher and took a post at a girls' grammar school, while continuing to apply for jobs in physics. The following year, she was offered the post of librarian at Australian Wireless Amalgamated (AWA). Once there, she made herself indispensable, taking on responsibility for editing AWA's journal and volunteering for research work before her skills were taken notice of and she was employed as a physicist. In 1941, during World War II, she was recruited as a radiophysicist at the Council for Scientific and Industrial Research (CSIR) to work on secret radar research. Over the next few years, she made some groundbreaking discoveries, including looking at deep-space phenomena and identifying several solar bursts.

After the war was over, Payne-Scott continued her research into solar bursts. She worked against a constant battle to challenge gender restrictions in the workplace, such as archaic dress codes, a ban on female (but not male) employees smoking and vastly unequal pay. In this letter, sent to the chairman of what was now called CSIRO, Ruby is responding to the way the status of female scientists changed after marriage. For years, her colleagues had thought she had a scandalous love life, living with a man without being married. Yet what she had recently revealed was that she and Bill Holman Hall were married – she had pretended not to be to try and save her career. Married women were automatically downgraded from full-time employees to 'temporary' employees.

Ruby Payne-Scott's coolly measured tone in this letter emphasises how little time she had for such archaic rules. What she wanted was to continue her work as a scientist without being distracted by side issues. The result of admitting to being married was that she was downgraded to temporary status, losing out financially, including being stripped of her pension.

In 1951, Ruby was 39 years old and a senior grade researcher, but she left the CSIRO because she was pregnant, and there was no maternity leave on offer. She gave birth to a son at the end of the year and a daughter two years later. Her son Peter Hall was an influential mathematician, while her daughter is the renowned artist Fiona Hall. Unable to return to her research, Ruby Payne-Scott went back to teaching. As a wife and mother, she found it impossible to find work as a radiophysicist again. She died in 1981 at the age of 68.

Radiophysics Laboratory
University grounds
Chippendale

20/2/50

Dear Dr. Ross

Your letter to me came while I was away on holidays, & in the rush of unprecedented solar activity of the last few weeks I seem to have mislaid it, so I will have to reply from memory.

Thankyou for your inquiries on my behalf, but when I spoke to you about my marriage I was in effect asking you whether the Executive realises that the customary demoting of women officers in their marriage to the status of "temporaries" does not appear to be required in the Act & whether the Executive agrees with this procedure or not. Whether or not there are any material disadvantages to the women concerned in this procedure, all the married women research officers I have met feel that their classification as "temporary" puts them at a considerable psychological disadvantage in their work.

Personally I feel no legal or moral obligation to have taken any other action than I have in making my marriage known. I have never denied to anyone who has asked me the fact that I am married, & it has gradually become common knowledge in the laboratory, particularly as many of the staff are my close neighbours at home! More recently I have stated the fact that I am married, among other information, in a form that I was asked to complete & return to Head Office. I have, of course, always stated it on my income-tax form. I have been informed by a solicitor friend that the Act does not make it obligatory on an officer to inform any official of C.S.I.R.O. of his or her marriage, unless they are asked for the information.

I should still be very interested to know whether the Executive is in agreement with the present procedure with regard to married women, which seems to go far beyond the simple statement in the Act that their employment may be continued where it seems desirable. I told you my story not in order to implicate you in any way but to demonstrate that the present procedure is ridiculous & can lead to ridiculous results.

With best wishes
Yours sincerely
Ruby Payne-Scott

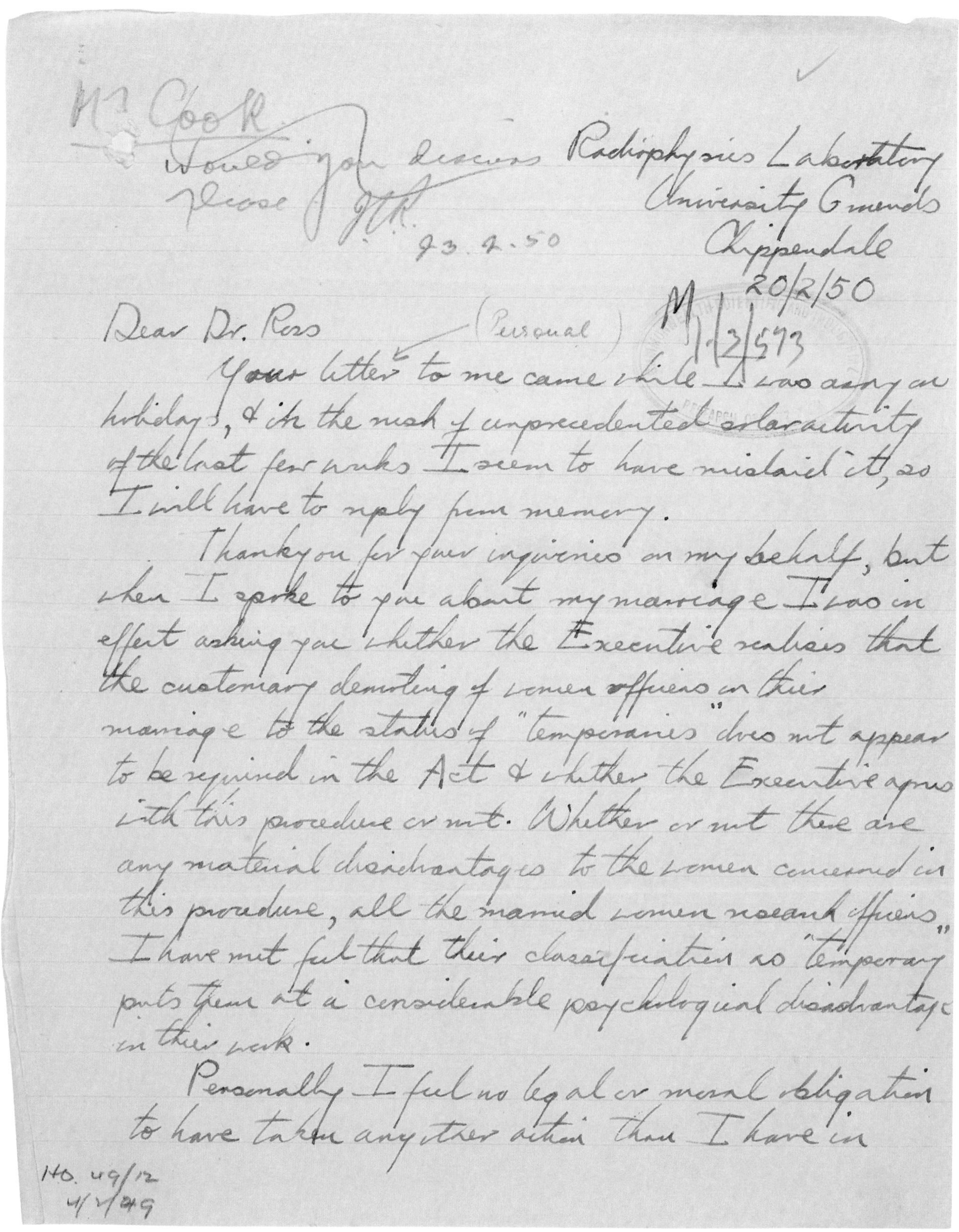

Mr Cook

Would you discuss
please J.P.K.

9·3·4·50

Radiophysics Laboratory
University Grounds
Chippendale
20/2/50

M 12/573

Dear Dr. Ross (Personal)

Your letter to me came while I was away on holidays, & in the rush of unprecedented solar activity of the last few weeks I seem to have mislaid it, so I will have to reply from memory.

Thank you for your inquiries on my behalf, but when I spoke to you about my marriage I was in effect asking you whether the Executive realises that the customary demoting of women officers on their marriage to the status of "temporaries" does not appear to be required in the Act & whether the Executive agrees with this procedure or not. Whether or not there are any material disadvantages to the women concerned in this procedure, all the married women research officers I have met feel that their classification as "temporary" puts them at a considerable psychological disadvantage in their work.

Personally I feel no legal or moral obligation to have taken any other action than I have in

140. 49/12
4/1/49

making my marriage known. I have never denied to anyone who has asked me the fact that I am married, & it has gradually become common knowledge in the laboratory, particularly as many of the staff are my close neighbours at home. More recently I have stated the fact that I am married, among other information, on a form that I was asked to complete & return to Head Office. I have, of course, always stated it on my income-tax forms. I have been informed by a solicitor friend that the Act does not make it obligatory on an officer to inform any official of C.S.I.R.O. of his or her marriage, unless they are asked for the information.

I should still be very interested to know whether the Executive is in agreement with the present procedure with regard to married women, which seems to go far beyond the simple statement in the Act that their employment may be continued where it seems desirable. I told you my story not in order to implicate you in any way but to demonstrate that the present procedure is ridiculous & can lead to ridiculous results.

With best wishes

yours sincerely
Ruby Payne-Scott

DOROTHY HODGKIN

Chemist, 1910–1994
To Linus Pauling, 3 May 1951

In 1964, Dorothy Crowfoot Hodgkin won the Nobel Prize for Chemistry, making her the only female British scientist to have been awarded a Nobel Prize. In addition to her formidable scientific career, she also made history by becoming the first woman ever to receive maternity pay from an Oxford college. Today, a Royal Society Fellowship in her name exists specifically to assist female scientists who want to raise children as well as pursue their career.

Dorothy Crowfoot was born in Cairo, Egypt, the daughter of a British couple who were living there for work. Later in Dorothy's childhood, they moved to Sudan, and it was here that she first discovered her interest in chemistry, encouraged by her mother, who was a keen botanist. Dorothy and her three younger sisters were then sent to live with their grandparents in England. At school, Dorothy was one of only two girls permitted to study chemistry, for which they had to join a class of boys. Her parents' shared passion was for archaeology, and when Dorothy joined them in Sudan, she helped with excavations and studied the pebbles and crystals that she found, something that would be reflected in her career. Later in life she mused that, in these early years, she almost gave up the dream of becoming a chemist in favour of becoming an archaeologist.

As a teenager, the writing that influenced Dorothy's life most strongly was Sir William Bragg's book, *Concerning the Nature of Things: Six Lectures delivered at the Royal Institution* (1925). This book was instrumental in determining her future career in chemistry rather than archaeology. In 1928, Dorothy became an undergraduate at Somerville College, Oxford; she was one of only four women studying for a degree in chemistry. Her research concerned X-ray crystallography, a then-new technique for determining the molecular structure of crystals. After graduating with first-class honours, she studied for her PhD at Cambridge, where she researched sterols (a kind of lipid) and other molecules. During this time, she achieved a scientific first: making an X-ray diffraction photograph of a protein, something that proved invaluable in her later research. Dorothy's university career and her brilliant research were indebted to another remarkable woman: her aunt, Dorothy Hood, who paid her university fees and all her student bills.

By the time she had finished her PhD, Oxford had persuaded Dorothy to come back. She returned to Somerville in 1934, but this time as a fellow – a young Margaret Roberts (later Thatcher) would be one of her students. Three years later she married the historian Thomas Hodgkin, who had recently returned from working in Palestine. Thomas also became a lecturer at Oxford and, between 1938 and 1946, they became parents to three children – a daughter and two sons. Dorothy's work at Oxford cemented her as a pioneer in her field. She mapped the structure of insulin, penicillin and vitamin B12, changing and saving the lives of millions of people all over the world.

Dorothy Hodgkin was always politically active, most notably as a leading member of the Pugwash Campaign, a body set up to campaign against nuclear weapons. This letter was sent to the American chemist Linus Pauling, also a fervent supporter of the anti-nuclear movement ever since the atomic bombing of Hiroshima and Nagasaki. His beliefs led to his passport being revoked. Dorothy Hodgkin stayed steadfast in her anti-nuclear views, and continued to attend conferences and travel overseas almost to the end of her life.

Opposite Top Dorothy Hodgkin at work in her laboratory in 1964, the year she won the Nobel Prize.

May 3rd. 1951

Dear Linus,

We were all shocked and angry and very sad that you could not come. Is there anything we can do? At the meeting we did not know for certain that you would not be coming till near the end when Adrian arrived since it was reported he was in Washington and trying to extricate you. So the time for immediate protests passed.

But we missed you a great deal in all the discussion and will do anything we can to make it possible for you to come some other time.

With all our best wishes, sympathy, & admiration.

Dorothy Hodgkin

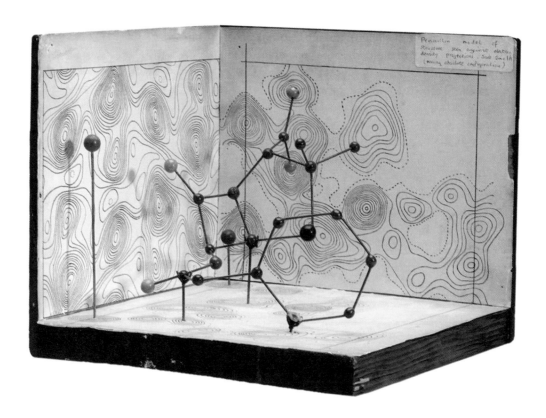

Above A model of a penicillin molecule, made by Hodgkin in 1945.

POWDER HILL HOUSE,
BOAR'S HILL,
OXFORD.
TEL. OXFORD 85530.

May 3rd. 1951

Dear Linus,

we were all shocked and angry and very sad that you could not come. Is there anything we can do? At the meeting we did not know for certain that you would not be coming till near the end when adrian arrived – since it was reported he was in Washington

and trying to extricate you. So the time for immediate protests passed.

But we missed you a great deal in all the discussion and will do anything we can to make it possible for you to come some other time.

With all our best wishes. Sympathy & admiration.

Dorothy Hodgkin.

NINA SIMONE

Musician, 1933–2003
To Langston Hughes, 6 July, 1966

Growing up in North Carolina, Eunice Wayman – who would later change her name to Nina Simone – was a child prodigy who could read music and perform from a very young age. Initially, she was known not for her singing but as a pianist. Eunice played the piano and the organ for the church at which her mother was a preacher, and she dreamed of becoming a concert pianist. But her ambition was to be thwarted by racism. After her family moved to Philadelphia, Eunice was accepted as a student at the prestigious Juilliard music school in New York. A year later, she auditioned at the Curtis Institute of Music in Philadelphia, and she was convinced the sole reason she was rejected was the colour of her skin. That hurt remained with her for the rest of her life. In a later interview she said, 'I knew I was good enough, but they turned me down. And it took me about six months to realize it was because I was black. I never really got over that jolt of racism.' Her frustration with such racial attitudes – something that affected her entire career – is reflected in this letter. It was sent to her friend, the poet and novelist Langston Hughes, and was written when Nina, her then-husband Andrew and their daughter Lisa were in London. Langston Hughes was a leader of the Jazz Poetry movement and at the heart of the Harlem Renaissance; he was also a central chronicler of the Civil Rights movement.

After her rejection from the Curtis Institute, Nina took a job playing piano in a bar in Atlantic City, which is when she adopted her stage name. It was while working at this bar that she also began to sing in public, with a voice that would soon become renowned all over the world. At the age of 24, she was signed to Bethlehem Records, before moving to Colpix Records. In 1959, 'I Loves You Porgy', a single from her first album *The Amazing Nina Simone*, became her breakthrough song. After making it into the mainstream, she was able to use her music to reflect her social conscience and wrote protest songs to express her fury at inequality, one of the most famous being 'Mississippi Goddam', written after the murder of four black children in Alabama. The single was released in 1964, and promptly banned by several of the southern states. It made her a leading voice in the struggle for Civil Rights. Her deep, expressive voice was instantly recognisable. Nina herself said of her singing style, 'Sometimes I sound like gravel, and sometimes I sound like coffee and cream.'

In the 1970s, Nina left her abusive husband, Andrew Stroud, and moved to Liberia. Later she travelled around Europe before settling in France. Over her long career, she released more than 40 albums. In the 1980s, her 1950s single 'My Baby Just Cares for Me' was used in a TV advert in the UK, prompting a renewed interest in her music and a new generation of fans. By the time of her death, on 21 April 2003, Nina had seen her music undergo yet another renaissance in the digital age. In the last decade of her life alone, Nina Simone sold more than 1 million CDs.

London,
Sunday night
July 6?

Dear Langston –

I've owed you this letter for some time now – so I'm finally doing it.

Thank you – thank you for the books (your autobiographies) you gave us – I'm reading "The Big Sea", right now and it gives me such pleasure – you have no idea! It is so funny – I read chapters over & over again – 'cause certain ones paint complete pictures for me and I get completely absorbed!

Then too, If I'm in a negative mood and want to get more negative (about the racial problem, I mean) if I want to get downright mean and violent I go straight to this book and there is also material for that. Amazing – I use the book – what I mean is I underline all meaningful sentences to me – I make comments in pencil about certain paragraphs etc. And as I said there is a wealth of knowledge concerning the negro problem, especially if one wants to trace the many many areas that we've had it rough in all these years – sometimes when I'm with white "liberals" who want to know why we're so bitter – I forget (I don't forget – I just get tongue-tied) how complete has been the white race's rejection of us all these years and then when this happens I go get your book. I'm looking forward to using it more & more in this way as times go on.

As a matter of fact, Langston, I feel sorta' tongue-tied now for there's so much I'd like to say to you and I can't possibly write as fast as I think and even if I did I'd be here all night writing this letter.

I know one thing – I've always admired you and been proud of you – respected you and felt honored to know you – but brother, you got a fan now! I'm going out and buy every book you've written – I had no idea I could enjoy you so. You see, reading isn't easy for me – but "The Big Sea" is so varied and so simply written that I don't have to force myself to concentrate – It grips my imagination immediately plus everything in it I identify with, even your going to sea and I've never been to sea –

Enough of this!... I enjoy it immensely – okay? 'Nough said.

Andrew, Lisa & I are in London – have been for two wks. Working at a club – the job is finished; we remain here another week for promotion & T.V. And then move on to France, Belgium, Spain for another two wks. Then home. No pleasure – just work.
Please let us see you sometime. We get back home August 6th or 7th

Love,
Nina

You know who nina is, don't you? I mean I didn't sign my last name!!? (Joke)
Andy sends love

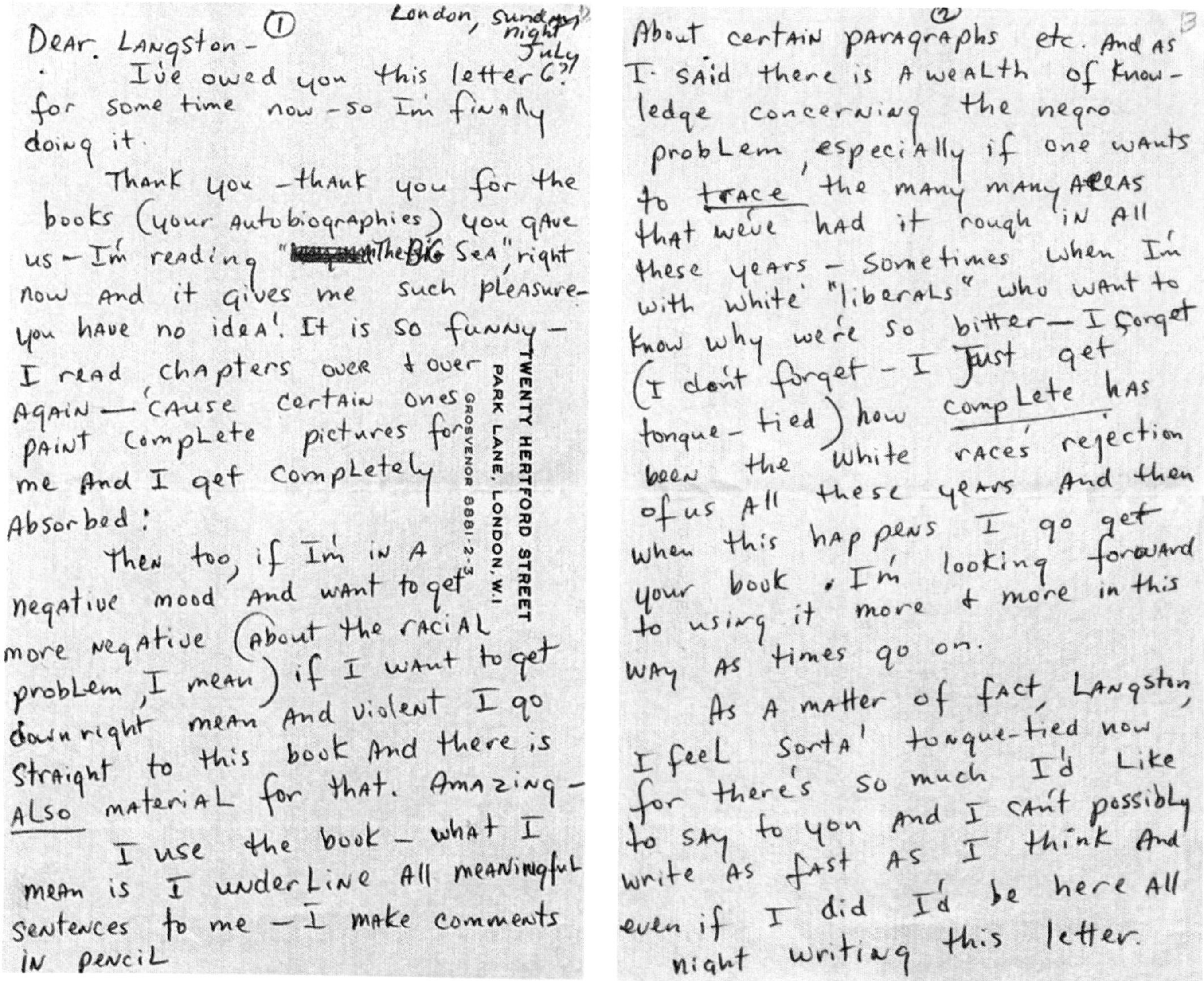

Dear Langston - ①   London, sunday
. I've owed you this letter 6?!   night
for some time now - so I'm finally   July
doing it.

Thank you - thank you for the
books (your autobiographies) you gave
us - I'm reading "~~~~~ The Big Sea", right
now and it gives me such pleasure-
you have no idea! It is so funny -
I read chapters over + over
again - 'cause certain ones
paint complete pictures for
me And I get completely
Absorbed!

Then too, if I'm in a
negative mood And want to get
more negative (about the racial
problem, I mean) if I want to get
down right mean and violent I go
straight to this book And there is
also material for that. Amazing -

I use the book - what I
mean is I underline all meaningful
sentences to me - I make comments
in pencil

GROSVENOR 8881-2-3
TWENTY HERTFORD STREET
PARK LANE, LONDON, W.I

About certain paragraphs etc. And as
I said there is a wealth of knowledge concerning the negro
problem, especially if one wants
to trace the many many areas
that we've had it rough in all
these years - Sometimes when I'm
with white "liberals" who want to
know why we're so bitter - I forget
(I don't forget - I just get
tongue-tied) how complete has
been the white races' rejection
of us all these years And then
when this happens I go get
your book. I'm looking forward
to using it more + more in this
way as times go on.

As a matter of fact, Langston,
I feel sorta' tongue-tied now
for there's so much I'd like
to say to you And I can't possibly
write as fast as I think And
even if I did I'd be here all
night writing this letter.

I know one thing ③ — I've Always Admired you And been proud of you — respected you And felt honored to know you — but brother, you got A FAN NOW! I'm going out And buy every book you've written — I had no idea I could enjoy you so. You see, reading isn't EASY for me — but "The Big Sea" is so vAried And so simply written that I don't have to force myself to concentrate — It grips my imAginAtion immediAtely plus everything in it I identify with, even your going to seA And I've never been to seA —
Enough of This! . . . ;
I enjoy it immensely — okey? 'Nough sAid.

Andrew, LisA + I Are in London — have been for Two wks. working At A club — The job is finished; we remAin here Another week for promotion + T.V. And then move on to FrAnce, Belgium,

④ SpAin for Another Two wks. — Then home. No pleAsure — just work. PleAse let us see you sometime. We get bAck home August 6th or 7th

TWENTY HERTFORD STREET
PARK LANE, LONDON, W.1
GROSVENOR 6881-2-3

Love,
Nina

you know who ninA is, don't you? I meAn I didn't sign my lAst nAme !!? (joke)
ANdy sends Love

BARBARA HEPWORTH

Artist, 1903–1975
To Ben Nicholson, 9 May 1968

Barbara Hepworth was born in Wakefield, West Yorkshire. Today, the place of her birth has an award-winning art gallery, named The Hepworth Wakefield, while her former home in St Ives, Cornwall, has become the Barbara Hepworth Museum and Sculpture Garden. Although Hepworth did not see herself as a feminist icon or pioneer, she and her work changed the way in which female sculptors were perceived and ended the perception of sculpting as a masculine art form.

In 1920, the year in which she turned 17, Barbara became a scholarship student at the Leeds School of Art. The following year, she was accepted to study at the Royal College of Art in London. At both art schools, one of her fellow students was the sculptor Henry Moore, who became a lifelong friend. Years later, Barbara recalled seeing signs on doors within the art school stating that the welding rooms were out of bounds to female students – something that Hepworth's own work would change. Unintentionally, she forged a path for all female artists to come.

Hepworth studied in London for three years, after which she was awarded a travel scholarship, enabling her to travel to Italy, where she learnt to carve marble from a master sculptor. During her year in Italy, she married fellow sculptor John Skeaping. They moved back to London, where their son Paul was born, and frequently exhibited their works together.

This letter was written to the artist Ben Nicholson, with whom Barbara fell in love while they were both still married to other people. In 1934, a year after she divorced Skeaping, Barbara gave birth to triplets: Sarah, Rachel and Simon. She married their father,

Nicholson, in 1938. This disarmingly honest letter, still full of affection, was written 17 years after their divorce.

Following her separation from Nicholson, Hepworth moved permanently into her studio in St Ives, and her home became renowned as an artistic centre. Her modernist sculptures are instantly recognisable – their flowing forms are heavily influenced by the natural landscapes and the shapes she found on the coastlines around her home.

Throughout her career, Hepworth was at the centre of European artistic life. She knew and exhibited with famous fellow artists, including Picasso, Miró, Brancusi, Arp, Braque, Mondrian, Calder, Kandinksy and of course her friend Henry Moore. She was often described as the world's foremost 'female sculptor', a title that infuriated her as she didn't believe her gender should make any difference to the importance of her work. Her global reputation saw her receive commissions for many important public works, which remain on display all over the world. She was awarded a CBE in 1958 and made a dame seven years later. Her numerous other awards included seven honorary degrees, being made a Fellow of the Royal College of Art, being made an honorary member of the American Academy of Arts and being named a Bard of Cornwall.

Although Barbara Hepworth left a huge body of work as her legacy, several of her works have been lost forever. During World War II, her London studio was damaged in a bombing raid, destroying the sculptures within. Many of her later works were also destroyed in the devastating fire at her home in St Ives, on 20 May 1975, which resulted in Hepworth's death.

Trewyn Studio   *May 9*
St. Ives   *1968*
Cornwall

My dear Ben – it was marvellous to be able to speak to you so clearly on the phone. I wanted to write to you immediately; but I realised how you would be inundated by letters from all your friends & 100's of fans – so I waited. You have no idea how delighted everybody has been about the O.M. You had a marvellous & such a warm press. All people were truly thrilled & they wrote as though you were just here & with real pride & affection.

Your Tate show will be a great affair & people are all anticipating it. You will be besieged – but don't resent it – because it will be an expression of true love & appreciation!

I have, myself, been richly rewarded by the high attendance at the Tate & the huge sale of catalogues. Also by the many moving letters from strangers all of whom loved 'touching' the sculptures altho' against orders. Next week the CAS give me a farewell party & then the awful business of dismantling the show! I felt so happy & 'on top' ten days ago, & the sun was shining, & I really felt I might be able to walk again, so I went up to Zennor to see Pat. It was gorgeous there but when I got back I found I had seriously damaged my good leg. I have been bandaged & splintered by it for 10 days & totally immobilised not having a leg to stand on! This has been the last straw but the Drs & physio therapist hope to get me to London; but it means a wheelchair again for my party which is a fearful blow. I so adore moving & it has been hard to bear these last 12 months.

But I must go – apart from the party in my honour – I have to see Stanley Lee (my cancer surgeon) & so does Herbert - & I hope to see Herbert for a while.

Your letter about my show & Catalogue & Brams book was most welcome & very fair & I thank you for it. I did a good talk on 3rd programme this week – I will send you a copy when I get the typscript. Your comment on our marriage not quite fair.

I love you as fiercely now as I did when I first met you, as I did when we conceived the children & as I did when you left here for good. It has never changed & never will. Now I'm so old & more than a decade has past this statement cannot hurt you & Feli or anybody else.

Continued overleaf

Continued from overleaf

I have tried all my life to be sophisticated & reasonable, with little effect. I am a pagan at heart & my full & mature life was being married to you. The first marriage was young & almost adolescent romantically. John has always been kind & I am grateful for his kindness. But I matured & was fulfilled when I met you. The whole time meant so much – but Bram knew (& all my friends have known) that I love you fiercely & always will. So dear Bram, with all his sensitivity wrote in a way that could not possibly cause you both distress nor expose my feeling which I have tried so hard to hide.

It doesn't matter now – but is bound to come out in my autobiography.

I can't help being a pagan. I can't help remembering the whole time the way you feel, speak, move & paint. It is all vivid & the sense of touch never more so.

In my crits, many have spoken of the sensuality contained in my sculptures despite the outward classical & disciplined exterior. All want to touch. That is as it should be.

Also, as it should be, has been the 12 (?) years I have lived utterly alone & will continue to do so. But the time for me is drawing short & I feel now that an admission of my true feeling of dedication to you & my work cannot hurt anybody.

I will continue to be a pagan trying outwardly to behave myself.

Have you read that marvellous book "On Aggression" by Konrad Lorenz? If so you will know what I mean. He is actually receiving an honorary doctorate with me next month at Oxford. I look forward to meeting him. I shall then be Dr x 4. I had to cancel my USA doctorate due to my illness. I only hope I can walk by next month. I so love movement & dancing

With love to you both *Barbara*

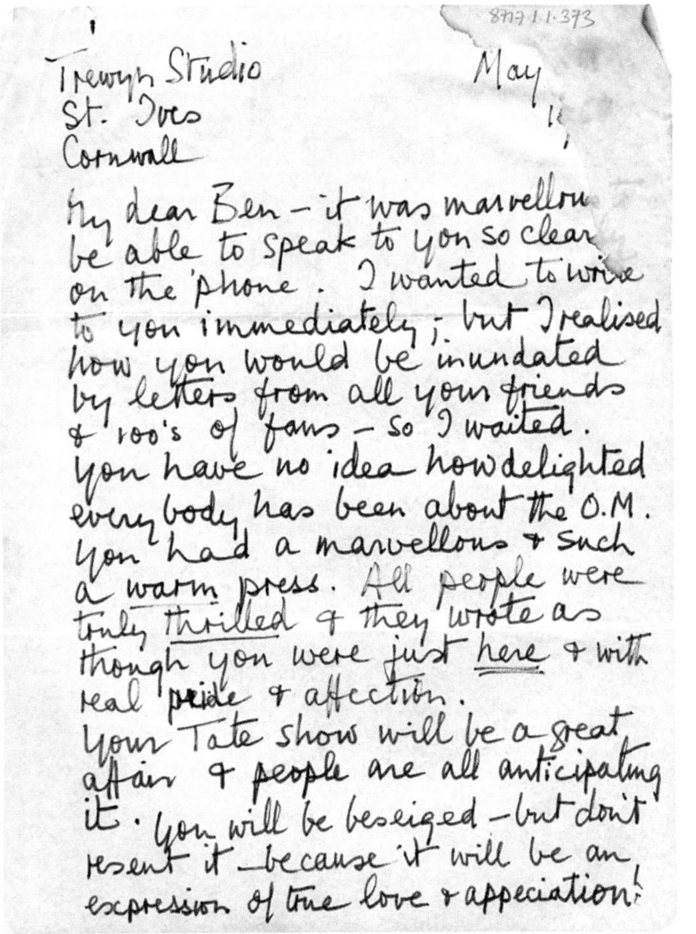

Trewyn Studio
St. Ives
Cornwall

May
1[?]

My dear Ben — it was marvellou[s]
be able to speak to you so clear[ly]
on the 'phone. I wanted to wire
to you immediately; but I realised
how you would be inundated
by letters from all your friends
& 100's of fans — so I waited.
You have no idea how delighted
everybody has been about the O.M.
You had a marvellous & such
a warm press. All people were
truly thrilled & they wrote as
though you were just here & with
real pride & affection.
Your Tate show will be a great
affair & people are all anticipating
it. You will be beseiged — but don't
resent it — because it will be an
expression of true love & appreciation!

I have, myself, been richly rewarded by
the high attendance at the Tate & the
huge sale of catalogues. Also by so
many moving letters from strangers
all of whom loved 'touching' the
sculptures altho' against orders.
Next week the CAS give me a
farewell party & then the awful
business of dismantling the show!
I felt so happy & 'on top' ten days
ago, & the sun was shining, & I
really felt I might be able to
walk again, so I went up to Zennor
to see Pat. It was gorgeous there
but when I got back I found I
had seriously damaged my good
leg. I have been bandaged &
splintered by it for 10 days &
totally immobilised not having
a leg to stand on! This has been
the last straw but the Dr's & physio
therapist hope to get me to
London; but it means a wheelchair

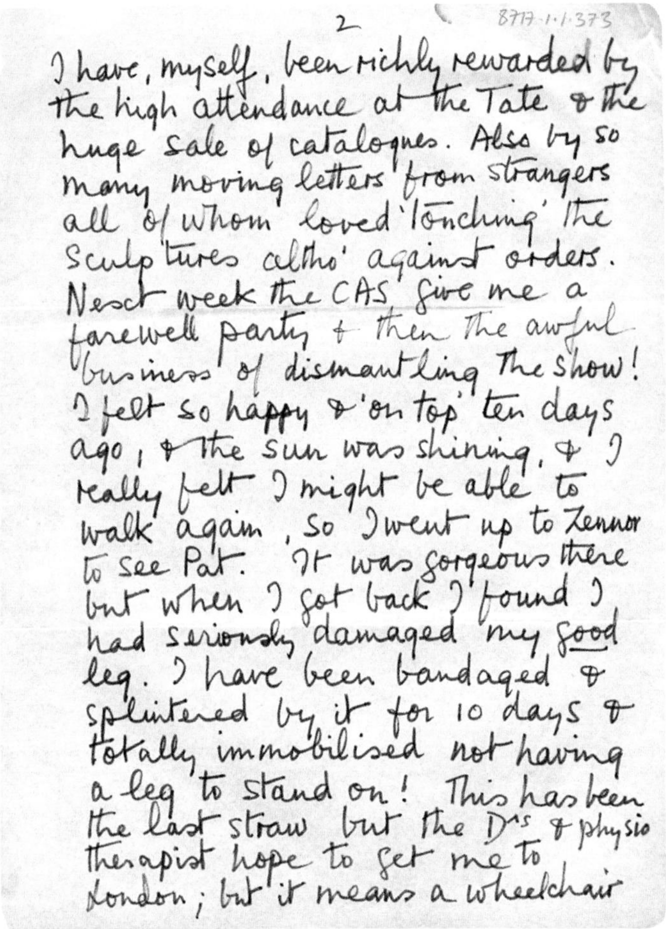

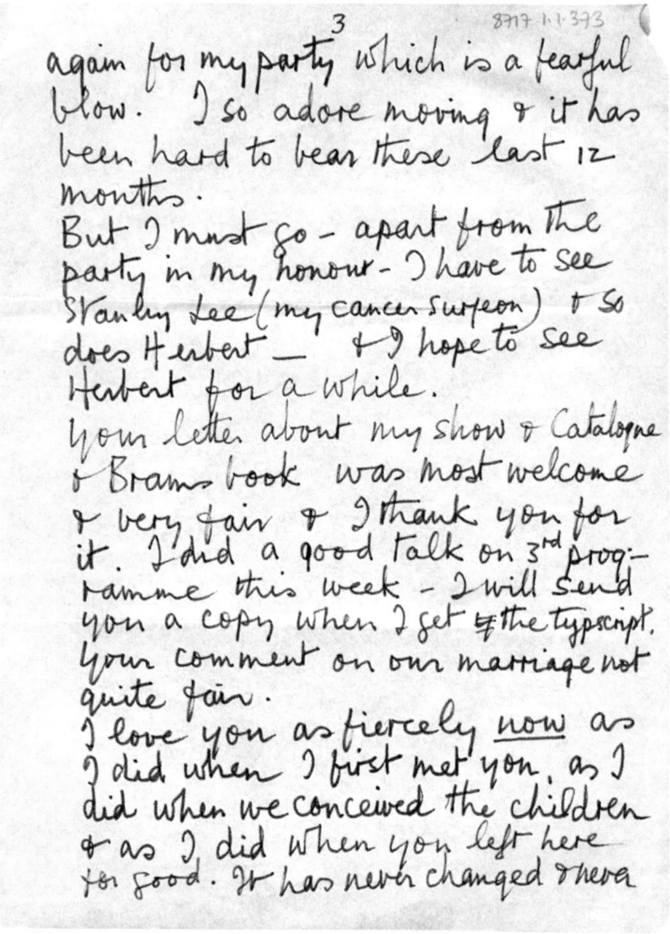

3

8717·1·1·373

again for my party which is a fearful
blow. I so adore moving & it has
been hard to bear these last 12
months.
But I must go – apart from the
party in my honour – I have to see
Stanley Lee (my cancer surgeon) & so
does Herbert — & I hope to see
Herbert for a while.
Your letter about my show & Catalogue
& Brams book was most welcome
& very fair & I thank you for
it. I did a good talk on 3rd programme this week – I will send
you a copy when I get the typescript.
Your comment on our marriage not
quite fair.
I love you as fiercely <u>now</u> as
I did when I first met you, as I
did when we conceived the children
& as I did when you left here
for good. It has never changed & never

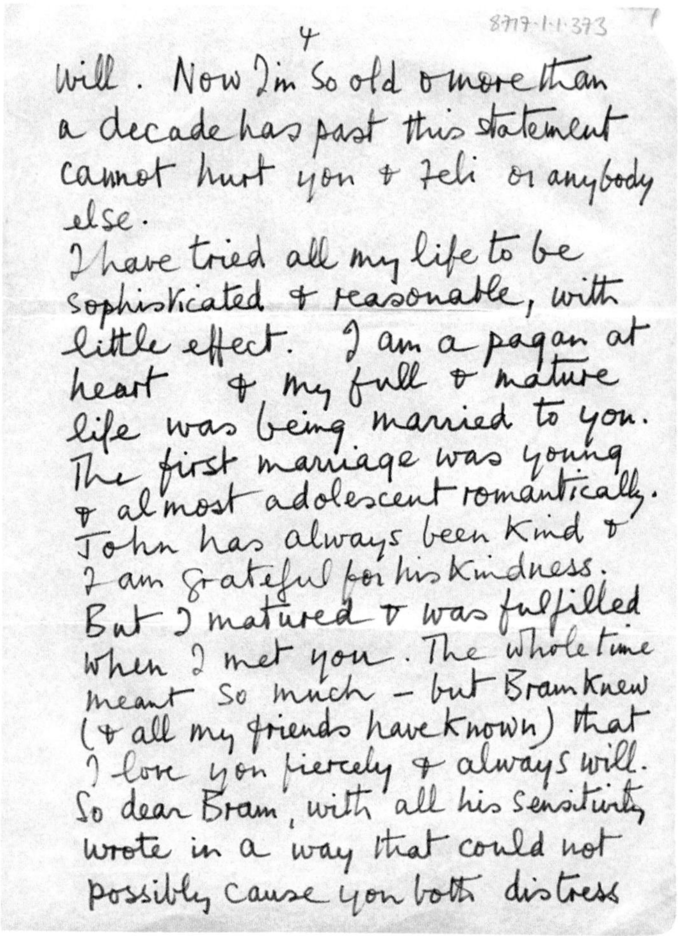

4

8717·1·1·373

will. Now I'm so old & more than
a decade has past this statement
cannot hurt you & Feli or anybody
else.
I have tried all my life to be
sophisticated & reasonable, with
little effect. I am a pagan at
heart & my full & mature
life was being married to you.
The first marriage was young
& almost adolescent romantically.
John has always been kind &
I am grateful for his kindness.
But I matured & was fulfilled
when I met you. The whole time
meant so much – but Bram knew
(& all my friends have known) that
I love you fiercely & always will.
So dear Bram, with all his sensitivity
wrote in a way that could not
possibly cause you both distress

5

8777.1.1.373

nor expose my feeling which I have
tried so hard to hide.
It doesn't matter now — but is
bound to come out in my
autobiography.
I can't help being a pagan. I can't
help remembering the whole time
the way you feel, speak, move & paint.
It is all vivid & the sense of
touch never more so.
In my crits. many have spoken
of the sensuality contained in
my sculptures despite the outward
classical & disciplined exterior.
All want to touch. That is
as it should be.
Also, as it should be, has been
the 12 (?) years I have lived
utterly alone & will continue to
do so. But the time for me is

6

8777.1.1.373

drawing short & I feel now that
an admission of my true feeling
of dedication to you & my
work cannot hurt anybody.

I will continue to be a pagan
trying outwardly to behave
myself.

Have you read that marvellous
book "On Aggression" by Konrad
Lorenz? If so you will know
what I mean.   He is actually
receiving an honorary doctorate
with me next month at Oxford.
I look forward to meeting him.
I shall then be D^ X 4. I had
to cancel my USA doctorate due
to my illness.   I only hope I can
walk by next month.   I so love
movement & dancing
With love to you both Barbara

SHIRLEY CHISHOLM

Politician, 1924–2005
To Don Edwards, 14 April 1971

In 1968, just four years after the end of segregation in the USA, Shirley Chisholm became the first African American woman to win a seat in the House of Representatives. She described her appointment as 'a new era in political history'. Four years later, she became the first woman and the first African American to seek nomination for the presidency of the United States – an attempt sabotaged by racism in the media, with Shirley blocked from almost all the televised debates. During her election campaign she wrote her autobiography, *Unbought and Unbossed*, which charted her progress through the political system. Forty years later it was updated and re-released.

Shirley Anita Chisholm (née St Hill) was born in Brooklyn, New York. Her father was from Guyana and her mother was from Barbados. Both her parents worked, and Shirley and her four younger sisters were expected to study hard at school and get good jobs. Shirley began her career as a nursery school teacher, studied for her master's degree and became involved with politics. In 1949, she married Conrad Q. Chisholm, a private investigator originally from Jamaica. They divorced in 1977, and she married Arthur Hardwick Jnr that same year.

By 1960, Shirley was working as a consultant in early childhood education for the city of New York. Four years later, she was voted into the New York City Legislature and four years after that she won her seat in Congress. Her election followed a campaign in which she commented, 'Our representative democracy is not working because the Congress that is supposed to represent the voters does not respond to their needs. I believe the chief reason for this is that it is ruled by a small group of old men.' In 1969, she gave a rousing speech at Howard University about her response to those who told African Americans to 'go back to Africa'. She said, 'We came here shackled in chains at our ankles and our wrists … Our roots are here, our blood and our sweat and our tears are here. And we're going to stay here. And we're going to fight.'

Shirley Chisholm fought her campaigns on the grounds that the country needed politicians with good morals and integrity, calling herself 'the candidate of the people'. She battled for the causes she believed in, famously opposing the Vietnam War and fighting for racial equality and, as this letter shows, gender equality. She co-founded the National Women's Political Caucus and the National Political Congress of Black Women and spent much of her career fostering and furthering the careers of other women in politics. In an interview, Shirley commented, 'Of my two handicaps, being a female put many more obstacles in my path than being black.'

In the early 1980s, Shirley Chisholm retired from Congress and returned to education, becoming a professor at Mount Holyoke College. In the 1990s, her name was put forward as a candidate for the position of US Ambassador to Jamaica, but her failing health meant she was unable to take up the position. She died on New Year's Day 2005, at the age of 80.

April 14, 1971

Congressman Don Edwards, Chairman
Subcommittee #4, House Judiciary Committee
2137 Rayburn House Office Building
Washington, D. C.

Dear Don:

As you know, I am deeply concerned about the hearings currently being held by your Subcommittee on the Equal Rights Amendment Force on the Status of Women Report.

In the past we haven't even been able to have a hearing on these issues and now group after group is coming in to me and the other women of Congress, and I am sure to you, to express their concern over the fact that they have not been able to testify on the opening day of the hearings but so many witnesses were scheduled and it was taking so long to get through the witness list that I decided to just file my statement.

I know that it is tedious and often boring to sit and listen to many, many statements on the same issues but it is equally important to realize the sensitivity of this issue. Many of these people who are asking to testify, especially the younger women have never had an opportunity to express their views before. And when the Committee indicates that they don't have time to hear them, the results are sometimes explosive...as for example the case of the group of women from George Washington.

The disruption on March 31 never would have occurred if those women had the opportunity to testify. I know that you have subsequently made arrangements so the GW group can be heard. I hope you will also provide that opportunity to other groups, especially groups representing our young women.

page 2
April 14, 1971

For example, I know that the Intercollegiate Associate of Women Students was very concerned that they did not have an opportunity to testify in person.

Your record in the field of Civil Rights has been exemplary. I hope you can use your position on the Judiciary Committee to help to create more understanding of and sympathy for the civil rights of women.

> Cordially,
> *Shirley Chisholm*
> Congresswoman

SHIRLEY CHISHOLM
12TH DISTRICT, NEW YORK

DISTRICT OFFICE:
587 EASTERN PARKWAY
BROOKLYN, NEW YORK 11216
(212) 596-3500

WASHINGTON OFFICE:
1108 LONGWORTH BUILDING
(202) 225-6231

Congress of the United States
House of Representatives
Washington, D.C. 20515

COMMITTEE:
VETERANS' AFFAIRS
SUBCOMMITTEE ON EDUCATION
AND TRAINING
SUBCOMMITTEE ON INSURANCE

MR. WESLEY McD. HOLDER
DISTRICT REPRESENTATIVE

April 14, 1971

Congressman Don Edwards, Chairman
Subcommittee #4, House Judiciary Committee
2137 Rayburn House Office Building
Washington, D. C.

Dear Don:

As you know, I am deeply concerned about the hearings
currently being held by your Subcommittee on the Equal Rights
Amendment Force on the Status of Women Report.

In the past we haven't even been able to have a hearing on
these issues and now group after group is coming in to me
and the other women of Congress, and I am sure to you, to
express their concern over the fact that they have not been
able to testify and were only able to file testimony. I,
myself, wished to testify on the opening day of the hearings
but so many witnesses were scheduled and it was taking so
long to get through the witness list that I decided to just
file my statement.

I know that it is tedious and often boring to sit and listen
to many, many statements on the same issues but it is equally
important to realize the sensitivity of this issue. Many of
these people who are asking to testify, especially the younger
women have never had an opportunity to express their views
before. And when the Committee indicates that they don't have
time to hear them, the results are sometimes explosive...as
for example the case of the group of women from George Washington.

The disruption on March 31 never would have occurred if those
women had had the opportunity to testify. I know that you
have subsequently made arrangements so the GW group can be
heard. I hope you will also provide that opportunity to
other groups, especially groups representing our young women.

page 2
April 14, 1971

For example, I know that the Intercollegiate Associate of Women Students was very concerned that they did not have an opportunity to testify in person.

Your record in the field of Civil Rights has been exemplary. I hope you can use your position on the Judiciary Committee to help to create more understanding of and sympathy for the civil rights of women.

Cordially,

SHIRLEY CHISHOLM
CONGRESSWOMAN

SC:pb

RUTH BADER GINSBURG

Lawyer and Supreme Court Justice, 1933–2020
To Emanuel Celler, 15 April 1971

Right from the beginning of her career, American lawyer Ruth Bader Ginsberg fought ceaselessly for equality, setting a trail that other women could follow. In this letter, she urges Congressman Emanuel Celler to vote for the Equal Rights Amendment. Her letter was sent following the passing of the Women's Equality Act, which – despite its name – had not secured equality. The Democrat Celler, who opposed the Equal Rights Amendment, would be beaten in the primary elections of 1972 by a female colleague.

Ruth Bader was born in Brooklyn, New York, to a Polish mother and Ukrainian father. Her parents were highly supportive of her education. Tragically, her mother Celia died the day before Ruth graduated from high school.

After studying at Cornell University, where one of her professors was the author Vladimir Nabokov, Ruth wanted to study law. At Cornell, she had met fellow student Martin Ginsburg and they married in 1954. Two years later, Ruth Bader Gisburg was accepted into Harvard Law School – one of only nine women in a class of 500. Her interview included being asked by the dean of the university to justify why he should offer her the place instead of giving it to a man. Once again, Ruth finished top of her class, yet she found it impossible to get a job. In a later interview she said she 'struck out on three grounds': she was female, Jewish and a mother. This experience made her determined to change the society in which she lived, and to do so by means of legislation.

In 1963, Ruth Bader Ginsburg joined the faculty of Rutgers Law School in New Jersey, where it was deemed acceptable for the university to tell her that, because she had a husband with a well-paid job, her salary would be lower than that of her male peers. She taught at Rutgers for nine years, creating a groundbreaking course on women and the law. This ensured that the upcoming generation of lawyers was primed to join the battle in which Ruth was constantly engaged. The year in which she wrote this letter, 1971, was also the year in which Bader Ginsburg made her first successful argument before the Supreme Court. It resulted in the court striking down a law on the grounds of sex discrimination for the very first time.

In 1972, Ruth Bader Ginsburg became the first woman to be appointed a professor at Columbia Law School in New York. In the same year, she helped to found the Women's Civil Rights Project at the American Civil Liberties Union (ACLU) and was appointed the ACLU's general counsel. In that role, she sought to weed out gender discrimination one law at a time. In 1993, she was nominated to her country's highest court, the Supreme Court, only the second woman to be appointed to the role. She remained in the Supreme Court for 27 years. Despite being diagnosed with cancer, Ruth Bader Ginsburg continued to work until the day she died. By the time of her death, at the age of 87, she had become a world-renowned figure.

Opposite Women march through Washington, DC, in 1970, demanding equal rights.

April 15, 1971

The Honorable Emanuel Celler
House of Representatives
Washington, D. C. 20515

Dear Congressman Celler:

I wish to urge your support and cooperation in expediting passage of the Equal Rights Amendment (H.J. Res. 208).

In this critical area of human rights it is regrettable that the United States has delayed assertion of a pace-setting role. Reporting on developments in his country, Sweden's Prime Minister stated during his stay in Washington last year:

> "Public opinion is nowadays so well informed that if a politician today should declare that women ought to have a different role than men [in economic and social life] he would be regarded to be of the stone age."

He emphasized that equal rights entailed emancipation of the man as much as the woman. Address by Mr. Olof Palme, the Women's National Democratic Club, Washington, D. C., June 8, 1970.

Although the Women's Equality Act of 1971 is a desirable supplement, it is not a substitute for the statement of basic rights represented by the Equal Rights Amendment.

I very much hope that you will do all that you can to assure that in this nation every person will be given equal opportunity to develop his or her individual talents. Application of this fundamental principle to women is long overdue.

Sincerely,

Ruth Bader Ginsburg
Professor of Law

file

RUTGERS UNIVERSITY · *The State University of New Jersey*

SCHOOL OF LAW · NEWARK
180 University Avenue
Newark, New Jersey 07102
Tel. 201-~~648-766~~
648-5486

N. J. Res 208
Sect 4

April 15, 1971

The Honorable Emanuel Celler
House of Representatives
Washington, D. C. 20515

Dear Congressman Celler:

I wish to urge your support and cooperation in expediting passage of the Equal Rights Amendment (H.J. Res.
208).

In this critical area of human rights it is regrettable that the United States has delayed assertion
of a pace-setting role. Reporting on developments in
his country, Sweden's Prime Minister stated during his
stay in Washington last year:

> "Public opinion is nowadays so well informed
> that if a politician today should declare
> that women ought to have a different role
> than men [in economic and social life] he
> would be regarded to be of the stone age."

He emphasized that equal rights entailed emancipation
of the man as much as the woman. Address by Mr. Olof
Palme, the Women's National Democratic Club, Washington,
D. C., June 8, 1970.

Although the Women's Equality Act of 1971 is a
desirable supplement, it is not a substitute for the
statement of basic rights represented by the Equal
Rights Amendment.

I very much hope that you will do all that you
can to assure that in this nation every person will be
given equal opportunity to develop his or her individual
talents. Application of this fundamental principle to
women is long overdue.

Sincerely,

Ruth Ginsburg

Ruth Bader Ginsburg
Professor of Law

RBG/em

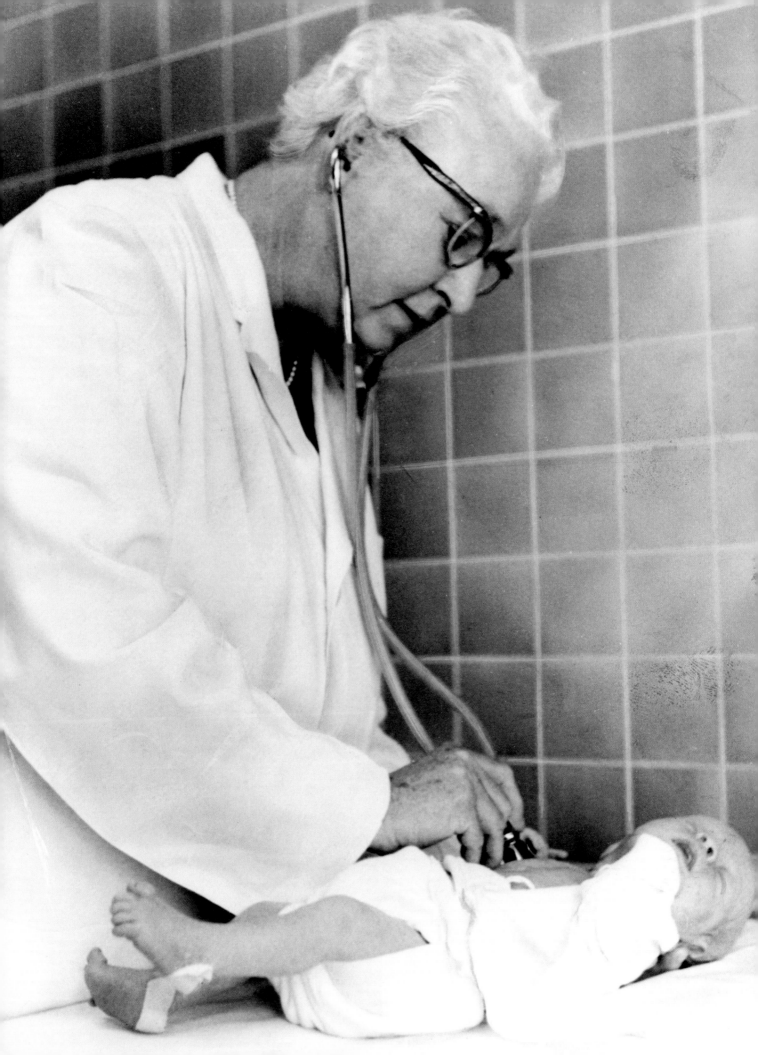

VIRGINIA APGAR

Physician, 1909–1974
To Dr R.S. Ikonen, 3 July 1974

As a child growing up in New Jersey, Virginia Apgar was encouraged in her studies by parents who took a keen interest in science. At an early age, Virginia was well aware of medical problems, as her older brother died of tuberculosis and her younger brother was often very unwell. She studied for an undergraduate degree in zoology at Mount Holyoke College, where she also excelled in music and sports. By the time she finished her degree, she had decided she wanted to become a doctor, and in 1929 she began medical school at Columbia University. She was one of only nine women in a class of 90 students. She graduated towards the top of her class.

Having initially intended to become a surgeon, Apgar was persuaded by the chair of surgery, Dr Alan Whipple, to change her field. He encouraged her to study anaesthesiology. Whipple had recognised Virginia's potential and intended to invite her back to teach future anaesthesiologists. At this time, there were many more trained surgeons than there were available jobs, and female surgeons were experiencing a great deal of prejudice. This would have made it a difficult career for a woman from a non-wealthy background to earn a living in, especially during the Great Depression. As an anaesthesiologist, Virginia quickly rose to the top of her field, despite the discipline not yet being taken seriously by many hospitals.

During her work in obstetrical anaesthesia, Virginia began to research the problems encountered by newborn babies. Her research led her to develop the groundbreaking work for which she is best remembered today, the Apgar score. This is a quick test with which a physician can assess the health of a newborn baby and measure its reactions to life outside the womb. Infant mortality was still high at this time, and Virginia believed that the rates of death were medically unjustifiable. She was the first woman to be appointed to the Executive Committee of the American Society of Anaesthetists, and the first woman to be made a full professor at the Columbia University College of Physicians and Surgeons. (The position of Chair, which was expected to be awarded to her, was given instead to a male colleague.)

Since its formulation in 1952, the Apgar score has become standard in hospitals all around the world and has dramatically reduced the number of infant deaths. In the 1950s, Virginia took a sabbatical from anaesthesiology to undertake a Master's degree in public health, after which she began research into the prevention of birth defects. She was later named Director of the Division of Congenital Defect at the National Foundation for Infantile Paralysis.

This letter was written a month before Virginia Apgar's death, in response to a Finnish physician who had referenced the Apgar score in their doctoral thesis and sent her a signed copy of the thesis. The letter shows how rightly proud and happy Virginia Apgar was that her work had produced such important results and was being recognised internationally.

Opposite Virginia Apgar examining a newborn baby in 1966. At the time she was a lecturer at Cornell University School of Medicine, where she taught teratology (the study of birth defects).

July 3, 1974

R.S. Ikonen, M.D.
Central Hosiptal of Tampere
33520 Tampere 52
Finland

Dear Doctor Ikonen:

Never before has a doctoral thesis been written about the newborn scoring system which I reported in 1952! I do hope it helps you attain your degree, and not the opposite.

It interests me to read how often the scoring system is expected to forecast conditions for which it was never intended. As stated in 1953, the system was devised, as described on page 260 of your reference #7, "as a basis for discussion and comparison of the results of obstetric practices, types of maternal pain relief and the effects of resuscitation." Actually, its uses were: 1) to predict infant mortality and 2) to point out to the physician the need for active resuscitation if the total score was four or less.

Now, 22 years later, the score is being examined for association with I.Q. at school age, behavioural disorders, fatal infant diseases such as Tay-Sachs, autism, and length of time in the intensive care unit! I would not expect that there would be either a positive or negative association with these parameters. However, it does no harm at all to investigate under what conditions the score is useful or useless.

Dr. Erich Saling of West Berlin, who has quantitated the degree of asphyxia and acid-base balance, and I are attempting to combine our methods and hope to have something published soon.

Thank you for the autographed thesis. Please give my best regards to Dr. Ahvenainen. I had hoped to visit you during the Helsinki meeting of the European Teratology Society, but had to go to California instead.

With best wishes.

Sincerely yours,

Virginia Apgar, M.D., M.P.H.

July 3, 1974

R.S. Ikonen, M.D.
Central Hospital of Tampere
33520 Tampere 52
Finland

Dear Doctor Ikonen:

Never before has a doctoral thesis been written about the newborn scoring system which I reported in 1952! I do hope it helped you attain your degree, and not the opposite.

It interests me to read how often the scoring system is expected to forecast conditions for which it was never intended. As stated in 1953, the system was devised, as described on page 260 of your reference #7, "as a basis for discussion and comparison of the results of obstetric practices, types of maternal pain relief and the effects of resuscitation." Actually, its uses were: 1) to predict infant mortality and 2) to point out to the physician the need for active resuscitation if the total score was four or less.

Now, 22 years later, the score is being examined for association with I.Q. at school age, behavioral disorders, fatal infant diseases such as Tay-Sachs, autism, and length of time in the intensive care unit! I would not expect that there would be either a positive or negative association with these parameters. However, it does no harm at all to investigate under what conditions the score is useful or useless.

Dr. Erich Saling of West Berlin, who has quantitated the degree of asphyxia and acid-base balance, and I are attempting to combine our methods and hope to have something published soon.

Thank you for the autographed thesis. Please give my best regards to Dr. Ahvenainen. I had hoped to visit you during the Helsinki meeting of the European Teratology Society, but had to go to California instead.

With best wishes.

Sincerely yours,

Virginia Apgar, M.D., M.P.H.

VA:bm

BOBBI GIBB

Athlete, artist and neuroscientist, b. 1942
To Art & Mental Health Group, Rhode Island, 20 May 2015

Bobbi Gibb first saw the Boston Marathon in 1964 and 'fell in love with it'. She had been a keen runner since childhood, and now she started a two-year training programme to enable her to run the marathon. When she wrote to the organisers to request an application form for the 1966 marathon, the reply she received stated that it was a men-only event and dismissed women as 'not physiologically able to run a marathon'. Thus began her quest to prove them wrong and in the process help to break down the prejudices that governed women's sports. In her training, Bobbi would regularly run up to 40 miles a day, yet the US Amateur Athletics Union at that time had a ban on women running distances of more than 1.5 miles.

In 1966, Bobbi was living in California, but she returned to Boston for the marathon. On the day, she dressed in her brother's running clothes, including a hood to obscure her face, and hid in some bushes near the starting point. After letting some of the runners go past, she joined the male runners and found that they, and the crowd of spectators, were welcoming and appreciative. The male runners promised that, if any of the officials noticed she was a woman and tried to eject her, they would not let them throw her out. When interviewed for the BBC's *Woman's Hour* radio programme in 2017, she said, 'I was trying to end this stupid war between the sexes… I was running with the men not against them.' Gibb finished the marathon in 3 hours, 21 minutes and 40 seconds, in the first third of the competitors.

After her historic marathon achievement, Bobbi concentrated on studying law and neuroscience, but her athletic achievement had paved the way for social change. In 1967, Kathrine Switzer received an official number to run the Boston Marathon, having been accepted in the belief that she was male. The discovery that a woman had entered officially aroused widespread outrage – and great publicity for women's sports. Bobbi also ran the marathon in 1967 and again in 1968, and she was the first woman to reach the finish line in both years. Five years later, the US Amateur Athletics Union finally changed its rules on women's distance running and women were able to enter the marathon without subterfuge.

In 1969, Bobbi Gibb graduated with a pre-med science degree. Later she revealed that she was turned down for medical school because of her gender. Instead of becoming a doctor, she studied law and was admitted to the Bar in 1978. She has since worked in the world of neuroscience, as an associate at the Cecil B. Day Neuromuscular Laboratory at the University of Massachussetts Medical Center. In addition to her sporting and scientific achievements, she has a side career as an artist, painting and sculpting. Her sculptures include runners and ballerinas, as well as busts of public figures including Mother Teresa and Albert Einstein. Her diverse achievements have led to her being described as a 'Renaissance woman'. In 2016, she was invited back to the Boston Marathon as a celebration of '50 Years of Women' at the event.

Opposite Bobbi Gibb pictured
shortly after completing the
1966 Boston Marathon.

From
Bobbi Gibb
Institute for the Study of Natural Systems
Cambridge, Massachusetts 02139

To
Art and Mental Health Group
Rhode Island 02860

May 20, 2015

Dear _____,

Thank you very much for inviting me to speak.

You indicated that as an introduction I should mention the Boston Marathon and a bit about running and continue with my career in art, law and neuroscience and then speak a bit about mental health, perhaps touching on books that I've written and other interests.

What about something like this?

In 1966, I was the first woman to ever run the Boston Marathon at a time when it was generally believed that women were not physically able to run the 26.2 mile distance. I'd first seen the Boston Marathon in 1964 and had fallen in love with it. I began to train myself. As part of my training I took a 3000 mile journey with my malamute puppy, Moot, across the entire continent, sleeping out at night under the stars and running in different places across the country. Finally when I wrote for my application in March of 1966 I received a letter from the race director informing me that the marathon was a men's division race, no women allowed, and that women were not "physiologically able" to run a marathon and they couldn't take the medical liability. At that time I was running forty miles at a stretch.

I then realized that it was more important than ever to run as a social statement. I knew if I could prove this prejudice and false belief about women wrong it would throw into doubt all the other prejudices and false beliefs that have been used for centuries to keep women down and prevent women from having the opportunities to become all they can become.

So I ran the race and finished ahead of two thirds of the men. The next day it was front-page headlines and word went out around the world that Bobbi Gibb, a "tidy blonde housewife", had done the impossible and run a marathon. It turned out to be a pivotal point in changing people's attitudes about women and in bringing attention to running as a way of life for everyone. In those days there were about three hundred men runners from all over the world. Boston was at that time the only major city marathon that I knew of. I came back in 1967 and finished about an hour ahead of the other woman competitor, and again in 1968 I finished first in a field of five women. These pre-sanctioned races are now called the women's pioneer division.

Running for me has always been not just physical but also spiritual. I love most to run through the woods and along the beaches in nature. I love nature. Nature is where my artwork comes from as well. I love to sculpture the human figure and bronze portrait busts of people. I paint nature, and now am painting more abstract paintings because when I close my eyes, especially when falling asleep, I see beautiful colored abstract patterns that continuously evolve, and change, and I want to share these with the world. Someday I would love to animate these paintings. There is some talk of my creating a life-sized sculpture to be placed along the marathon route. I've created dozens of smaller sculptures of athletes and busts and I'm excited to create more life-sized sculptures.

Running and art come from the same place, a love of the universe and a celebration of life. Being alive is such an amazing experience. We have little notion of why or how all this wonder and glory got here and why and how we ourselves are here on this small planet circling a star somewhere in one of millions of galaxies. It is a miracle of gigantic proportions.

I studied law and became an attorney as a way of being more effective in bringing about social change and improving our environment and our health. I ended up practicing intellectual property law, while working in neuroscience with Professor Lettvin at the Massachusetts Institute of Technology in Cambridge.

In 1976 I started the Institute for the Study of Natural Systems. This includes living systems, economic and social systems, which are ultimately imbedded in nature and dependent on nature for resources, and for life itself. I wrote The Art of Inflation in the late 70's with novel insights into the causes and cures of inflation. I wrote The Art of Economics, now in the process of rewriting, from a very basic standpoint that is easily understood, starting with the Givens of Nature and the operation of human ingenuity on the Givens of Nature to create resources, goods and services. I pointed out that nothing is a resource until the human mind invents a way to use it. And conversely everything is a resource once human ingenuity discovers a way to use it. I also co-produced a film on Amory Lovins in 1980, called Lovins on the Soft Path, on alternative energy and a green economy, which is still relevant today.

Since then I've raised a family, and written a book on my experiences from 1964 to 1966 training for and running that first marathon, called Wind in the Fire, a Personal Journey. I've also written a book called 26.2 Essays, a New World View, on my thoughts on a diversity of topics from birth, to economics, to cosmology and the mind, and a smaller book called To Boston with Love. I'm currently working on several more books and someday hope to make a film.

So that is a brief summary of some of the things I'm doing. I hope this is ok?

This is what I propose for my talk for June 17, 2015 on mental health. What do you think?

What is mental health? Mental health is the health of the mind. But what is the mind? We live in a culture that historically has divided existence into two distinct categories: mind or spirit on the one hand and body or the material and physical on the other hand.

Mind has been thought of as an insubstantial, invisible substance that inhabits the mechanical brain, sort of like the ghost in the machine. In our culture the mind or spirit has been thought to be superior to the body and the body has been subjugated to the mind or spirit in this worldview. Indeed our creation myths attribute the power of creation to a supernatural deity that rules the physical universe. This same prototype has been used to conceptualize not only the ascendency of a supernatural male figure over the natural world, but also to justify the absolute rule of kings over subjects. According to our cultural myths man was given dominion over the earth and all its creatures.

So mind has been thought of as spirit as a supernatural entity, as an invisible king that rules the body, as the little man in there who perceives, intends and is in charge of things. We conceive of who we are as a little man, in our heads, watching the TV screen and making decisions about what the body will do. We talk about our hands, our heart and our brain as if this supernatural ascendant being owns the rest of us.

The more I studied neuroscience the more I became aware that the fact is that there is no such thing as mind. That is to say, mind is not a thing at all. Mind is the word we use to refer to the inner subjective view of the brain of its own processes. Stunningly, there is no insubstantial entity inhabiting the brain. The brain is all there is. This is astounding and if we think about it deeply we see that this new paradigm overturns our beliefs in a multitude of ways.

First of all in the field of medicine it means that when we talk about mental illness what we are now talking about are diseases of the brain. This demystifies the entire field of mental science. We are no longer treating an invisible entity; we are treating an organ of the body as real and physical as the liver or the heart.

Much progress has been made on recognizing that many aberrations in human behavior are simply brain dysfunctions that can be alleviated and allow people to live happy, normal lives.

A growing understanding, in the areas of political and legal consequences of brain disorders, indicates that criminal, terrorist acts, gang wars, drug related violence and other disruptive acts are often caused by people who are suffering diseases of the brain.

A fresh look at history from the perspective of brain science reveals that much of the historic violence and bloodshed that has characterized human behavior has been instigated by people who were suffering psychotic breaks with reality. And indeed, it has long been my contention that war, itself may be seen as a mass psychosis.

Second, this new view that the brain is all there is changes the way we think of the body because now we see that the brain is the body and now we understand that this part of the body is capable of having subjective experiences, that is, of being conscious. This is remarkable! Think about it. We look at the brain and what do we see? We see a pinkish grey soft substance crinkled up into many folds. Indeed, the ancients thought the brain was some sort of radiator for cooling the body.

There is no clue, looking at this unlikely organ from the outside, that it has anything to do with subjective experience. But the astounding reality is that this rather messy looking mass from the inside is having a conscious experience.

And what is it having a conscious experience of? Not some invisible other worldly entity. Rather, the brain is having a conscious experience of its own activity.

This is amazing!!! How is this possible? How can a material object that is made up of cells, which are made up of molecules, possibly have a conscious subjective experience of its own activities ... and yet it does!!!

Our third conclusion, based on our new realization, is that the universe, in its fundamental nature, cannot be purely materialistic, as material has been understood. Matter is taken to be the hard, solid bits of things out there in the external extended world. We talk about the ultimate, or smallest, particle that physicists have been searching for. And we conceive of an objective universe in which mindless particles are shuttled about by forces and everything can be explained in terms of mass, energy, space and time. But such a universe would never be able to evolve consciousness. We know there is consciousness because that is what we directly experience.

This leads us to our fourth conclusion. Our own consciousness is all that we ever experience. We speak of the blue sky, the green grass, the hot sun, the sweet sugar, as if these qualities are attributes of the objective physical world out there. Indeed philosophers refer to these qualities as secondary qualities of objects. The more I studied neuroscience the more I came to see that none of these qualities exist at all in the external world. All we know is what our brains construct from the bits of information abstracted by our sense organs from the bits of energy that they receive. We then project these constructs back on to the world.

We can never know what is out there directly. All we know are the models that our brains make. This is our subjective experience, this inner view of the activities of our brains as it processes information and creates its models of the world.

And, this leads us to our fifth conclusion and one that I've been working on and writing about for decades. The solution to the mind body problem is that the ultimate substance is neither material nor mind but a unified being that includes and explains attributes of what we previously have called mind and body. What can this unitary substance possibly be? No one knows. But clearly we see that body is the mind and mind is the body. This means that what we have taken to be the physical universe is also spiritual in the sense that we have attributed to spirit this property of subjective experience, intelligence and a transcendent type of being.

Our sixth conclusion, then, has to be that existence is not divided into the natural physical universe and the transcendent spiritual universe, but rather that the natural is transcendent, and transcendent is perfectly natural. This returns the intelligence, the glory, the sacredness and holiness that we have ascribed to the transcendent back to nature where it belongs. Nature then in its largest sense contains what we have called the spiritual and the transcendent. This means that our earth is sacred and our universe is holy and so are we. We can reclaim our birthright as transcendent beings in a transcendent universe that is perfectly natural.

We are floating in intergalactic space right now, through unimaginable eons of time and unending space. There is nothing separating us right now from the furthermost reaches of the universe. Our bodies and brains are made of atoms that were forged in the cores of ancient supernovas. The iron in our blood is the same iron that forms the hot planetary core of our earth. We are part of nature.

Most of the time we don't think about this deep reality of our being because we are so caught up in our daily lives of getting to work, paying our bills, taking care of our families and social obligations, but the reality of our connection with all human beings, all living creatures and with the totality of the cosmos, in which we have our being, and out of which we have evolved, remains the fundamental reality of our existence. When we consciously realize this deep reality, we feel love because we know we are part of this deep connection with everything.

So realizing the connection that is embodied in the fact of our cosmos and the interconnection of all the diverse parts of the cosmos fills us with love. This connectedness in the cosmos into a unitary whole is the most powerful thing there is. So, in this sense, love is the most powerful thing there is. If we say that love is connection then love is fundamental to existence.

Out of that love, a new sense of wonder and caring will come into being, and this new consciousness will heal the earth and heal the human heart. A new appreciation of truth will burgeon forth, healing the human mind. When this happens, humanity will take a giant step towards a transformation that will end wars and bring peace to the world for centuries to come.

Indeed this advancement to a new consciousness is the only way that human beings will be able to continue to live and to flourish on the earth, on this beautiful planet that is floating in this infinite cosmos... a cosmos that is continuously being born out of a love so vast that it is beyond our comprehension.

Looking forward to seeing you soon!!!

Many Regards,

Bobbi

Greta Thunberg
@GretaThunberg

When the haters go after your looks and differences, it means they have nowhere left to go. And then you know you're winning!
I have Aspergers and that means I'm sometimes a bit different from the norm. And – given the right circumstances – being different is a superpower.
#aspiepower

10:44 PM • Aug 31, 2019

GRETA THUNBERG

Environmental activist, b. 2003
Tweet, 31 August 2019

In August 2018, 15-year-old Swedish schoolgirl Greta Thunberg went on strike. She stopped going to school and sat outside the Swedish Parliament holding a home-made placard bearing the words 'Skolstrejk för llimatet' (School strike for the climate). This simple action gave birth to a new activism and the #FridaysForFuture movement, which was taken up by schoolchildren – and the media – all over the globe.

Greta grew up in Stockholm, Sweden, the elder daughter of an opera singer mother and an actor father. She is also related to the Nobel-Prize-winning chemist Svante Arrhenius, a climate-change pioneer who predicted the greenhouse effect and global warming way back in the 1890s.

Greta began learning about climate change at primary school and became so traumatised about what was being done to the planet, and the refusal by those in power to take the issue seriously, that for some time she stopped speaking. Then she decided to take action. As Greta writes in this tweet, she has Asperger's Syndrome, for which she has suffered abuse, most publicly from former US president Donald Trump – but Greta considers her condition in a different light. For her, Asperger's syndrome is her 'superpower'. She sees the world, she says, not in many shades and tones and colours, but in black and white – and 'there are no grey areas when it comes to climate change'.

By the end of 2018, more than 20,000 young people had joined the school strike. Greta met many of the strikers, travelling only by train and boat, as she refuses to travel by plane or non-electric car. She has since been invited to conferences all over the world. On 23 September 2019, she made history at the United Nations summit in New York (which she travelled to by yacht). In her furious speech, the 16-year-old excoriated world leaders for their refusal to take climate change seriously and for their lack of any real action about the issue. She spoke on behalf of young people all over the world, including the words: 'You have stolen my dreams and my childhood with your empty words. And yet I'm one of the lucky ones. People are suffering. People are dying. Entire ecosystems are collapsing. We are in the beginning of a mass extinction, and all you can talk about is money and fairy tales of eternal economic growth. How dare you!'

In 2020, *I Am Greta*, a documentary about the teenager, premiered at the Venice Film Festival. Due to the Covid-19 pandemic, Greta was not able to appear in person, but via a video link she praised the film, declaring that it showed her as she really was: 'Not the angry, naïve child who sits in the United Nations general assembly screaming at world leaders. Because that's not the person I am. … [It] definitely made me seem like a more shy, nerdy person, which is the person I am.' She also appreciated the fact that the documentary debunked conspiracy theories about her being manipulated by other people, saying, 'In the movie you can see … that I do, of course, speak for myself and decide everything for myself.'

Opposite Top Greta Thunberg standing in front of the Swedish parliament building with a sign saying 'School strike for the climate' in Stockholm in 2018.

BEVERLEY DITSIE

Activist and filmmaker, b. 1971
To the world's LGBTQ+ population, 24 October 2019

This letter is addressed to everyone who has shared in Beverley Ditsie's personal struggle. The writer's beginnings came in a place and time of acute crisis. Born in Soweto, the daughter of Eaglette Ditsie, a famous singer who regularly toured South Africa, Beverley Palesa Ditsie was five years old in June 1976, when police killed 176 people, many of them children, protesting the forced teaching of Afrikaans in the township schools. She grew up with an awareness of an unjust system, one that classified her and her family as 'coloureds', thereby giving them better access to schools, hospitals and transport than 'black' people. It was a classification that she and her family rejected. Her fury was given a focus when, in 1986, on the tenth anniversary of the massacre, she joined the Student Representative Council to fight apartheid.

In Johannesburg a year later, Bev Ditsie met Simon Nkoli, who was campaigning for gay rights in South Africa, having been acquitted in the Delmas Treason Trial (a three-year-long trial of 22 anti-apartheid activists). In Nkoli, she found what she had felt was missing in the anti-apartheid struggle – respect for her queerness that meant fighting for freedom not only as a black person, but also as a gay woman.

Nkoli became Bev's mentor and friend and, together with Linda Ngcobo, they founded the Gay and Lesbian Organisation of Witwatersrand (GLOW), which was instrumental in promoting LGBTQ+ rights. As a result in part of their efforts, post-apartheid South Africa's new constitution became the first in world history to mention sexual orientation and its expression as a human right.

In 1995, Bev was invited to the UN Women's Conference in Beijing – the other delegates being almost entirely male. When the lesbian caucus was given just five minutes to speak, Bev was chosen to talk. In those few minutes, she advanced the cause of gay rights by years, asking that the conference 'recognise that discrimination based on sexual orientation is a violation of basic human rights' and insisting that LGBTQ+ rights must be enshrined in law.

While much of her activism now takes place online, in the late 1990s, Bev Ditsie took part in a reality TV show similar to *Big Brother*, in which eight people lived together for six months. A fellow contestant told her, 'I used to beat up gays, because as far as I'm concerned you don't belong on Earth.' The two of them had become friends by the end of the show, but regular encounters with such hatred have taken their toll.

Bev has also put herself behind the camera, writing and directing over 20 documentaries, including *Simon and I* (2002), which charts Nkoli's political and personal life, from the Dalmas trial to his death from AIDS aged 41 in 1998. A more recent documentary, put together in lockdown, is *Lesbians Free Everyone – The Beijing Perspective*, which first screened in October 2020, marking the 25th anniversary of her address.

This recent letter demonstrates Ditsie's disappointment with the current situation in South Africa, where the Rainbow Nation that came together with Nelson Mandela in an arc of hope has faded to a disappointment of grey. With regard to the renaming of the Pride March to the Pride Parade, she insists that, although there is much to celebrate, there is still so much to protest. Bev Ditsie continues to march, and in her very person, she makes a change for the better, 'For Everyone'.

A love letter to my queer family

By Bev Ditsie 24 October 2019

My Dearest Family – across the entire queer spectrum

My name is Bev Ditsie.

I am one of the founders of the first Pride March in 1990, and an alumni of one of the first multiracial/multicultural LGBTIQA organisations on the continent, the Gay and Lesbian Organisation of the Witwatersrand, GLOW.

This love letter is long overdue, I know.

I've been silently and not so silently watching and listening to the debates, the recriminations, denials and PR spin in relation to Pride, and silently bleeding while deflecting the annual obligatory requests for media interviews.

For the past 20 years or so, this time of the year has been a very painful time for me.

This is the time where I am reminded of my failure as an activist and leader, and our collective failure not just as LGBTIQA people/organisations/movements, but also as a country.

This is the time of the year where I mourn the loss of the dream that began the first Pride March in 1990.

Allow me to be nostalgic. This is, after all, a love letter.

The handful of us, inspired by the unbanning of all liberation movements and freedom fighters like Nelson Mandela and our founder and leader, Simon Nkoli, were brimming with hope when this march was conceived.

We were from different backgrounds, different races, ages, genders, orientations, abilities etc. and it didn't matter. We were a mish-mash of diverse people unified by one goal, to be seen, heard, and one day to be treated with the dignity and respect that is enjoyed by all other human beings.

To this end, visibility, particularly black visibility, would be key. Gay people had been relegated to living in the shadows, in the margins, living in shame and subjected to all sorts of abuses and injustices and we had had enough.

Even further, the accepted notion from our black families and communities was (and still is) that we are unAfrican and trying to adopt some mindless, pointless Western existence – or even worse, an existence whose intention is to destroy Africa and Africanism – a preposterous idea considering many of us love our traditions and cultures and are part of the fabric of this soil. We understood that Pride was a political act, an act of protest at these injustices as well as a celebration of our existence.

We were no longer begging for our freedom. We were taking it.

To ensure the inclusivity that we generally didn't feel in our everyday life, we decided the entire event would be free. GLOW held fundraising events throughout the year and those members who could, also contributed an annual membership fee.

Accessibility to the event was another key factor. The city of Johannesburg has always attracted people from all corners of the country, and the centre of Johannesburg was normally accessible by at least one mode of transport. Braamfontein was our starting point. It also made sense to go through Hillbrow. This suburb signified freedom for the young white folk, for the queer folk, as well as a new kind of freedom for the black person as it was one of the first suburbs to allow black people access to both housing and entertainment. And yes, that's also where the gay bars were found.

Everyone at GLOW understood we were fighting an intersectional fight. New word, I know, but we understood we were waging a struggle that recognised all our struggles. Across gender, race, social standing or economic status.

Everyone had a vision of this freedom, even if we could not articulate it at the time.

"Today, we are here to show the world that we here in SA have been oppressed for too long, and we are tired. We are here to show the world that we are proud of who we are." I said on that podium.

Edwin Cameron (now a retired Constitutional Court judge) said: "Criminal law is for criminals. Gays and lesbians are not criminals".

Simon clinched it when he spoke about being black and gay and fighting for the liberation of his entire being. "I am black, I am gay, I cannot separate the two parts of myself into secondary or primary struggle. They are one".

Donne Rundle read the manifesto of demands. It was a march after all.

I don't remember what Hendrik Pretorius said. I remember there was something that sounded like an apology to Simon (Nkoli). This created a buzz in the space. I was only 17 years old, and new to the politics, but I soon learned the significance of this almost apology.

In the early 1980s when Simon was first arrested as a student activist, he sought support from the only gay organisation that existed at the time, the Gay Association of South Africa – Gasa.

Gasa responded by saying it does not support terrorists.

I was already reading and learning from warriors like Audre Lorde, and was reminded of her saying that: "Gay white men were not here to change the status quo, but to belong to it." Why would they want to change anything? To be white, male and able-bodied was (and still is) a position of power and privilege, especially in apartheid South Africa, so of course, Gasa was simply fighting to belong, while Simon and all of us, wanted to topple the whole damn system.

That "apology" created a buzz because it acknowledged many things that normally remain unsaid. We marched that year, and every year after, in defiance, in celebration, in Pride and in protest.

And even after the new Constitution was adopted in 1996, ensuring our rights, the violence and intimidation continued unabated, especially for those of us in the townships, rural areas, in homophobic homes and communities.

We marched to continue to reclaim our dignity and our rightful space in society.

So, you can imagine my shock sometime in the mid-1990s when the Pride committee, made up of mostly white men, started suggesting that the march should be changed from Pride March to Pride Parade. I don't remember who else was there, but I remember distinctly Paul Stobbs, then chair of the committee, saying that queer people were now free and there was no longer a need to protest.

I remembered Audre Lorde's words:

I remember even saying: You have always been free. But I am not. I am not sure if I said this out loud, or if I was even heard.

By the late 1990s, the Pride March became the Pride Parade, changing routes, charging entrance fees, changing the fundamental essence of what the first Pride March stood for.

Gay White South Africa could finally openly celebrate their freedom without being encumbered by the rest of us and our struggles.

There were two occasions when there was an attempt at an alternative. One was in 1999 when Pride started and ended in Newtown. It was a heroic compromise that began when the inaugural international lesbian and gay association conference was held in Johannesburg. The next occasion was in 2004 when a different committee took over. This route started in Braamfontein, went through Hillbrow and ended back in Braamfontein, at a gay hub then called Heartland. There was real palpable fear during that Parade, and not unjustified. There was a feeling of hostility in the air, and this was exacerbated when someone threw a bottle at the revellers from a balcony. Someone was injured.

While some argued that that was the exact reason why the route had been changed to the relative safety of suburbia, with its high walls, others argued that that's exactly why the route needed to stay.

Of course, the inevitable happened. The Rosebank route was loved by many, but obviously missed the point. Zoo Lake, even after fighting the entrance fee, became another mess with its exclusionary policies – including choice of entertainment, expensive refreshments and once again, the sense of hostility and exclusion. Our people rectified this very easily. We stopped "parading" and gathered on the other side of the fence from the main event. We were there, but on our own terms.

Annually, the violations, discrimination, gang rapes and murders in the townships continued unabated, while Pride continued to celebrate in suburbia.

Most of you probably know what happened in 2012 when the One in Nine campaign disrupted Pride. By the time I arrived on Jan Smuts Avenue some of the womxn were already at the Rosebank Police Station. A few had been injured and were taken to hospital. The bruises were not just physical.

What will stay with me for the rest of my life is not Tanya Harford – then chair and main organiser – screaming at my sisters from the driving seat of her convertible Jeep: "This is my Pride, this is my route", but the white man next to her, zap signs in the air, yelling at her to: "Drive over them, don't stop, run them over." This is before the fists started flying.

Later, Tanya Harford said she didn't realise that the 12 or so black womxn standing on Jan Smuts Avenue were queer. She just saw black bodies, and they spelled danger. She also insisted there was no way to stop the momentum of the Parade for a moment of silence. Well, having been to Marches and Parades in many parts of the world, in hostile and friendly places, I can tell you that is a lie.

Also, the continuing insistence that Pride cannot be both political and celebratory is also a lie rooted in racist, elitist privilege and a refusal to even try. She decided to cancel Pride the next year. Besides the fact that it was never hers to cancel, many of us didn't really care. Well, at least, I had convinced myself that I had stopped caring.

The People's Pride was established in 2013 and organised a few very political Marches. It was awesome to see some of the people, who had also personally boycotted the Parade. But the people's pride is struggling. Understandably, this is a labour of love, and the politics take everything out of you. It is commendable that Soweto Pride has tenaciously held on, against so many odds.

So I'm sure you are asking why I wrote this lengthy letter. That's because I keep thinking that I don't care for the Johannesburg Pride Parade.

Yet, every single year, spring brings with it a fresh wave of anguish.

I refuse to do interviews, but when I do accept to talk to one person or another, I find myself saying the same thing over and over again. White gay and middle-class queer people have everything to celebrate. Let them.

I am personally not concerned with them.

I'm just sad for all the black queers that have not, and might never experience the feeling of community, of belonging, the feeling of Pride in its fullness.

This is why I cannot call for or even support the boycott of Pride. I cannot in good conscience deprive anyone of the experience, even if it is tainted with a sense of mistrust and hostility.

I have been sad for 20 years.

So this year I have decided to do something different.

I have decided to celebrate.

My friends and I will be having a picnic at Zoo Lake to commemorate this day. We will have our cooler boxes, our little fireplaces and I actually intend to enjoy this day.

Those of you going to the Johannesburg Pride Parade, enjoy yourselves. You know what this is about, and why you are there. Take up the space. Make it yours. After all, it belongs to you, whether you are from Alex or Camps Bay.

Those of you who would like to celebrate with us, you're welcome.

Happy Pride

I love you all so much. Please be safe.

Yours Always
Dr Bev Palesa Ditsie (Hon, CGU, CAL, USA).

P.S. To the Johannesburg Pride Parade organisers

Please rectify the information on your pages. Johannesburg Pride Parade was not born in 1990 (September or October). *The Lesbian and Gay Pride March* was born in 1990 and this was not just an event, it was a movement, a philosophy born of an understanding of all our intersectional struggles.

The concept of the *Parade* was established in 1994. This is an entirely different, de-politicized, elitist concept born of the ignorance and lack of care for other less privileged members of this so-called community.

In claiming to be born in 1990, you are in essence erasing me, Simon Nkoli, Donne Rundle, Terry Myburg, Roy Shepherd, Edwin Cameron, Paul Mokgethi, Phybia Dlamini, Lesley Mtambo, Mark Gevisser, Andrew Lindsey, Gerry Davidson, Diane, Patience, Tshidi, Linda, Zaza, and all those who sacrificed themselves in all sorts of ways to make that first Pride March a possibility, people you have not consulted with or interacted with in any way while you make these claims.

So while this rewriting of history makes for great PR, it is, in fact, an act of erasure. Please rectify it.

INDEX

ACKNOWLEDGEMENTS AND CREDITS

The author would like to thank all those at Welbeck Books and Tall Tree Books who worked on this title in such extraordinary times, including Rob Colson, Issy Wilkinson and Georgia Goodall, as well as all those working in the archives and picture libraries.